Hawthorne in England

Selections from *Our Old Home*
and *The English Note-Books*

Hawthorne in England

Selections from *Our Old Home*

and *The English Note-Books*

Edited by CUSHING STROUT

Cornell Paperbacks

Cornell University Press

ITHACA, NEW YORK

CORNELL UNIVERSITY PRESS

First published 1965

Library of Congress Catalog Card Number: 65–15775

PRINTED IN THE UNITED STATES OF AMERICA
BY W. F. HUMPHREY PRESS

Editor's Note

EMERSON spoke at Harvard in 1837 on the duty of the American scholar, no longer apprenticed to the learning of other lands, to turn his attention to the domestic realities of the here and now, "the meal in the firkin and the milk in the pan." He hoped that this advice would nurture the growth of native intellectual independence. Yet the imaginations of America's classic writers would also be nourished by their experience of Europe and by their brooding reflection upon the encounter between the native dream of an innocent New World and the complicated reality of a more experienced Old World, which both charmed and repelled the American mind. Our own engagement with Europe since 1941 has cast this theme into high relief.

Irving and Longfellow began the literary discovery of Europe; Melville and Cooper carried it to a far more critical, realistic stage. Two years after Cooper's death Nathaniel Hawthorne, as a reward for his campaign biography of his old friend Franklin Pierce, was made American consul at Liverpool. From the spring of 1853 to the winter of 1858 he kept a journal of this experience, and in 1862 he consoled himself in the midst of his country's fratricidal conflict by artfully fashioning reflective essays out of the raw ore of his notebooks. Published in 1863 and dedicated to Pierce, whose political reputation was at its nadir in the North, *Our Old Home* ran afoul of the passions of war; his friends dropped off, Hawthorne complained, "like autumn leaves." One hundred years later *Our Old Home* can gain its deserved respect, no longer obscured by the political controversy provoked by Hawthorne's loyalty to Pierce.

Hawthorne originally had hoped to make a work of fiction out of his English experience, as he had drawn upon his year and a half in Italy for *The Marble Faun*. In 1859 he had finished that romance at Leamington, where "the fogs of old England" had put him into "working trim." Back in America, however, he found "the Present, the Immediate, the Actual," too much for him. He could produce only confused and incomplete sketches of a story *(Dr. Grimshawe's Secret)* based on the legend of a bloody footstep at Smithell's Hall in England. The novel was to have told the tale of an American's misguided effort to claim an English estate to which he was entitled as a descendant of an Englishman who had fled long ago to this country. The idea was emblematic of Hawthorne's sense of his own relation to England. "It is our forefathers' land," he wrote in his notebook — "our land, for I will not give up such a precious inheritance." The ambiguities of this Yankee piety are richly expressed in *Our Old Home,* which thus becomes a valuable substitute for his unfinished novel.

Born on the Fourth of July, Hawthorne was a sturdy patriot, committed like the protagonists of his aborted romance, "the Adam and Eve of a new epoch," to being a missionary for "a new social faith." A Yankee of Puritan ancestors, an enthusiastic Democrat, and a writer of Gothic romances, he had a complex sensibility, richly compounded for appreciating subtleties. His discriminating eye makes these essays on England much more than the record of a sentimental journey. They reflect a probing comparison of the Old World with the New, of traditional hierarchical

society with modern democratic life, and it is not surprising
that Henry James, the master of "the international theme,"
found *Our Old Home* "the best written" of all the productions of this "good American," who was "exquisitely provincial." These recollections eloquently reveal an American
writer coming to terms with his English heritage. If the
terms sometimes seem too romantic for us — he often said
he could not understand history until it was at least a hundred years old — the task still remains an obligation and an
opportunity to balance sympathy and judgment with his poise.

For admirers of Hawthorne's art these pages generously
display a vivifying eye, a quiet humor, and a reflective mind,
disciplined to his purpose at a time of devastating national
crisis. James warmly appreciated these aspects of *Our Old
Home,* but he felt that it sometimes suffered from being
the work of "a shy and susceptible man, with nothing at
stake, mentally, in his appreciation of the country." Hawthorne was too much the detached stranger in a country in
which "it is easiest for a stranger to remain a stranger." Yet
despite his sense of "being a stranger and an alien" in England — as Hawthorne wrote in his journal when he felt no
sympathy with English excitement over the Crimean War in
1854 — he flirted several times with the idea of settling there.
Politics made the difference. If only "our old home" were
a republic, he remarked, Americans might easily settle there.
"I shall never again be so free," he wrote his publisher,
"as I have been in England and Italy." Watching his country
embroiled in a series of crises over the issue of slavery, he
complained that the United States, though fit for many excellent purposes, was certainly "not fit to live in." On his
return to America he found that his mind had, for the purposes
of fiction, "lost its temper and its fine edge." Three months
before his journey with General Pierce to New Hampshire,
from which he never returned, he wrote his publisher: "If
I could but go to England now, I think that the sea-voyage
and the 'old Home' might set me all right." English critics

quite mistakenly thought him bitter against their countrymen. "I would as soon," Hawthorne protested, "hate my
own people." Surely James is right, in qualifying his own
criticism, to point out "the tender side of the book," which
contains "more charming and affectionate things than ... had
ever before been written about a country not the writer's own."

I have used the text of the Riverside Edition, eliminating
only parenthetical or repetitive material and the long account
of the mad Delia Bacon, whose scholarly fantasies about the
authorship of Shakespeare's plays aroused Hawthorne's chiv-
alrous sympathies. The chapter, "Recollections of a Gifted
Woman," might now better be called "Shakespeare Country."
I have added some passages from *The English Note-Books*,
in the same edition, because they help to round out Hawthorne's view of English life.

The only complete version of the notebooks is Randall
Stewart's edition, published in 1941 by the Modern Language
Association. The various versions of Hawthorne's aborted
romance about the American in England can be found in
Edward H. Davidson's edition of *Dr. Grimshawe's Secret*, pub-
lished in 1954 by Harvard University Press. Cornell Uni-
versity Press has recently published in paperback Henry
James's justly famous essay on Hawthorne. I have also drawn
above on letters cited in my *The American Image of the
Old World*, published in 1963 by Harper and Row.

CUSHING STROUT

Ithaca, New York
November 1964

Contents

Our Old Home

To A Friend

[from the Dedication to Franklin Pierce]

I ONCE hoped, indeed, that so slight a volume would not be all that I might write. These and other sketches, with which in a somewhat rougher form than I have given them here, my journal was copiously filled, were intended for the side-scenes and backgrounds and exterior adornment of a work of fiction of which the plan had imperfectly developed itself in my mind, and into which I ambitiously proposed to convey more of various modes of truth than I could have grasped by a direct effort. Of course, I should not mention this abortive project, only that it has been utterly thrown aside and will never now be accomplished. The Present, the Immediate, the Actual, has proved too potent for me. It takes away not only my scanty faculty, but even my desire for imaginative composition, and leaves me sadly content to scatter a thousand peaceful fantasies upon the hurricane that is sweeping us all along with it, possibly, into a Limbo where our nation and its polity may be as literally the fragments of a shattered dream as my unwritten Romance. But I have far better hopes for our dear country; and for my individual share of the catastrophe, I afflict myself little, or not at all, and shall easily find room for the abortive work on a certain ideal shelf, where are reposited many other

shadowy volumes of mine, more in number, and very much
superior in quality, to those which I have succeeded in rendering actual.

To return to these poor Sketches: some of my friends have
told me that they evince an asperity of sentiment towards
the English people which I ought not to feel, and which
it is highly inexpedient to express. The charge surprises
me, because, if it be true, I have written from a shallower
mood than I supposed. I seldom came into personal relations with an Englishman without beginning to like him,
and feeling my favorable impression wax stronger with the
progress of the acquaintance. I never stood in an English
crowd without being conscious of hereditary sympathies.
Nevertheless, it is undeniable that an American is continually thrown upon his national antagonism by some acrid
quality in the moral atmosphere of England. These people
think so loftily of themselves, and so contemptuously of
everybody else, that it requires more generosity than I possess to keep always in perfectly good-humor with them.
Jotting down the little acrimonies of the moment in my
journal, and transferring them thence (when they happened
to be tolerably well expressed) to these pages, it is very possible that I may have said things which a profound observer
of national character would hesitate to sanction, though
never any, I verily believe, that had not more or less of
truth. If they be true, there is no reason in the world why
they should not be said. Not an Englishman of them all
ever spared America for courtesy's sake or kindness; nor, in
my opinion, would it contribute in the least to our mutual
advantage and comfort if we were to besmear one another
all over with butter and honey. At any rate, we must not
judge of an Englishman's susceptibilities by our own, which
likewise, I trust, are of a far less sensitive texture than formerly.

Consular Experiences

THE Consulate of the United States, in my day, was located in Washington Buildings (a shabby and smoke-stained edifice of four stories high, thus illustriously named in honor of our national establishment), at the lower corner of Brunswick Street, contiguous to the Goree Arcade, and in the neighborhood of some of the oldest docks. This was by no means a polite or elegant portion of England's great commercial city, nor were the apartments of the American official so splendid as to indicate the assumption of much consular pomp on his part. A narrow and ill-lighted staircase gave access to an equally narrow and ill-lighted passageway on the first floor, at the extremity of which, surmounting a door-frame, appeared an exceedingly stiff pictorial representation of the Goose and Gridiron, according to the English idea of those ever-to-be-honored symbols. The staircase and passageway were often thronged, of a morning, with a set of beggarly and piratical-looking scoundrels (I do no wrong to our own countrymen in styling them so, for not one in twenty was a genuine American), purporting to belong to our mercantile marine, and chiefly composed of Liverpool Blackballers and the scum of every maritime nation on earth; such being the seamen by whose assistance we then disputed

the navigation of the world with England.*   These specimens
of a most unfortunate class of people were shipwrecked crews
in quest of bed, board, and clothing; invalids asking permits for the hospital; bruised and bloody wretches complain-
ing of ill-treatment by their officers; drunkards, desperadoes,
vagabonds, and cheats, perplexingly intermingled with an
uncertain proportion of reasonably honest men.   All of them
(save here and there a poor devil of a kidnapped landsman
in his shore-going rags) wore red flannel shirts, in which
they had sweltered or shivered throughout the voyage, and
all required consular assistance in one form or another.

Any respectable visitor, if he could make up his mind to
elbow a passage among these sea-monsters, was admitted into
an outer office, where he found more of the same species,
explaining their respective wants or grievances to the Vice-
Consul and clerks, while their shipmates awaited their turn
outside the door.   Passing through this exterior court, the
stranger was ushered into an inner privacy, where sat
the Consul himself, ready to give personal attention to
such peculiarly difficult and more important cases as might
demand the exercise of (what we will courteously suppose
to be) his own higher judicial or administrative sagacity.

It was an apartment of very moderate size, painted in imitation of oak, and duskily lighted by two windows looking
across a by-street at the rough brick-side of an immense cotton warehouse, a plainer and uglier structure than ever was
built in America.   On the walls of the room hung a large
map of the United States (as they were, twenty years ago,
but seem little likely to be, twenty years hence), and a similar one of Great Britain, with its territory so provokingly
compact, that we may expect it to sink sooner than sunder.
Farther adornments were some rude engravings of our naval
victories in the War of 1812, together with the Tennessee

---

*[Liverpool was the major port for British export trade with America.
Irving had earlier worked for his brothers' business there, and Melville's
Redburn describes a sailor's disillusioning first voyage to the city.   It was
virtually an Anglo-American connecting link to New York.]

State House, and a Hudson River steamer, and a colored, life-size lithograph of General Taylor, with an honest hideousness of aspect, occupying the place of honor above the mantel-piece. On the top of a bookcase stood a fierce and terrible bust of General Jackson, pilloried in a military collar which rose above his ears, and frowning forth immitigably at any Englishman who might happen to cross the threshold. I am afraid, however, that the truculence of the old General's expression was utterly thrown away on this stolid and obdurate race of men; for, when they occasionally inquired whom this work of art represented, I was mortified to find that the younger ones had never heard of the Battle of New Orleans, and that their elders had either forgotten it altogether, or contrived to misremember, and twist it wrong end foremost into something like an English victory. They have caught from the old Romans (whom they resemble in so many other characteristics) this excellent method of keeping the national glory intact by sweeping all defeats and humiliations clean out of their memory. Nevertheless, my patriotism forbade me to take down either the bust or the pictures, both because it seemed no more than right that an American Consulate (being a little patch of our nationality imbedded into the soil and institutions of England) should fairly represent the American taste in the fine arts, and because these decorations reminded me so delightfully of an old-fashioned American barber's shop.

One truly English object was a barometer hanging on the wall, generally indicating one or another degree of disagreeable weather, and so seldom pointing to Fair, that I began to consider that portion of its circle as made superfluously. The deep chimney, with its grate of bituminous coal, was English too, as was also the chill temperature that sometimes called for a fire at midsummer, and the foggy or smoky atmosphere which often, between November and March, compelled me to set the gas aflame at noonday. I am not aware of omitting anything important in the above descriptive inventory, unless it be some book-shelves filled with octavo volumes of the American Statutes, and a good many pigeon-holes stuffed with dusty communications from former Secretaries of State, and other official documents of similar value, constituting part of the archives of the Consulate, which I might have done my successor a favor by flinging into the coal-grate.   Yes; there was one other article demanding prominent notice: the consular copy of the New Testament, bound in black morocco, and greasy, I fear, with a daily succession of perjured kisses; at least, I can hardly hope that all the ten thousand oaths, administered by me between two breaths, to all sorts of people and on all manner of worldly business, were reckoned by the swearer as if taken at his soul's peril.

Such, in short, was the dusky and stifled chamber in which I spent wearily a considerable portion of more than four good years of my existence. At first, to be quite frank with the reader, I looked upon it as not altogether fit to be tenanted by the commercial representative of so great and prosperous a country as the United States then were; and I should speedily have transferred my headquarters to airier and loftier apartments, except for the prudent consideration that my government would have left me thus to support its dignity at my own personal expense. Besides, a long line of distinguished predecessors, of whom the latest is now a gallant general under the Union banner, had found the locality good enough for them; it might certainly be tolerated, therefore, by an individual so little ambitious of external magnificence as myself. So I settled quietly down, striking some of my roots into such soil as I could find, adapting myself to circumstances, and with so much success, that, though from first to last I hated the very sight of the little room, I should yet have felt a singular kind of reluctance in changing it for a better.

Hither, in the course of my incumbency, came a great variety of visitors, principally Americans, but including almost every other nationality on earth, especially the distressed and downfallen ones, like those of Poland and Hungary.

Italian bandits (for so they looked), proscribed conspirators from Old Spain, Spanish-Americans, Cubans who professed to have stood by Lopez, and narrowly escaped his fate, scarred French soldiers of the Second Republic, — in a word, all sufferers, or pretended ones, in the cause of Liberty, all people homeless in the widest sense, those who never had a country, or had lost it, those whom their native land had impatiently flung off for planning a better system of things than they were born to, — a multitude of these, and, doubtless, an equal number of jail-birds, outwardly of the same feather, sought the American Consulate, in hopes of at least a bit of bread, and, perhaps, to beg a passage to the blessed shores of Freedom. In most cases there was nothing, and in any case distressingly little, to be done for them; neither was I of a proselyting disposition, nor desired to make my Consulate a nucleus for the vagrant discontents of other lands. And yet it was a proud thought, a forcible appeal to the sympathies of an American, that these unfortunates claimed the privileges of citizenship in our Republic on the strength of the very same noble misdemeanors that had rendered them outlaws to their native despotisms. So I gave them what small help I could. Methinks the true patriots and martyr-spirits of the whole world should have been conscious of a pang near the heart, when a deadly blow was aimed at the vitality of a country which they have felt to be their own in the last resort.

As for my countrymen, I grew better acquainted with many of our national characteristics during those four years than in all my preceding life. Whether brought more strikingly out by the contrast with English manners, or that my Yankee friends assumed an extra peculiarity from a sense of defiant patriotism, so it was that their tones, sentiments, and behavior, even their figures and cast of countenance, all seemed chiselled in sharper angles than ever I had imagined them to be at home. It impressed me with an odd idea of having somehow lost the property of my own person, when I occasionally heard one of them speaking of me as

"my Consul"! They often came to the Consulate in parties
of half a dozen or more, on no business whatever, but merely
to subject their public servant to a rigid examination, and
see how he was getting on with his duties. These inter-
views were rather formidable, being characterized by a
certain stiffness which I felt to be sufficiently irksome at the
moment, though it looks laughable enough in the retrospect.
It is my firm belief that these fellow-citizens, possessing a
native tendency to organization, generally halted outside
of the door, to elect a speaker, chairman, or moderator, and
thus approached me with all the formalities of a deputation
from the American people. After salutations on both sides, —
abrupt, awful, and severe on their part, and deprecatory
on mine, — and the national ceremony of shaking hands
being duly gone through with, the interview proceeded by
a series of calm and well-considered questions or remarks
from the spokesman (no other of the guests vouchsafing to
utter a word), and diplomatic responses from the Consul,
who sometimes found the investigation a little more search-
ing than he liked. I flatter myself, however, that, by much
practice, I attained considerable skill in this kind of intercourse, the art of which lies in passing off commonplaces
for new and valuable truths, and talking trash and empti-
ness in such a way that a pretty acute auditor might mistake
it for something solid. If there be any better method of
dealing with such junctures, — when talk is to be created
out of nothing, and within the scope of several minds at once,
so that you cannot apply yourself to your interlocutor's individuality, — I have not learned it.

Sitting, as it were, in the gateway between the Old World
and the New, where the steamers and packets landed the
greater part of our wandering countrymen, and received them
again when their wanderings were done, I saw that no
people on earth have such vagabond habits as ourselves. The
Continental races never travel at all if they can help it; nor
does an Englishman ever think of stirring abroad, unless

he has the money to spare, or proposes to himself some definite advantage from the journey; but it seemed to me that nothing was more common than for a young American deliberately to spend all his resources in an aesthetic peregrination about Europe, returning with pockets nearly empty to begin the world in earnest. It happened, indeed, much oftener than was at all agreeable to myself, that their funds held out just long enough to bring them to the door of my Consulate, where they entered as if with an undeniable right to its shelter and protection, and required at my hands to be sent home again. In my first simplicity, — finding them gentlemanly in manners, passably educated, and only tempted a little beyond their means by a laudable desire of improving and refining themselves, or perhaps for the sake of getting better artistic instruction in music, painting, or sculpture than our country could supply, — I sometimes took charge of them on my private responsibility, since our government gives itself no trouble about its stray children, except the seafaring class. But, after a few such experiments, discovering that none of these estimable and ingenuous young men, however trustworthy they might appear ever dreamed of reimbursing the Consul, I deemed it expedient to take another course with them. Applying myself to some friendly shipmaster, I engaged homeward passages on their behalf, with the understanding that they were to make themselves serviceable on shipboard; and I remember several very pathetic appeals from painters and musicians, touching the damage which their artistic fingers were likely to incur from handling the ropes. But my observation of so many heavier troubles left me very little tenderness for their finger ends. In time I grew to be reasonably hard-hearted, though it never was quite possible to leave a countryman with no shelter save an English poorhouse, when, as he invariably averred, he had only to set foot on his native soil to be possessed of ample funds. It was my ultimate conclusion, however, that American ingenuity may be pretty safely left to itself,

and that, one way or another, a Yankee vagabond is certain to turn up at his own threshold, if he has any, without
help of a Consul, and perhaps be taught a lesson of foresight that may profit him hereafter.

Among these stray Americans, I met with no other case
so remarkable as that of an old man, who was in the habit
of visiting me once in a few months, and soberly affirmed
that he had been wandering about England more than a
quarter of a century (precisely twenty-seven years, I think),
and all the while doing his utmost to get home again.
Herman Melville, in his excellent novel or biography of
"Israel Potter," has an idea somewhat similar to this. The
individual now in question was a mild and patient, but very
ragged and pitiable old fellow, shabby beyond description,
lean and hungry-looking, but with a large and somewhat red
nose. He made no complaint of his ill-fortune, but only
repeated in a quiet voice, with a pathos of which he was
himself evidently unconscious, "I want to get home to Ninety-
Second Street, Philadelphia." He described himself as a
printer by trade, and said that he had come over when he
was a younger man, in the hope of bettering himself, and
for the sake of seeing the Old Country, but had never since
been rich enough to pay his homeward passage. His manner and accent did not quite convince me that he was an
American, and I told him so; but he steadfastly affirmed,
"Sir, I was born and have lived in Ninety-Second Street,
Philadelphia," and then went on to describe some public
edifices and other local objects with which he used to be
familiar, adding, with a simplicity that touched me very
closely, "Sir, I had rather be there than here!" Though
I still manifested a lingering doubt, he took no offence,
replying with the same mild depression as at first, and insisting again and again on Ninety-Second Street. Up to the
time when I saw him, he still got a little occasional job-
work at his trade, but subsisted mainly on such charity as
he met with in his wanderings, shifting from place to place

continually, and asking assistance to convey him to his native land. Possibly he was an impostor, one of the multitudinous shapes of English vagabondism, and told his falsehood with such powerful simplicity, because, by many repetitions, he had convinced himself of its truth. But if, as I believe, the tale was fact, how very strange and sad was this old man's fate! Homeless on a foreign shore, looking always towards his country, coming again and again to the point whence so many were setting sail for it, — so many who would soon tread in Ninety-Second Street, — losing, in this long series of years, some of the distinctive characteristics of an American, and at last dying and surrendering his clay to be a portion of the soil whence he could not escape in his lifetime.

He appeared to see that he had moved me, but did not attempt to press his advantage with any new argument, or any varied form of entreaty. He had but scanty and scattered thoughts in his gray head, and in the intervals of those, like the refrain of an old ballad, came in the monotonous burden of his appeal, "If I could only find myself in Ninety-Second Street, Philadelphia!" But even his desire of getting home had ceased to be an ardent one (if, indeed, it had not always partaken of the dreamy sluggishness of his character), although it remained his only locomotive impulse, and perhaps the sole principle of life that kept his blood from actual torpor.

The poor old fellow's story seemed to me almost as worthy of being chanted in immortal song as that of Odysseus or Evangeline. I took his case into deep consideration, but dared not incur the moral responsibility of sending him across the sea, at his age, after so many years of exile, when the very tradition of him had passed away, to find his friends dead, or forgetful, or irretrievably vanished, and the whole country become more truly a foreign land to him than England was now — and even Ninety-Second Street, in the weed-like decay and growth of our localities, made over anew and grown unrecognizable by his old eyes. That street, so patiently longed for, had transferred itself to the New Jerusalem, and he must seek it there, contenting his slow heart, meanwhile, with the smoke-begrimed thoroughfares of English towns, or the green country lanes and by-paths with which his wanderings had made him familiar; for doubtless he had a beaten track, and was the "long-remembered beggar" now, with food and a roughly hospitable greeting ready for him at many a farm-house door, and his choice of lodging under a score of haystacks. In America, nothing awaited him but that worst form of disappointment which comes under the guise of a long-cherished and late-accomplished purpose, and then a year or two of dry and barren sojourn in an almshouse, and death among strangers at last, where he had imagined a circle of familiar faces. So I contented myself with giving him alms, which he thankfully accepted, and went away with bent shoulders and an aspect of gentle forlornness; returning upon his orbit, however, after a few months, to tell the same sad and quiet story of his abode in England for more than twenty-seven years, in all which time he had been endeavoring, and still endeavored as patiently as ever, to find his way home to Ninety-Second Street, Philadelphia.

I recollect another case, of a more ridiculous order, but still with a foolish kind of pathos entangled in it, which impresses me now more forcibly than it did at the moment. One day, a queer, stupid, good-natured, fat-faced individual came into my private room, dressed in a sky-blue, cut-away coat and mixed trousers, both garments worn and shabby, and rather too small for his overgrown bulk. After a little preliminary talk, he turned out to be a country shopkeeper (from Connecticut, I think), who had left a flourishing business, and come over to England purposely and solely to have an interview with the Queen. Some years before he had named his two children, one for her Majesty and the other for Prince Albert, and had transmitted photographs of the little people, as well as of his wife and himself, to the illustrious godmother. The Queen had gratefully acknowledged the favor in a letter under the hand of her private secretary. Now the shopkeeper, like a great many other Americans, had long cherished a fantastic notion that he was one of the rightful heirs of a rich English estate; and on the strength of her Majesty's letter and the hopes of royal patronage which it inspired, he had shut up his little country-store and come over to claim his inheritance. On the voyage, a German fellow-passenger had relieved him of his money on pretence of getting it favorably exchanged, and had disappeared immediately on the ship's arrival; so that the poor fellow was compelled to pawn all his clothes, except the remarkably shabby ones in which I beheld him, and in which (as he himself hinted, with a melancholy, yet good-natured smile) he did not look altogether fit to see the Queen. I agreed with him that the bobtailed coat and mixed trousers constituted a very odd-looking court-dress, and suggested that it was doubtless his present purpose to get back to Connecticut as fast as possible. But no! The resolve to see the Queen was as strong in him as ever; and it was marvellous the pertinacity with which he clung to it amid raggedness and starvation, and the earnestness of his supplication that I would supply him with funds for a suitable appearance at Windsor Castle.

I never had so satisfactory a perception of a complete booby before in my life; and it caused me to feel kindly towards him, and yet impatient and exasperated on behalf of common-sense, which could not possibly tolerate that such an unimaginable donkey should exist. I laid his absurdity before him in the very plainest terms, but without either exciting his anger or shaking his resolution. "Oh my dear man," quoth he, with good-natured, placid, simple, and tearful stubbornness, "if you could but enter into my feelings and see the matter from beginning to end as I see it!" To confess the truth, I have since felt that I was hard-hearted to the poor simpleton, and that there was more weight in his remonstrance than I chose to be sensible of, at the time; for, like many men who have been in the habit of making playthings or tools of their imagination and sensibility, I was too rigidly tenacious of what was reasonable in the affairs of real life. And even absurdity has its rights, when, as in this case, it has absorbed a human being's entire nature and purposes. I ought to have transmitted him to Mr. Buchanan, in London, who, being a good-natured old gentleman, and anxious, just then, to gratify the universal Yankee nation, might, for the joke's sake, have got him admittance to the Queen, who had fairly laid herself open to his visit, and has received hundreds of our countrymen on infinitely slighter grounds. But I was inexorable, being turned to flint by the insufferable proximity of a fool, and refused to interfere with his business in any way except to procure him a passage home. I can see his face of mild, ridiculous despair at this moment, and appreciate, better than I could then, how awfully cruel he must have felt my obduracy to be. For years and years, the idea of an interview with Queen Victoria had haunted his poor foolish mind; and now, when he really stood on English ground, and the palace-door was hanging ajar for him, he was expected to turn back, a penniless and bamboozled simpleton, merely because an iron-hearted Consul refused to lend him thirty shillings (so low had his demand ultimately sunk) to buy a second-class ticket on the rail for London!

He visited the Consulate several times afterwards, subsisting on a pittance that I allowed him in the hope of gradually starving him back to Connecticut, assailing me with the old petition at every opportunity, looking shabbier at every visit, but still thoroughly good-tempered, mildly stubborn, and smiling through his tears, not without a perception of the ludicrousness of his own position. Finally, he disappeared altogether, and whither he had wandered, and whether he ever saw the Queen, or wasted quite away in the endeavor, I never knew; but I remember unfolding the "Times," about that period, with a daily dread of reading an account of a ragged Yankee's attempt to steal into Buckingham Palace, and how he smiled tearfully at his captors, and besought them to introduce him to her Majesty. I submit to Mr. Secretary Seward that he ought to make diplomatic remonstrances to the British Ministry, and require them to take such order that the Queen shall not any longer bewilder the wits of our poor compatriots by responding to their epistles and thanking them for their photographs.

One circumstance in the foregoing incident — I mean the unhappy storekeeper's notion of establishing his claim to an English estate — was common to a great many other applications, personal or by letter, with which I was favored by my countrymen. The cause of this peculiar insanity lies deep in the Anglo-American heart. After all these bloody wars and vindictive animosities, we have still an unspeakable yearning towards England. When our forefathers left the old home, they pulled up many of their roots, but trailed along with them others, which were never snapt asunder by the tug of such a lengthening distance, nor have been torn out of the original soil by the violence of subsequent struggles, nor severed by the edge of the sword. Even so late as these days, they remain entangled with our heart-strings, and might often have influenced our national cause like the tiller-ropes of a ship, if the rough gripe of England had been capable of managing so sensitive a kind of machinery. It has required nothing less than the boorishness, the stolidity, the self-sufficiency, the contemptuous jealousy, the half-sagacity, invariably blind of one eye and often distorted of the other, that characterize this strange people, to compel us to be a great nation in our own right, instead of continuing virtually, if not in name, a province of their small island. What pains did they take to shake us off, and have ever since taken to keep us wide apart from them! It might seem their folly, but was really their fate, or, rather, the Providence of God, who has doubtless a work for us to do, in which the massive materiality of the English character would have been too ponderous a dead-weight upon our progress. And, besides, if England had been wise enough to twine our new vigor round about her ancient strength, her power would have been too firmly established ever to yield, in its due season, to the otherwise immutable law of imperial vicissitude. The earth might then have beheld the intolerable spectacle of a sovereignty and institutions, imperfect, but indestructible.

Nationally, there has ceased to be any peril of so inauspicious and yet outwardly attractive an amalgamation. But as an individual, the American is often conscious of the deep-rooted sympathies that belong more fitly to times gone by, and feels a blind pathetic tendency to wander back again, which makes itself evident in such wild dreams as I have alluded to above, about English inheritances. A mere coincidence of names (the Yankee one, perhaps, having been assumed by legislative permission), a supposititious pedigree, a silver mug on which an anciently engraved coat of arms has been half scrubbed out, a seal with an uncertain crest, an old yellow letter or document in faded ink, the more scantily legible the better, — rubbish of this kind, found in a neglected drawer, has been potent enough to turn the brain of many an honest Republican, especially if assisted by an advertisement for lost heirs, cut out of a British newspaper. There is no estimating or believing, till we come into a position to know it, what foolery lurks latent in the breasts of very sensible people. Remembering such sober extravagances, I should not be at all surprised to find that I am myself guilty of some unsuspected absurdity, that may appear to me the most substantial trait in my character.

I might fill many pages with instances of this diseased American appetite for English soil. A respectable-looking woman, well advanced in life, of sour aspect, exceedingly homely, but decidedly New-Englandish in figure and manners, came to my office with a great bundle of documents, at the very first glimpse of which I apprehended something terrible. Nor was I mistaken. The bundle contained evidences of her indubitable claim to the site on which Castle Street, the Town Hall, the Exchange, and all the principal business part of Liverpool have long been situated; and, with considerable peremptoriness, the good lady signified her expectation that I should take charge of her suit, and prosecute it to judgment; not, however, on the equitable condition of receiving half the value of the property recovered (which, in case of complete success, would have made both of us ten or twenty fold millionnaires), but without recompense or reimbursement of legal expenses, solely as an incident of my official duty. Another time came two ladies, bearing a letter of emphatic introduction from his Excellency the Governor of their native State, who testified in most satisfactory terms to their social respectability. They were claimants of a great estate in Cheshire, and announced themselves as blood-relatives of Queen Victoria, — a point, however, which they deemed it expedient to keep in the background until their territorial rights should be established, apprehending that the Lord High Chancellor might otherwise be less likely to come to a fair decision in respect to them, from a probable disinclination to admit new members into the royal kin. Upon my honor, I imagine that they had an eye to the possibility of the eventual succession of one or both of them to the crown of Great Britain through superiority of title over the Brunswick line; although, being maiden ladies, like their predecessor Elizabeth, they could hardly have hoped to establish a lasting dynasty upon the throne. It proves, I trust, a certain disinterestedness on my part, that, encountering them thus in the dawn of their fortunes, I forbore to put in a plea for a future dukedom.

Another visitor of the same class was a gentleman of refined manners, handsome figure, and remarkably intellectual aspect. Like many men of an adventurous cast, he had

so quiet a deportment, and such an apparent disinclination
to general sociability, that you would have fancied him
moving always along some peaceful and secluded walk of
life.   Yet, literally from his first hour, he had been tossed
upon the surges of a most varied and tumultuous existence,
having been born at sea, of American parentage, but on
board of a Spanish vessel, and spending many of the subsequent years in voyages, travels, and outlandish incidents
and vicissitudes, which, methought, had hardly been par-
alleled since the days of Gulliver or De Foe.   When his dignified reserve was overcome, he had the faculty of narrating
these adventures with wonderful eloquence, working up his
descriptive sketches with such intuitive perception of the
picturesque points that the whole was thrown forward with
a positively illusive effect, like matters of your own visual
experience.   In fact, they were so admirably done that I
could never more than half believe them, because the genuine affairs of life are not apt to transact themselves so
artistically.   Many of his scenes were laid in the East, and
among those seldom-visited archipelagoes of the Indian
Ocean, so that there was an Oriental fragrance breathing
through his talk, and an odor of the Spice Islands still lingering in his garments.   He had much to say of the delightful
qualities of the Malay pirates, who, indeed, carry on a pred-
atory warfare against the ships of all civilized nations, and
cut every Christian throat among their prisoners; but (except for deeds of that character, which are the rule and
habit of their life, and matter of religion and conscience
with them) they are a gentle-natured people, of primitive
innocence and integrity.

But his best story was about a race of men (if men they
were) who seemed so fully to realize Swift's wicked fable of
the Yahoos, that my friend was much exercised with psy-
chological speculations whether or no they had any souls.
They dwelt in the wilds of Ceylon, like other savage beasts,
hairy, and spotted with tufts of fur, filthy, shameless, weap-

onless (though warlike in their individual bent), tool-less,
houseless, language-less, except for a few guttural sounds,
hideously dissonant, whereby they held some rudest kind
of communication among themselves. They lacked both
memory and foresight, and were wholly destitute of government, social institutions, or law or rulership of any description, except the immediate tyranny of the strongest; radi-
cally untamable, moreover, save that the people of the country managed to subject a few of the less ferocious and stupid
ones to outdoor servitude among their other cattle. They
were beastly in almost all their attributes, and that to such
a degree that the observer, losing sight of any link betwixt
them and manhood, could generally witness their brutali-
ties without greater horror than at those of some disagreeable quadruped in a menagerie. And yet, at times, comparing what were the lowest general traits in his own race
with what was highest in these abominable monsters, he
found a ghastly similitude that half compelled him to
recognize them as human brethren.

After these Gulliverian researches, my agreeable acquaintance had fallen under the ban of the Dutch government,
and had suffered (this, at least, being matter of fact) nearly
two years' imprisonment, with confiscation of a large amount
of property, for which Mr. Belmont, our minister at the
Hague, had just made a peremptory demand of reimbursement and damages. Meanwhile, since arriving in England
on his way to the United States, he had been providentially
led to inquire into the circumstances of his birth on shipboard, and had discovered that not himself alone, but another
baby, had come into the world during the same voyage of
the prolific vessel, and that there were almost irrefragable
reasons for believing that these two children had been as-
signed to the wrong mothers. Many reminiscences of his
early days confirmed him in the idea that his nominal parents were aware of the exchange. The family to which he
felt authorized to attribute his lineage was that of a noble-

man, in the picture-gallery of whose country-seat (whence
if I mistake not, our adventurous friend had just returned)
he had discovered a portrait bearing a striking resemblance
to himself. As soon as he should have reported the out-
rageous action of the Dutch government to President Pierce
and the Secretary of State, and recovered the confiscated
property, he purposed to return to England and establish
his claim to the nobleman's title and estate.

I had accepted his Oriental fantasies (which, indeed, to
do him justice, have been recorded by scientific societies
among the genuine phenomena of natural history), not as
matters of indubitable credence, but as allowable specimens of
an imaginative traveller's vivid coloring and rich embroidery
on the coarse texture and dull neutral tints of truth. The English romance was among the latest communications that he intrusted to my private ear; and as soon as I heard the first
chapter, — so wonderfully akin to what I might have wrought
out of my own head, not unpractised in such figments, — I
began to repent having made myself responsible for the future nobleman's passage homeward in the next Collins
steamer. Nevertheless, should his English rent-roll fall a
little behindhand, his Dutch claim for a hundred thousand
dollars was certainly in the hands of our government, and
might at least be valuable to the extent of thirty pounds,
which I had engaged to pay on his behalf. But I have reason
to fear that his Dutch riches turned out to be Dutch gilt
or fairy gold, and his English country-seat a mere castle
in the air, — which I exceedingly regret, for he was a delightful companion and a very gentlemanly man.

A Consul, in his position of universal responsibility, the
general adviser and helper, sometimes finds himself compelled to assume the guardianship of personages who, in
their own sphere, are supposed capable of superintending
the highest interests of whole communities. An elderly
Irishman, a naturalized citizen, once put the desire and expectation of all our penniless vagabonds into a very suit-

able phrase, by pathetically entreating me to be a "father to him"; and, simple as I sit scribbling here, I have acted a father's part, not only by scores of such unthrifty old children as himself, but by a progeny of far loftier pretensions. It may be well for persons who are conscious of any radical weakness in their character, any besetting sin, any unlawful propensity, any unhallowed impulse, which (while surrounded with the manifold restraints that protect a man from that treacherous and lifelong enemy, his lower self, in the circle of society where he is at home) they may have succeeded in keeping under the lock and key of strictest propriety, — it may be well for them, before seeking the perilous freedom of a distant land, released from the watchful eyes of neighborhoods and coteries, lightened of that wearisome burden, an immaculate name, and blissfully obscure after years of local prominence, — it may be well for such individuals to know that when they set foot on a foreign shore, the long-imprisoned Evil, scenting a wild license in the unaccustomed atmosphere, is apt to grow riotous in its iron cage. It rattles the rusty barriers with gigantic turbulence, and if there be an infirm joint anywhere in the framework, it breaks madly forth, compressing the mischief of a lifetime into a little space.

A parcel of letters had been accumulating at the Consulate for two or three weeks, directed to a certain Doctor of Divinity, who had left America by a sailing-packet and was still upon the sea. In due time, the vessel arrived, and the reverend Doctor paid me a visit. He was a fine-looking middle-aged gentleman, a perfect model of clerical propriety, scholar-like, yet with the air of a man of the world rather than a student, though overspread with the graceful sanctity of a popular metropolitan divine, a part of whose duty it might be to exemplify the natural accordance between Christianity and good-breeding. He seemed a little excited, as an American is apt to be on first arriving in England, but conversed with intelligence as well as animation, making himself so agreeable that his visit stood out in considerable relief from the monotony of my daily commonplace. As I learned from authentic sources, he was somewhat distinguished in his own region for fervor and eloquence in the pulpit, but was now compelled to relinquish it temporarily for the purpose of renovating his impaired health by an extensive tour in Europe. Promising to dine with me, he took up his bundles of letters and went away.

The Doctor, however, failed to make his appearance at dinner-time, or to apologize the next day for his absence; and in the course of a day or two more, I forgot all about him, concluding that he must have set forth on his Continental travels, the plan of which he had sketched out at our interview. But, by and by, I received a call from the master of the vessel in which he had arrived. He was in some alarm about his passenger, whose luggage remained on shipboard, but of whom nothing had been heard or seen since the moment of his departure from the Consulate. We conferred together, the captain and I, about the expediency of setting the police on the traces (if any were to be found) of our vanished friend; but it struck me that the good captain was singularly reticent, and that there was something a little mysterious in a few points that he hinted at rather than expressed; so that, scrutinizing the affair carefully, I surmised that the intimacy of life on shipboard might have taught him more about the reverend gentleman than, for some reason or other, he deemed it prudent to reveal. At home, in our native country, I would have looked to the Doctor's personal safety and left his reputation to take care of itself, knowing that the good fame of a thousand saintly clergymen would amply dazzle out any lamentable spot on a single brother's character. But in scornful and invidious England, on the idea that the credit of the sacred office was measurably intrusted to my discretion, I could not endure, for the sake of American Doctors of Divinity generally, that this particular Doctor should cut an ignoble figure in the police reports of the English newspapers, except at the last necessity. The clerical body, I flatter myself, will acknowledge that I acted on their own principle. Besides, it was now too late; the mischief and violence, if any had been impending, were not of a kind which it requires the better part of a week to perpetrate; and to sum up the entire matter, I felt certain, from a good deal of somewhat similar experience, that, if the missing Doctor still breathed this vital air, he would turn up at the Consulate as soon as his money should be stolen or spent.

Precisely a week after this reverend person's disappearance, there came to my office a tall, middle-aged gentleman in a blue military surtout, braided at the seams, but out at elbows, and as shabby as if the wearer had been bivouacking in it throughout a Crimean campaign. It was buttoned up to the very chin, except where three or four of the buttons were lost; nor was there any glimpse of a white shirt-collar illuminating the rusty black cravat. A grisly mustache was just beginning to roughen the stranger's upper lip. He looked disreputable to the last degree, but still had a ruined air of good society glimmering about him, like a few specks of polish on a sword-blade that has lain corroding in a mud-puddle. I took him to be some American marine officer, of dissipated habits, or perhaps a cashiered British major, stumbling into the wrong quarters through the unrectified bewilderment of the last night's debauch. He greeted me, however, with polite familiarity, as though we had been previously acquainted; whereupon I drew coldly back (as sensible people naturally do, whether from strangers or former friends, when too evidently at odds with fortune) and requested to know who my visitor might be, and what was his business at the Consulate. "Am I then so changed?" he exclaimed with a vast depth of tragic intonation; and after a little blind and bewildered talk, behold! the truth flashed upon me. It was the Doctor of Divinity! If I had meditated a scene or a *coup de theâtre,* I could not have contrived a

more effectual one than by this simple and genuine difficulty
of recognition. The poor Divine must have felt that he had
lost his personal identity through the misadventures of one
little week. And, to say the truth, he did look as if, like
Job, on account of his especial sanctity, he had been delivered over to the direst temptations of Satan, and proving
weaker than the man of Uz, the Arch Enemy had been
empowered to drag him through Tophet, transforming him,
in the process, from the most decorous clergyman into the
rowdiest and dirtiest of disbanded officers. I never fath-
omed the mystery of his military costume, but conjectured
that a lurking sense of fitness had induced him to exchange
his clerical garments for this habit of a sinner; nor can I
tell precisely into what pitfall, not more of vice than terrible calamity, he had precipitated himself, — being more
than satisfied to know that the outcasts of society can sink
no lower than this poor, desecrated wretch had sunk.

The opportunity, I presume, does not often happen to a
layman, of administering moral and religious reproof to
a Doctor of Divinity; but finding the occasion thrust upon
me, and the hereditary Puritan waxing strong in my breast,
I deemed it a matter of conscience not to let it pass entirely
unimproved. The truth is, I was unspeakably shocked and
disgusted. Not, however, that I was then to learn that
clergymen are made of the same flesh and blood as other
people, and perhaps lack one small safeguard which the rest
of us possess, because they are aware of their own pecca-
bility, and therefore cannot look up to the clerical class for
the proof of the possibility of a pure life on earth, with such
reverential confidence as we are prone to do. But I remembered the innocent faith of my boyhood, and the good old
silver-headed clergyman, who seemed to me as much a saint
then on earth as he is now in heaven, and partly for whose
sake, through all these darkening years, I retain a devout,
though not intact nor unwavering respect for the entire
fraternity. What a hideous wrong, therefore, had the back-

slider inflicted on his brethren, and still more on me, who much needed whatever fragments of broken reverence (broken, not as concerned religion, but its earthly institutions and professors) it might yet be possible to patch into a sacred image! Should all pulpits and communion-tables have thenceforth a stain upon them, and the guilty one go unrebuked for it? So I spoke to the unhappy man as I never thought myself warranted in speaking to any other mortal, hitting him hard, doing my utmost to find out his vulnerable part, and prick him into the depths of it. And not without more effect than I had dreamed of, or desired!

No doubt, the novelty of the Doctor's reversed position, thus standing up to receive such a fulmination as the clergy have heretofore arrogated the exclusive right of inflicting, might give additional weight and sting to the words which I found utterance for. But there was another reason (which, had I in the least suspected it, would have closed my lips at once) for his feeling morbidly sensitive to the cruel rebuke that I administered. The unfortunate man had come to me, laboring under one of the consequences of his riotous outbreak, in the shape of delirium tremens; he bore a hell within the compass of his own breast, all the torments of which blazed up with tenfold inveteracy when I thus took upon myself the Devil's office of stirring up the red-hot embers. His emotions, as well as the external movement and expression of them by voice, countenance, and gesture, were terribly exaggerated by the tremendous vibration of nerves resulting from the disease. It was the deepest tragedy I ever witnessed. I know sufficiently, from that one experience, how a condemned soul would manifest its agonies; and for the future, if I have anything to do with sinners, I mean to operate upon them through sympathy and not rebuke. What had I to do with rebuking him? The disease, long latent in his heart, had shown itself in a frightful eruption on the surface of his life. That was all! Is it a thing to scold the sufferer for?

To conclude this wretched story, the poor Doctor of Divinity, having been robbed of all his money in this little airing beyond the limits of propriety, was easily persuaded to give up the intended tour and return to his bereaved flock, who, very probably, were thereafter conscious of an increased unction in his soul-stirring eloquence, without suspecting the awful depths into which their pastor had dived in quest of it. His voice is now silent. I leave it to members of his own profession to decide whether it was better for him thus to sin outright, and so to be let into the miserable secret what manner of man he was, or to have gone through life outwardly unspotted, making the first discovery of his latent evil at the judgment-seat. It has occurred to me that his dire calamity, as both he and I regarded it, might have been the only method by which precisely such a man as himself, and so situated, could be redeemed. He has learned, ere now, how that matter stood.

For a man, with a natural tendency to meddle with other people's business, there could not possibly be a more congenial sphere than the Liverpool Consulate. For myself, I had never been in the habit of feeling that I could sufficiently comprehend any particular conjunction of circumstances with human character, to justify me in thrusting in my awkward agency among the intricate and unintelligible machinery of Providence. I have always hated to give advice, especially when there is a prospect of its being taken. It is only one-eyed people who love to advise, or have any spontaneous promptitude of action. When a man opens both his eyes, he generally sees about as many reasons for acting in any one way as in any other, and quite as many for acting in neither; and is therefore likely to leave his friends to regulate their own conduct, and also to remain quiet as regards his especial affairs till necessity shall prick him onward. Nevertheless, the world and individuals flourish upon a constant succession of blunders. The secret of English practical success lies in their characteristic faculty of shutting one eye, whereby they get so distinct and decided a view of what immediately concerns them that they go stumbling towards it over a hundred insurmountable obstacles, and achieve a magnificent triumph without ever being aware of half its difficulties. If General McClellan could but have shut his left eye, the right one would long ago have guided us into Richmond. Meanwhile, I have strayed far away from the Consulate, where, as I was about to say, I was compelled, in spite of my disinclination, to impart both advice and assistance in multifarious affairs that did not personally concern me, and presume that I effected about as little mischief as other men in similar contingencies. The duties of the office carried me to prisons, police-courts, hospitals, lunatic asylums, coroner's inquests, death-beds, funerals, and brought me in contact with insane people, criminals, ruined speculators, wild adventurers, diplomatists, brother-consuls, and all manner of simpletons and unfortunates, in greater number and variety than I had ever dreamed of as pertaining to America; in addition to whom there was an equivalent multitude of English rogues, dexterously counterfeiting the genuine Yankee article. It required great discrimination not to be taken in by these last-mentioned scoundrels; for they knew how to imitate our national traits, had been at great pains to instruct themselves as regarded American localities, and were not readily to be caught by a cross-examination as to the topographical features, public institutions, or prominent inhabitants of the places where they pretended to belong. The best shibboleth I ever hit upon lay in the pronunciation of the word "been" which the English invariably make to rhyme with "green," and we Northerners, at least (in accordance, I think, with the custom of Shakespeare's time), universally pronounce "bin."

All the matters that I have been treating of, however, were merely incidental, and quite distinct from the real business of the office. A great part of the wear and tear of mind and temper resulted from the bad relations between the seamen and officers of American ships. Scarcely a morning passed, but that some sailor came to show the marks of his ill-usage on shipboard. Often, it was a whole crew of them, each with his broken head or livid bruise, and all testifying with one voice to a constant series of savage outrages during the voyage; or, it might be, they laid an accusation of actual murder, perpetrated by the first or second officers, with many blows of steel-knuckles, a rope's end, or a marline-spike, or by the captain, in the twinkling of an eye, with a shot of his pistol. Taking the seamen's view of the case, you would suppose that the gibbet was hungry for the murderers. Listening to the captain's defence, you would seem to discover that he and his officers were the humanest of mortals, but were driven to a wholesome severity by the mutinous conduct of the crew, who, moreover, had themselves slain their comrade in the drunken riot and confusion of the first day or two after they were shipped. Looked at judicially, there appeared to be no right side to the matter, nor any right side possible in so thoroughly vicious a system as that of the American mercantile marine. The Consul could do little, except to take depositions, hold forth the greasy Testament to be profaned anew with perjured kisses, and, in a few instances of murder or manslaughter, carry the case before an English magistrate, who generally decided that the evidence was too contradictory to authorize the transmission of the accused for trial in America. The newspapers all over England contained paragraphs, inveighing against the cruelties of American shipmasters. The British Parliament took up the matter (for nobody is so humane as John Bull, when his benevolent propensities are to be gratified by finding fault with his neighbor), and caused Lord John Russell to remonstrate with our government on the outrages for which it was responsible before the world, and which it failed to prevent or punish. The American Secretary of State, old General Cass, responded, with perfectly astounding ignorance of the subject, to the effect that the statements of outrages had probably been exaggerated, that the present laws of the United States were quite adequate to deal with them, and that the interference of the British Minister was uncalled for.

The truth is, that the state of affairs was really very horrible, and could be met by no laws at that time (or I presume now) in existence. I once thought of writing a pamphlet on the subject, but quitted the Consulate before finding time to effect my purpose; and all that phase of my life immediately assumed so dream-like a consistency that I despaired of making it seem solid or tangible to the public. And now it looks distant and dim, like troubles of a century ago. The origin of the evil lay in the character of the seamen, scarcely any of whom were American, but the off-scourings and refuse of all the seaports of the world, such stuff as piracy is made of, together with a considerable intermixture of returning emigrants, and a sprinkling of absolutely kidnapped American citizens. Even with such material the ships were very inadequately manned. The shipmaster found himself upon the deep, with a vast responsibility of property and human life upon his hands, and no means of salvation except by compelling his inefficient and demoralized crew to heavier exertions than could reasonably be required of the same number of able seamen. By law he had been intrusted with no discretion of judicious punishment; he therefore habitually left the whole matter of discipline to his irresponsible mates, men often of scarcely a superior quality to the crew. Hence ensued a great mass of petty outrages, unjustifiable assaults, shameful indignities, and nameless cruelty, demoralizing alike to the perpetrators and the sufferers; these enormities fell into the ocean between the two countries, and could be punished in neither. Many miserable stories come back upon my memory as I write; wrongs that were immense, but for which nobody could be held responsible, and which, indeed, the closer you looked into them, the more they lost the aspect of wilful misdoing, and assumed that of an inevitable calamity. It was the fault of a system, the misfortune of an individual. Be that as it may, however, there will be no possibility of dealing effectually with these troubles as long as we deem it inconsistent with our national dignity or interests to allow the English courts, under such restrictions as may seem fit, a jurisdiction over offences perpetrated on board our vessels in mid-ocean.

In such a life as this, the American shipmaster develops himself into a man of iron energies, dauntless courage, and inexhaustible resource, at the expense, it must be acknowledged, of some of the higher and gentler traits which might do him excellent service in maintaining his authority. The class has deteriorated of late years on account of the narrower field of selection, owing chiefly to the diminution of that excellent body of respectably educated New England seamen, from the flower of whom the officers used to be recruited. Yet I found them, in many cases, very agreeable and intelligent companions, with less nonsense about them than landsmen usually have, eschewers of fine-spun theories, delighting in square and tangible ideas, but occasionally infested with prejudices that stuck to their brains like barnacles to a ship's bottom. I never could flatter myself that I was a general favorite with them. One or two, perhaps, even now, would scarcely meet me on amicable terms. Endowed universally with a great pertinacity of will, they especially disliked the interference of a consul with their management on shipboard; notwithstanding which I thrust in my very limited authority at every available opening, and did the utmost that lay in my power, though with lamentably small effect, towards enforcing a better kind of discipline. They thought, no doubt (and on plausible grounds enough, but scarcely appreciating just that one little grain of hard New England sense, oddly thrown in among the flimsier composition of the Consul's character), that he, a landsman, a bookman, and, as people said of him, a fanciful recluse, could not possibly understand anything of the difficulties or the necessities of a shipmaster's position. But their cold regards were rather acceptable than otherwise, for it is exceedingly awkward to assume a judicial austerity in the morning towards a man with whom you have been hobnobbing over night.

With the technical details of the business of that great Consulate (for great it then was, though now, I fear, wofully fallen off, and perhaps never to be revived in anything like its former extent), I did not much interfere. They could safely be left to the treatment of two as faithful, upright, and competent subordinates, both Englishmen, as ever a man was fortunate enough to meet with, in a line of life altogether new and strange to him. I had come over with instructions to supply both their places with Americans, but, possessing a happy faculty of knowing my own interest and the public's, I quietly kept hold of them, being little inclined to open the consular doors to a spy of the State Department or an intriguer for my own office. The venerable Vice-Consul, Mr. Pearce, had witnessed the successive arrivals of a score of newly-appointed Consuls, shadowy and short-lived dignitaries, and carried his reminiscences back to the epoch of Consul Maury, who was appointed by Washington, and has acquired almost the grandeur of a mythical personage in the annals of the Consulate. The principal clerk, Mr. Wilding, who has since succeeded to the Vice-Consulship, was a man of English integrity, — not that the English are more honest than ourselves, but only there is a certain sturdy reliableness common among them, which we do not quite so invariably manifest in just these subordinate positions, — of English integrity, combined with American acuteness of intellect, quick-wittedness, and diversity of talent. It seemed an immense pity that he should wear out his life at a desk, without a step in advance from year's end to year's end, when, had it been his luck to be born on our side of the water, his bright faculties and clear prob-

ity would have insured him eminent success in whatever path
he might adopt. Meanwhile, it would have been a sore
mischance to me, had any better fortune on his part deprived
me of Mr. Wilding's services.

A fair amount of common-sense, some acquaintance with
the United States Statutes, an insight into character, a tact
of management, a general knowledge of the world, and a
reasonable but not too inveterately decided preference for his
own will and judgment over those of interested people, —
these natural attributes and moderate acquirements will
enable a consul to perform many of his duties respectably,
but not to dispense with a great variety of other qualifications, only attainable by long experience. Yet, I think, few
consuls are so well accomplished. An appointment of whatever grade, in the diplomatic or consular service of America,
is too often what the English call a "job"; that is to say, it
is made on private and personal grounds, without a paramount eye to the public good or the gentleman's especial
fitness for the position. It is not too much to say (of course
allowing for a brilliant exception here and there), that an
American never is thoroughly qualified for a foreign post,
nor has time to make himself so, before the revolution of
the political wheel discards him from his office. Our country wrongs itself by permitting such a system of unsuitable
appointments, and, still more, of removals for no cause,
just when the incumbent might be beginning to ripen into
usefulness. Mere ignorance of official detail is of comparatively small moment; though it is considered indispensable,
I presume, that a man in any private capacity shall be thoroughly acquainted with the machinery and operation of his
business, and shall not necessarily lose his position on having attained such knowledge. But there are so many more
important things to be thought of, in the qualifications of a
foreign resident, that his technical dexterity or clumsiness
is hardly worth mentioning.

One great part of a consul's duty, for example, should

consist in building up for himself a recognized position in the society where he resides, so that his local influence might be felt in behalf of his own country, and, so far as they are compatible (as they generally are to the utmost extent), for the interests of both nations. The foreign city should know that it has a permanent inhabitant and a hearty well-wisher in him. There are many conjunctures (and one of them is now upon us) where a long-established, honored, and trusted American citizen, holding a public position under our government in such a town as Liverpool, might go far towards swaying and directing the sympathies of the inhabitants. He might throw his own weight into the balance against mischief-makers; he might have set his foot on the first little spark of malignant purpose, which the next wind may blow into a national war. But we wilfully give up all advantages of this kind. The position is totally beyond the attainment of an American; there to-day, bristling all over with the porcupine quills of our Republic, and gone to-morrow, just as he is becoming sensible of the broader and more generous patriotism which might almost amalgamate with that of England, without losing an atom of its native force and flavor. In the changes that appear to await us, and some of which, at least, can hardly fail to be for good, let us hope for a reform in this matter.

For myself, as the gentle reader would spare me the trouble of saying, I was not at all the kind of man to grow into such an ideal Consul as I have here suggested. I never in my life desired to be burdened with public influence. I disliked my office from the first, and never came into any good accordance with it. Its dignity, so far as it had any, was an encumbrance; the attentions it drew upon me (such as invitations to Mayors' banquets and public celebrations of all kinds, where, to my horror, I found myself expected to stand up and speak) were — as I may say without incivility or ingratitude, because there is nothing personal in that sort of hospitality — a bore. The official business was irksome, and often painful. There was nothing pleasant about the whole affair, except the emoluments; and even those, never too bountifully reaped, were diminished by more than half in the second or third year of my incumbency. All this being true, I was quite prepared, in advance of the inauguration of Mr. Buchanan, to send in my resignation. When my successor arrived, I drew the long, delightful breath which first made me thoroughly sensible what an unnatural life I had been leading, and compelled me to admire myself for having battled with it so sturdily. The new-comer proved to be a very genial and agreeable gentleman, an F. F. V.,* and, as he pleasantly acknowledged, a Southern Fire-Eater, — an announcement to which I responded, with similar good-humor and self-complacency, by parading my descent from an ancient line of Massachusetts Puritans. Since our brief acquaintanceship, my fire-eating friend has had ample opportunities to banquet on his favorite diet, hot and hot, in the Confederate service. For myself, as soon as I was out of office, the retrospect began to look unreal. I could scarcely believe that it was I, — that figure whom they called a Consul, — but a sort of Double Ganger, who had been permitted to assume my aspect, under which he went through his shadowy duties with a tolerable show of efficiency, while my real self had lain, as regarded my proper mode of being and acting, in a state of suspended animation.

The same sense of illusion still pursues me. There is some mistake in this matter. I have been writing about another man's consular experiences, with which, through some mysterious medium of transmitted ideas, I find myself intimately acquainted, but in which I cannot possibly have had a personal interest. Is it not a dream altogether? The figure of that poor Doctor of Divinity looks wonderfully lifelike; so do those of the Oriental adventurer with the

*[First Family of Virginia.]

visionary coronet above his brow, and the moonstruck visitor of the Queen, and the poor old wanderer, seeking his native country through English highways and byways for almost thirty years; and so would a hundred others that I might summon up with similar distinctness. But were they more than shadows? Surely, I think not. Nor are these present pages a bit of intrusive autobiography. Let not the reader wrong me by supposing it. I never should have written with half such unreserve, had it been a portion of this life congenial with my nature, which I am living now, instead of a series of incidents and characters entirely apart from my own concerns, and on which the qualities personally proper to me could have had no bearing. Almost the only real incidents, as I see them now, were the visits of a young English friend, a scholar and a literary amateur, between whom and myself there sprung up an affectionate, and, I trust, not transitory regard. He used to come and sit or stand by my fireside, talking vivaciously and eloquently with me about literature and life, his own national characteristics and mine, with such kindly endurance of the many rough republicanisms wherewith I assailed him, and such frank and amiable assertion of all sorts of English prejudices and mistakes, that I understood his countrymen infinitely the better for him, and was almost prepared to love the intensest Englishman of them all, for his sake. It would gratify my cherished remembrance of this dear friend, if I could manage, without offending him, or letting the public know it, to introduce his name upon my page. Bright was the illumination of my dusky little apartment, as often as he made his appearance there!

The English sketches which I have been offering to the public comprise a few of the more external, and therefore more readily manageable, things that I took note of, in many escapes from the imprisonment of my consular servitude. Liverpool, though not very delightful as a place of residence, is a most convenient and admirable point to get away from.

London is only five hours off by the fast train. Chester, the most curious town in England, with its encompassing wall, its ancient rows, and its venerable cathedral, is close at hand. North Wales, with all its hills and ponds, its noble sea-scenery, its multitude of gray castles and strange old villages, may be glanced at in a summer day or two. The lakes and mountains of Cumberland and Westmoreland may be reached before dinner-time. The haunted and legendary Isle of Man, a little kingdom by itself, lies within the scope of an afternoon's voyage. Edinburgh or Glasgow are attainable overnight, and Loch Lomond betimes in the morning. Visiting these famous localities, and a great many others, I hope that I do not compromise my American patriotism by acknowledging that I was often conscious of a fervent hereditary attachment to the native soil of our forefathers, and felt it to be our own Old Home.

Leamington Spa

IN the course of several visits and stays of considerable length we acquired a homelike feeling towards Leamington, and came back thither again and again, chiefly because we had been there before. Wandering and wayside people, such as we had long since become, retain a few of the instincts that belong to a more settled way of life, and often prefer familiar and commonplace objects (for the very reason that they are so) to the dreary strangeness of scenes that might be thought much better worth the seeing. There is a small nest of a place in Leamington — at No. 10 Lansdowne Circus — upon which, to this day, my reminiscences are apt to settle as one of the cosiest nooks in England or in the world; not that it had any special charm of its own, but only that we stayed long enough to know it well, and even to grow a little tired of it. In my opinion, the very tediousness of home and friends makes a part of what we love them for; if it be not mixed in sufficiently with the other elements of life, there may be mad enjoyment, but no happiness.

The modest abode to which I have alluded forms one of a circular range of pretty, moderate-sized, two-story houses, all built on nearly the same plan, and each provided with its little grass-plot, its flowers, its tufts of box trimmed into globes and

other fantastic shapes, and its verdant hedges shutting the
house in from the common drive, and dividing it from its
equally cosey neighbors.   Coming out of the door, and taking
a turn round the circle of sister-dwellings, it is difficult to find
your way back by any distinguishing individuality of your
own habitation.   In the centre of the Circus is a space fenced
in with iron railing, a small play-place and sylvan retreat for
the children of the precinct, permeated by brief paths through
the fresh English grass, and shadowed by various shrubbery;
amid which, if you like, you may fancy yourself in a deep
seclusion, though probably the mark of eye-shot from the
windows of all the surrounding houses.   But, in truth, with
regard to the rest of the town and the world at large, an abode
here is a genuine seclusion; for the ordinary stream of life
does not run through this little, quiet pool, and few or none
of the inhabitants seem to be troubled with any business or
outside activities.   I used to set them down as half-pay officers,
dowagers of narrow income, elderly maiden ladies, and other
people of respectability, but small account, such as hang on
the world's skirts, rather than actually belong to it.   The quiet
of the place was seldom disturbed, except by the grocer and
butcher, who came to receive orders; or by the cabs, hackney-
coaches, and Bath-chairs, in which the ladies took an infrequent
airing; or the livery-steed which the retired captain sometimes
bestrode for a morning ride; or by the red-coated postman
who went his rounds twice a day to deliver letters, and again
in the evening, ringing a hand-bell, to take letters for the mail.
In merely mentioning these slight interruptions of its sluggish
stillness, I seem to myself to disturb too much the atmosphere
of quiet that brooded over the spot; whereas its impression
upon me was, that the world had never found the way hither,
or had forgotten it, and that the fortunate inhabitants were the
only ones who possessed the spell-word of admittance.   Nothing
could have suited me better, at the time; for I had been holding a position of public servitude, which imposed upon me

(among a great many lighter duties) the ponderous necessity of being universally civil and sociable.

Nevertheless, if a man were seeking the bustle of society, he might find it more readily in Leamington than in most other English towns. It is a permanent watering-place, a sort of institution to which I do not know any close parallel in American life: for such places as Saratoga bloom only for the summer-season, and offer a thousand dissimilitudes even then; while Leamington seems to be always in flower, and serves as a home to the homeless all the year round. Its original nucleus, the plausible excuse for the town's coming into prosperous existence, lies in the fiction of a chalybeate well, which, indeed, is so far a reality that out of its magical depths have gushed streets, groves, gardens, mansions, shops, and churches, and spread themselves along the banks of the little river Leam. This miracle accomplished, the beneficent fountain has retired beneath a pump-room, and appears to have given up all pretensions to the remedial virtues formerly attributed to it. I know not whether its waters are ever tasted nowadays; but not the less does Leamington — in pleasant Warwickshire, at the very midmost point of England, in a good hunting neighborhood, and surrounded by country-seats and castles — continue to be a resort of transient visitors, and the more permanent abode of a class of genteel, unoccupied, well-to-do, but not very wealthy people, such as are hardly known among ourselves. Persons who have no country-houses, and whose fortunes are inadequate to a London expenditure, find here, I suppose, a sort of town and country life in one.

In its present aspect the town is of no great age. In contrast with the antiquity of many places in its neighborhood, it has a bright, new face, and seems almost to smile even amid the sombreness of an English autumn. Nevertheless, it is hundreds upon hundreds of years old, if we reckon up that sleepy lapse of time during which it existed as a small village of thatched houses, clustered round a priory; and it would still have been precisely such a rural village, but for a certain Dr. Jephson, who lived within the memory of man, and who found out the magic well, and foresaw what fairy wealth might be made to flow from it. A public garden has been laid out along the margin of the Leam, and called the Jephson Garden, in honor of him who created the prosperity of his native spot. A little way within the garden-gate there is a circular temple of Grecian architecture, beneath the dome of which stands a marble statue of the good Doctor, very well executed, and representing him with a face of fussy activity and benevolence: just the kind of man, if luck favored him, to build up the fortunes of those about him, or, quite as probably, to blight his whole neighborhood by some disastrous speculation.

The Jephson Garden is very beautiful, like most other English pleasure-grounds; for, aided by their moist climate and not too fervid sun, the landscape gardeners excel in converting flat or tame surfaces into attractive scenery, chiefly through the skilful arrangement of trees and shrubbery. An Englishman aims at this effect even in the little patches under the windows of a suburban villa and achieves it on a larger scale in a tract of many acres. The Garden is shadowed with trees of a fine growth, standing alone, or in dusky groves and dense entanglements, pervaded by woodland paths; and emerging from these pleasant glooms, we come upon a breadth of sunshine, where the greensward — so vividly green that it has a kind of lustre in it — is spotted with beds of gemlike flowers. Rustic chairs and benches are scattered about, some of them ponderously fashioned out of the stumps of obtruncated trees, and others more artfully made with intertwining branches, or perhaps an imitation of such frail handiwork in iron. In a central part of the Garden is an archery-ground, where laughing maidens practise at the butts, generally missing their ostensible mark, but, by the mere grace of their action, sending an unseen shaft into some young man's heart. There is space, moreover, within these precincts, for an artificial lake, with a little green island in the midst of it; both lake and island being the haunt of swans, whose aspect and movement in the water are most beautiful and stately, — most infirm, disjointed, and decrepit, when, unadvisedly, they see fit to emerge, and try to walk upon dry land. In the latter case, they look like a breed of uncommonly ill-contrived geese; and I record the matter here for the sake of the moral, — that we should never pass judgment on the merits of any person or thing, unless we behold them in the sphere and circumstances to which they are specially adapted. In still another part of the Garden there is a labyrinthine maze formed of an intricacy of hedge-bordered walks, involving himself in which, a man might wander for hours inextricably within a circuit of only a few yards. It seemed to me a sad emblem of the mental and moral perplexities in which we sometimes go astray, petty in scope, yet large enough to entangle a lifetime, and bewilder us with a weary movement, but no genuine progress.

The Leam, — the "high complexioned Leam," as Drayton calls it, — after drowsing across the principal street of the town, beneath a handsome bridge, skirts along the margin of the Garden without any perceptible flow. Heretofore I had fancied the Concord the laziest river in the world, but now assign that amiable distinction to the little English stream. Its water is by no means transparent, but has a greenish, goose-puddly hue, which, however, accords well with the other coloring and characteristics of the scene, and is disagreeable neither to sight nor smell. Certainly, this river is a perfect feature of that gentle picturesqueness in which England is so rich, sleeping, as it does, beneath a margin of willows that droop into its bosom, and other trees, of deeper verdure than our own country can boast, inclining lovingly over it. On the Garden-side it is bordered by a shadowy, secluded grove, with winding paths among it boskiness, affording many a peep at the river's imperceptible lapse and tranquil gleam; and on the opposite shore stands the priory-church, with its churchyard full of shrubbery and tombstones.

The business portion of the town clusters about the banks of the Leam, and is naturally densest around the well to which the modern settlement owes its existence. Here are the commercial inns, the post-office, the furniture-dealers, the ironmongers, and all the heavy and homely establishments that connect themselves even with the airiest modes of human life; while upward from the river, by a long and gentle ascent, rises the principal street, which is very bright and cheerful in its physiognomy, and adorned with shop-fronts almost as splendid as those of London, though on a diminutive scale. There are likewise side-streets and cross-streets, many of which are bordered with the beautiful Warwickshire elm, a most unusual kind of adornment for an English town; and spacious avenues, wide enough to afford room for stately groves, with foot-paths running beneath the lofty shade, and rooks cawing and chattering so high in the tree-tops that their voices get musical before reaching the earth. The houses are mostly built in blocks and ranges, in which every separate tenement is a repetition of its fellow, though the architecture of the different ranges is sufficiently various. Some of them are almost palatial in size and sumptuousness of arrangement. Then, on the outskirts of the town, there are detached villas, enclosed within that separate domain of high stone fence and embowered shrubbery which an Englishman so loves to build and plant around his abode, presenting to the public only an iron gate, with a gravelled carriage-drive winding away towards the half-hidden mansion. Whether in street or suburb, Leamington may fairly be called beautiful, and, at some points, magnificent; but by and by you become doubtfully suspicious of a somewhat unreal finery: it is pretentious, though not glaringly so; it has been built with malice aforethought, as a place of gentility and enjoyment. Moreover, splendid as the houses look, and comfortable as they often are, there is a nameless something about them, betokening that they have not grown out of human hearts, but are the creations of a skilfully applied human intellect: no man has reared any one of them, whether stately or humble, to be his life-long residence, wherein to bring up his children, who are to inherit it as a home. They are nicely contrived lodging-houses, one and all, — the best as well as the shabbiest of them, — and therefore inevitably lack some nameless property that a home should have. This was the case with our own little snuggery in Lansdowne Circus, as with all the rest; it had not grown out of anybody's individual need, but was built to let or sell, and was therefore like a ready-made garment, — a tolerable fit, but only tolerable.

All these blocks, ranges, and detached villas are adorned with the finest and most aristocratic names that I have found anywhere in England, except perhaps, in Bath, which is the great metropolis of that second-class gentility with which watering-places are chiefly populated. Lansdowne Crescent, Lansdowne Circus, Lansdowne Terrace, Regent Street, Warwick Street, Clarendon Street, the Upper and Lower Parade: such are a few of the designations. Parade, indeed, is a well-chosen name for the principal street, along which the population of the idle town draws itself out for daily review and display. I only wish that my descriptive powers would enable me to throw off a picture of the scene at a sunny noontide, individualizing each character with a touch; the great people alighting from their carriages at the principal shop-doors; the elderly ladies and infirm Indian officers drawn along in Bath-chairs; the comely, rather than pretty, English girls, with their deep, healthy bloom, which an American taste is apt to deem fitter for a milkmaid than for a lady; the mustached gentlemen with frogged surtouts and a military air; the nursemaids and chubby children, but no chubbier than our own, and scampering on slenderer legs; the sturdy figure of John Bull in all varieties and of all ages, but ever with the stamp of authenticity somewhere about him.

To say the truth, I have been holding the pen over my paper, purposing to write a descriptive paragraph or two about the throng on the principal Parade of Leamington, so arranging it as to present a sketch of the British out-of-door aspect on a morning walk of gentility; but I find no personages quite

sufficiently distinct and individual in my memory to supply
the materials of such a panorama.   Oddly enough, the only
figure that comes fairly forth to my mind's eye is that of a
dowager, one of hundreds whom I used to marvel at, all over
England, but who have scarcely a representative among our
own ladies of autumnal life, so thin, careworn, and frail, as
age usually makes the latter.

I have heard a good deal of the tenacity with which English
ladies retain their personal beauty to a late period of life; but
(not to suggest that an American eye needs use and cultivation
before it can quite appreciate the charm of English beauty
at any age) it strikes me that an English lady of fifty is apt
to become a creature less refined and delicate, so far as her
physique goes, than anything that we Western people class
under the name of woman.   She has an awful ponderosity of
frame, not pulpy, like the looser development of our few fat
women, but massive with solid beef and streaky tallow; so
that (though struggling manfully against the idea) you inevitably think of her as made up of steaks and sirloins.   When
she walks, her advance is elephantine.   When she sits down,
it is on a great round space of her Maker's footstool, where
she looks as if nothing could ever move her.   She imposes
awe and respect by the muchness of her personality, to such
a degree that you probably credit her with far greater moral
and intellectual force than she can fairly claim.   Her visage
is usually grim and stern, seldom positively forbidding, yet
calmly terrible, not merely by its breadth and weight of feature,
but because it seems to express so much well-founded self-
reliance, such acquaintance with the world, its toils, troubles,
and dangers, and such sturdy capacity for trampling down a
foe.   Without anything positively salient, or actively offensive,
or, indeed, unjustly formidable to her neighbors, she has the
effect of a seventy-four gun-ship in time of peace; for, while
you assure yourself that there is no real danger, you cannot
help thinking how tremendous would be her onset if pug-
naciously inclined, and how futile the effort to inflict any

counter-injury. She certainly looks ten-fold — nay, a hundred-fold — better able to take care of herself than our slender-framed and haggard womankind; but I have not found reason to suppose that the English dowager of fifty has actually greater courage, fortitude, and strength of character than our women of similar age, or even a tougher physical endurance than they. Morally, she is strong, I suspect, only in society, and in the common routine of social affairs, and would be found powerless and timid in any exceptional strait that might call for energy outside of the conventionalities amid which she has grown up.

You can meet this figure in the street, and live, and even smile at the recollection. But conceive of her in a ball-room, with the bare, brawny arms that she invariably displays there, and all the other corresponding development, such as is beautiful in the maiden blossom, but a spectacle to howl at in such an over-blown cabbage-rose as this.

Yet, somewhere in this enormous bulk there must be hidden the modest, slender, violet-nature of a girl, whom an alien mass of earthliness has unkindly overgrown; for an English maiden in her teens, though very seldom so pretty as our own damsels, possesses, to say the truth, a certain charm of half-blossom, and delicately folded leaves, and tender womanhood shielded by maidenly reserves, with which, somehow or other, our American girls often fail to adorn themselves during an appreciable moment. It is a pity that the English violet should grow into such an outrageously developed peony as I have attempted to describe. I wonder whether a middle-aged husband ought to be considered as legally married to all the accretions that have overgrown the slenderness of his bride, since he led her to the altar, and which make her so much more than he ever bargained for! Is it not a sounder view of the case, that the matrimonial bond cannot be held to include the three fourths of the wife that had no existence when the ceremony was performed? And as a matter of conscience and good morals, ought not an English married pair to insist upon the celebration of a silver-wedding at the end of twenty-five years, in order to legalize and mutually appropriate that corporeal growth of which both parties have individually come into possession since they were pronounced one flesh?

The chief enjoyment of my several visits to Leamington lay in rural walks about the neighborhood, and in jaunts to places of note and interest, which are particularly abundant in that region. The high-roads are made pleasant to the traveller by a border of trees, and often afford him the hospitality of a wayside bench beneath a comfortable shade. But a fresher delight is to be found in the foot-paths, which go wandering away from stile to stile, along hedges, and across broad fields, and through wooded parks, leading you to little hamlets of thatched cottages, ancient, solitary farm-houses, picturesque old mills, streamlets, pools, and all those quiet, secret, unexpected, yet strangely familiar features of English scenery that Tennyson shows us in his idyls and eclogues. These by-paths admit the wayfarer into the very heart of rural life, and yet do not burden him with a sense of intrusiveness. He has a right to go whithersoever they lead him; for, with all their shaded privacy, they are as much the property of the public as the dusty high-road itself, and even by an older tenure. Their antiquity probably exceeds that of the Roman ways; the footsteps of the aboriginal Britons first wore away the grass, and the natural flow of intercourse between village and village has kept the track bare ever since. An American farmer would plough across any such path, and obliterate it with his hills of potatoes and Indian corn; but here it is protected by law, and still more by the sacredness that inevitably springs up, in this soil, along the well-defined footprints of centuries. Old associations are sure to be fragrant herbs in English nostrils; we pull them up as weeds.

I remember such a path, the access to which is from Lovers' Grove, a range of tall old oaks and elms on a high hill-top, whence there is a view of Warwick Castle, and a wide extent of landscape, beautiful, though bedimmed with English mist.

This particular foot-path, however, is not a remarkably good specimen of its kind, since it leads into no hollows and seclusions, and soon terminates in a high-road. It connects Leamington by a short cut with the small neighboring village of Lillington, a place which impresses an American observer with its many points of contrast to the rural aspects of his own country. The village consists chiefly of one row of contiguous dwellings, separated only by party-walls, but ill-matched among themselves, being of different heights, and apparently of various ages, though all are of an antiquity which we should call venerable. Some of the windows are leaden-framed lattices opening on hinges. These houses are mostly built of gray stone; but others, in the same range, are of brick, and one or two are in a very old fashion, — Elizabethan, or still older, — having a ponderous frame-work of oak, painted black, and filled in with plastered stone or bricks. Judging by the patches of repair, the oak seems to be the more durable part of the structure. Some of the roofs are covered with earthen tiles; others (more decayed and poverty-stricken) with thatch, out of which sprouts a luxurious vegetation of grass, house-leeks, and yellow flowers. What especially strikes an American is the lack of that insulated space, the intervening gardens, grass-plots, orchards, broad-spreading shade-trees, which occur between our own village-houses. These English dwellings have no such separate surroundings; they all grow together, like the cells of a honeycomb.

Beyond the first row of houses, and hidden from it by a turn of the road, there was another row (or block, as we should call it) of small old cottages, stuck one against another, with their thatched roofs forming a single contiguity. These, I presume, were the habitations of the poorest order of rustic laborers; and the narrow precincts of each cottage, as well as the close neighborhood of the whole, gave the impression of a stifled, unhealthy atmosphere among the occupants. It seemed impossible that there should be a cleanly reserve, a proper self-respect among individuals, or a wholesome un-

familiarity between families where human life was crowded
and massed into such intimate communities as these. Nevertheless, not to look beyond the outside, I never saw a prettier
rural scene than was presented by this range of contiguous
huts. For in front of the whole row was a luxuriant and
well-trimmed hawthorn hedge, and belonging to each cottage
was a little square of garden-ground, separated from its neighbors by a line of the same verdant fence. The gardens were
chockfull, not of esculent vegetables, but of flowers, familiar
ones, but very bright-colored, and shrubs of box, some of which
were trimmed into artistic shapes; and I remember, before
one door, a representation of Warwick Castle, made of oyster-
shells. The cottagers evidently loved the little nests in which
they dwelt, and did their best to make them beautiful, and
succeeded more than tolerably well, — so kindly did nature
help their humble efforts with its verdure, flowers, moss,
lichens, and the green things that grew out of the thatch.
Through some of the open doorways we saw plump children
rolling about on the stone floors, and their mothers, by no
means very pretty, but as happy-looking as mothers generally
are; and while we gazed at these domestic matters an old
woman rushed wildly out of one of the gates, upholding a
shovel, on which she clanged and clattered with a key. At
first we fancied that she intended an onslaught against ourselves, but soon discovered that a more dangerous enemy was
abroad; for the old lady's bees had swarmed, and the air was
full of them, whizzing by our heads like bullets.

Not far from these two rows of houses and cottages, a green
lane, overshadowed with trees, turned aside from the main
road, and tended towards a square, gray tower, the battlements
of which were just high enough to be visible above the foliage.
Wending our way thitherward, we found the very picture and
ideal of a country church and churchyard. The tower seemed
to be of Norman architecture, low, massive, and crowned with
battlements. The body of the church was of very modest
dimensions, and the eaves so low that I could touch them

with my walking-stick. We looked into the windows and beheld the dim and quiet interior, a narrow space, but venerable
with the consecration of many centuries, and keeping its sanctity as entire and inviolate as that of a vast cathedral. The
nave was divided from the side aisles of the church by pointed
arches resting on very sturdy pillars: it was good to see how
solemnly they held themselves to their age-long task of supporting that lowly roof. There was a small organ, suited in size
to the vaulted hollow, which it weekly filled with religious
sound. On the opposite wall of the church, between two
windows, was a mural tablet of white marble, with an inscription in black letters, — the only such memorial that I could
discern, although many dead people doubtless lay beneath the
floor, and had paved it with their ancient tombstones, as is
customary in old English churches. There were no modern
painted windows, flaring with raw colors, nor other gorgeous
adornments, such as the present taste for mediaeval restoration often patches upon the decorous simplicity of the gray
village-church. It is probably the worshipping-place of no
more distinguished a congregation than the farmers and
peasantry who inhabit the houses and cottages which I have
just described. Had the lord of the manor been one of the
parishioners, there would have been an eminent pew near the
chancel, walled high about, curtained, and softly cushioned,
warmed by a fireplace of its own, and distinguished by hereditary tablets and escutcheons on the enclosed stone pillar.

A well-trodden path led across the churchyard, and the gate
being on the latch, we entered, and walked round among the
graves and monuments. The latter were chiefly head-stones,
none of which were very old, so far as was discoverable by the
dates; some, indeed, in so ancient a cemetery, were disagreeably
new, with inscriptions glittering like sunshine in gold letters.
The ground must have been dug over and over again, innumerable times, until the soil is made up of what was once
human clay, out of which have sprung successive crops of gravestones, that flourish their allotted time, and disappear, like

the weeds and flowers in their briefer period. The English climate is very unfavorable to the endurance of memorials in the open air. Twenty years of it suffice to give as much antiquity of aspect, whether to tombstone or edifice, as a hundred years of our own drier atmosphere, — so soon do the drizzly rains and constant moisture corrode the surface of marble or freestone. Sculptured edges lose their sharpness in a year or two; yellow lichens overspread a beloved name, and obliterate it while it is yet fresh upon some survivor's heart. Time gnaws an English gravestone with wonderful appetite; and when the inscription is quite illegible, the sexton takes the useless slab away, and perhaps makes a hearthstone of it, and digs up the unripe bones which it ineffectually tried to memorialize, and gives the bed to another sleeper. In the Charter Street burial-ground at Salem, and in the old graveyard on the hill at Ipswich, I have seen more ancient gravestones, with legible inscriptions on them, than in any English churchyard.

And yet this same ungenial climate, hostile as it generally is to the long remembrance of departed people, has sometimes a lovely way of dealing with the records on certain monuments that lie horizontally in the open air. The rain falls into the deep incisions of the letters, and has scarcely time to be dried away before another shower sprinkles the flat stone again, and replenishes those little reservoirs. The unseen, mysterious seeds of mosses find their way into the lettered furrows, and are made to germinate by the continual moisture and watery sunshine of the English sky; and by and by, in a year, or two years, or many years, behold the complete inscription —

HERE LYETH THE BODY,

and all the rest of the tender falsehood — beautifully embossed in raised letters of living green, a bas-relief of velvet moss on the marble slab! It becomes more legible, under the skyey influences, after the world has forgotten the deceased, than when it was fresh from the stone-cutter's hands. It outlives the grief of friends. I first saw an example of this in Beb-

bington churchyard, in Cheshire, and thought, that Nature
must needs have had a special tenderness for the person (no
noted man, however, in the world's history) so long ago laid
beneath that stone, since she took such wonderful pains to
"keep his memory green." Perhaps the proverbial phrase just
quoted may have had its origin in the natural phenomenon
here described.

While we rested ourselves on a horizontal monument, which
was elevated just high enough to be a convenient seat, I
observed that one of the gravestones lay very close to the
church, — so close that the droppings of the eaves would fall
upon it. It seemed as if the inmate of that grave had desired
to creep under the church-wall. On closer inspection, we
found an almost illegible epitaph on the stone, and with
difficulty made out this forlorn verse: —

> "Poorly lived,
> And poorly died,
> Poorly buried,
> And no one cried."

It would be hard to compress the story of a cold and luckless
life, death, and burial into fewer words, or more impressive
ones; at least, we found them impressive, perhaps because we
had to re-create the inscription by scraping away the lichens
from the faintly traced letters. The grave was on the shady
and damp side of the church, endwise towards it, the head-
stone being within about three feet of the foundation-wall;
so that, unless the poor man was a dwarf, he must have been
doubled up to fit him into his final resting-place. No wonder
that his epitaph murmured against so poor a burial as this!
His name, as well as I could make it out, was Treeo, — John
Treeo, I think, — and he died in 1810, at the age of seventy-
four. The gravestone is so overgrown with grass and weeds,
so covered with unsightly lichens, and so crumbly with time
and foul weather, that it is questionable whether anybody
will ever be at the trouble of deciphering it again. But there
is a quaint and sad kind of enjoyment in defeating (to such

slight degree as my pen may do it) the probabilities of oblivion
for poor John Treeo, and asking a little sympathy for him,
half a century after his death, and making him better and
more widely known, at least, than any other slumberer in
Lillington churchyard: he having been, as appearances go, the
outcast of them all.

You find similar old churches and villages in all the neighboring country, at the distance of every two or three miles;
and I describe them, not as being rare, but because they are so
common and characteristic. The village of Whitnash, within
twenty minutes' walk of Leamington, looks as secluded, as
rural, and as little disturbed by the fashions of to-day, as if
Dr. Jephson had never developed all those Parades and Crescents out of his magic well. I used to wonder whether the
inhabitants had ever yet heard of railways, or, at their slow
rate of progress, had even reached the epoch of stage-coaches.
As you approach the village, while it is yet unseen, you observe
a tall, overshadowing canopy of elm-tree tops, beneath which
you almost hesitate to follow the public road, on account of
the remoteness that seems to exist between the precincts of this
old-world community and the thronged modern street out of
which you have so recently emerged. Venturing onward, however, you soon find yourself in the heart of Whitnash, and
see an irregular ring of ancient rustic dwellings surrounding
the village-green, on one side of which stands the church, with
its square Norman tower and battlements, while close adjoining is the vicarage, made picturesque by peaks and gables.
At first glimpse, none of the houses appear to be less than two
or three centuries old, and they are of the ancient, wooden-
framed fashion, with thatched roofs, which give them the air
of birds' nests, thereby assimilating them closely to the simplicity of nature.

The church-tower is mossy and much gnawed by time; it
has narrow loopholes up and down its front and sides, and an
arched window over the low portal, set with small panes of
glass, cracked, dim, and irregular, through which a by-gone

age is peeping out into the day-light. Some of those old, grotesque faces, called gargoyles, are seen on the projections of the architecture. The churchyard is very small, and is encompassed by a gray stone fence that looks as ancient as the church itself. In front of the tower, on the village-green, is a yew-tree of incalculable age, with a vast circumference of trunk, but a very scanty head of foliage; though its boughs still keep some of the vitality which, perhaps, was in its early prime when the Saxon invaders founded Whitnash. A thousand years is no extraordinary antiquity in the lifetime of a yew. We were pleasantly startled, however, by discovering an exuberance of more youthful life than we had thought possible in so old a tree; for the faces of two children laughed at us out of an opening in the trunk, which had become hollow with long decay. On one side of the yew stood a framework of worm-eaten timber, the use and meaning of which puzzled me exceedingly, till I made it out to be the village-stocks; a public institution that, in its day, had doubtless hampered many a pair of shank-bones, now crumbling in the adjacent churchyard. It is not to be supposed, however, that this old-fashioned mode of punishment is still in vogue among the good people of Whitnash. The vicar of the parish has antiquarian propensities, and had probably dragged the stocks out of some dusty hiding-place and set them up on the former site as a curiosity.

I disquiet myself in vain with the effort to hit upon some characteristic feature, or assemblage of features, that shall convey to the reader the influence of hoar antiquity lingering into the present daylight, as I so often felt it in these old English scenes. It is only an American who can feel it; and even he begins to find himself growing insensible to its effect, after a long residence in England. But while you are still new in the old country, it thrills you with strange emotion to think that this little church of Whitnash, humble as it seems, stood for ages under the Catholic faith, and has not materially changed since Wickliffe's days, and that it looked as gray now as in Bloody Mary's time, and that Cromwell's troopers broke off the stone noses of those same gargoyles that are now grinning in your face. So, too, with the immemorial yew-tree; you see its great roots grasping hold of the earth like gigantic claws, clinging so sturdily that no effort of time can wrench them away; and there being life in the old tree, you feel all the more as if a contemporary witness were telling you of the things that have been. It has lived among men, and been a familiar object to them, and seen them brought to be christened and married and buried in the neighboring church and churchyard, through so many centuries, that it knows all about our race, so far as fifty generations of the Whitnash people can supply such knowledge.

And, after all, what a weary life it must have been for the old tree! Tedious beyond imagination! Such, I think, is the final impression on the mind of an American visitor, when his delight at finding something permanent begins to yield to his Western love of change, and he becomes sensible of the heavy air of a spot where the forefathers and foremothers have grown up together, intermarried, and died, through a long succession of lives, without any intermixture of new elements, till family features and character are all run in the same inevitable mould. Life is there fossilized in its greenest leaf. The man who died yesterday or ever so long ago walks the village-street to-day, and chooses the same wife that he married a hundred years since, and must be buried again to-morrow under the same kindred dust that has already covered him half a score of times. The stone threshold of his cottage is worn away with his hobnailed footsteps, shuffling over it from the reign of the first Plantagenet to that of Victoria. Better than this is the lot of our restless countrymen, whose modern instinct bids them tend always towards "fresh woods and pastures new." Rather than such monotony of sluggish ages, loitering on a village-green, toiling in hereditary fields, listening to the parson's drone lengthened through centuries in the gray Norman church, let us welcome whatever change may come, — change of place, social customs, political institutions, modes of worship, — trusting that, if all present things shall vanish, they will but make room for better systems, and for a higher type of man to clothe his life in them, and to fling them off in turn.

Nevertheless, while an American willingly accepts growth and change as the law of his own national and private existence, he has a singular tenderness for the stone-incrusted institutions of the mother-country. The reason may be (though I should prefer a more generous explanation) that he recognizes the tendency of these hardened forms to stiffen her joints and fetter her ankles, in the race and rivalry of improvement. I hated to see so much as a twig of ivy wrenched away from an old wall in England. Yet change is at work, even in such a village as Whitnash. At a subsequent visit, looking more critically at the irregular circle of dwellings that surround the yew-tree and confront the church, I perceived that some of the houses must have been built within no long time, although the thatch, the quaint gables, and the old oaken framework of the others diffused an air of antiquity over the whole assemblage. The church itself was undergoing repair and restoration, which is but another name for change. Masons were making patch-work on the front of the tower, and were sawing a slab of stone and piling up bricks to strengthen the side-wall, or possibly to enlarge the ancient edifice by an additional aisle. Moreover, they had dug an immense pit in the churchyard, long and broad, and fifteen feet deep, two thirds of which profundity were discolored by human decay, and mixed up with crumbly bones. What this excavation was intended for I could nowise imagine, unless it were the very pit in which Longfellow bids the "Dead Past bury its dead," and Whitnash, of all places in the world, were going to avail itself of our poet's suggestion. If so, it must needs be confessed that many picturesque and delightful things would be thrown into the hole, and covered out of sight forever. . . .

Almost always, in visiting such scenes as I have been attempting to describe, I had a singular sense of having been there

before.   The ivy-grown English churches (even that of Beb-
bington, the first that I beheld) were quite as familiar to me,
when fresh from home, as the old wooden meeting-house in
Salem, which used, on wintry Sabbaths, to be the frozen pur-
gatory of my childhood.   This was a bewildering, yet very
delightful emotion fluttering about me like a faint summer
wind, and filling my imagination with a thousand half-remem-
brances, which looked as vivid as sunshine at a side-glance, but
faded quite away whenever I attempted to grasp and define
them.   Of course, the explanation of the mystery was, that
history, poetry, and fiction, books of travel, and the talk of
tourists, had given me pretty accurate preconceptions of the
common objects of English scenery, and these, being long ago
vivified by a youthful fancy, had insensibly taken their places
among the images of things actually seen.   Yet the illusion
was often so powerful, that I almost doubted whether such
airy remembrances might not be a sort of innate idea, the
print of a recollection in some ancestral mind, transmitted,
with fainter and fainter impress through several descents, to
my own.   I felt, indeed, like the stalwart progenitor in person,
returning to the hereditary haunts after more than two hundred years, and finding the church, the hall, the farm-house,
the cottage, hardly changed during his long absence, — the
same shady by-paths and hedge-lanes, the same veiled sky, and
green lustre of the lawns and fields, — while his own affinities
for these things, a little obscured by disuse, were reviving at
every step.

An American is not very apt to love the English people, as
a whole, on whatever length of acquaintance.   I fancy that
they would value our regard, and even reciprocate it in their
ungracious way, if we could give it to them in spite of all
rebuffs; but they are beset by a curious and inevitable infelicity,
which compels them, as it were, to keep up what they seem to
consider a wholesome bitterness of feeling between themselves
and all other nationalities, especially that of America.   They
will never confess it; nevertheless, it is as essential a tonic to

them as their bitter ale. Therefore, — and possibly, too, from a similar narrowness in his own character, — an American seldom feels quite as if he were at home among the English people. If he do so, he has ceased to be an American. But it requires no long residence to make him love their island, and appreciate it as thoroughly as they themselves do. For my part, I used to wish that we could annex it, transferring their thirty millions of inhabitants to some convenient wilderness in the great West, and putting half or a quarter as many of ourselves into their places. The change would be beneficial to both parties. We, in our dry atmosphere, are getting too nervous, haggard, dyspeptic, extenuated, unsubstantial, theoretic, and need to be made grosser. John Bull, on the other hand, has grown bulbous, long-bodied, short-legged, heavy-witted, material, and, in a word, too intensely English. In a few more centuries he will be the earthliest creature that ever the earth saw. Heretofore Providence has obviated such a result by timely intermixtures of alien races with the old English stock; so that each successive conquest of England has proved a victory by the revivification and improvement of its native manhood. Cannot America and England hit upon some scheme to secure even greater advantages to both nations?

About Warwick

BETWEEN bright, new Leamington, the growth of the present century, and rusty Warwick, founded by King Cymbeline in the twilight ages, a thousand years before the mediaeval darkness, there are two roads, either of which may be measured by a sober-paced pedestrian in less than half an hour.

One of these avenues flows out of the midst of the smart parades and crescents of the former town, — along by hedges and beneath the shadow of great elms, past stuccoed Elizabethan villas and wayside alehouses, and through a hamlet of modern aspect, — and runs straight into the principal thoroughfare of Warwick. The battlemented turrets of the castle, embowered half-way up in foliage, and the tall, slender tower of St. Mary's Church, rising from among clustered roofs, have been visible almost from the commencement of the walk. Near the entrance of the town stands St. John's School-House, a picturesque old edifice of stone, with four peaked gables in a row, alternately plain and ornamented, and wide, projecting windows, and a spacious and venerable porch, all overgrown with moss and ivy, and shut in from the world by a high stone fence, not less mossy than the gabled front. There is an iron gate, through the rusty open-work of which you see a grassy lawn, and almost expect to meet the shy, curious eyes of the

little boys of past generations, peeping forth from their infan-
tile antiquity into the strangeness of our present life. I find
a peculiar charm in these long-established English schools,
where the school-boy of to-day sits side by side, as it were,
with his great-grandsire, on the same old benches, and often,
I believe, thumbs a later, but unimproved edition of the same
old grammar or arithmetic. The new-fangled notions of a
Yankee school-committee would madden many a pedagogue,
and shake down the roof of many a time-honored seat of learning, in the mother-country.

At this point, however, we will turn back, in order to follow
up the other road from Leamington, which was the one that
I loved best to take. It pursues a straight and level course,
bordered by wide gravel-walks and overhung by the frequent
elm, with here a cottage and there a villa; on one side a wooden
plantation, and on the other a rich field of grass or grain;
until, turning at right angles, it brings you to an arched bridge
over the Avon. Its parapet is a balustrade carved out of freestone, into the soft substance of which a multitude of persons
have engraved their names or initials, many of them now
illegible, while others, more deeply cut, are illuminated with
fresh green moss. These tokens indicate a famous spot; and
casting our eyes along the smooth gleam and shadow of the
quiet stream, through a vista of willows that droop on either
side into the water, we behold the gray magnificence of Warwick Castle, uplifting itself among stately trees, and rearing
its turrets high above their loftiest branches. We can scarcely
think the scene real, so completely do those machicolated
towers, the long line of battlements, the massive buttresses,
the high-windowed walls, shape out our indistinct ideas of the
antique time. It might rather seem as if the sleepy river (being
Shakespeare's Avon, and often, no doubt, the mirror of his
gorgeous visions) were dreaming, now of a lordly residence
that stood here many centuries ago; and this fantasy is strength-
ened, when you observe that the image in the tranquil water
has all the distinctness of the actual structure. Either might

be the reflection of the other. Wherever Time has gnawed one of the stones, you see the mark of his tooth just as plainly in the sunken reflection. Each is so perfect, that the upper vision seems a castle in the air, and the lower one an old stronghold of feudalism, miraculously kept from decay in an enchanted river.

A ruinous and ivy-grown bridge, that projects from the bank a little on the hither side of the castle, has the effect of making the scene appear more entirely apart from the every-day world, for it ends abruptly in the middle of the stream, — so that, if a cavalcade of the knights and ladies of romance should issue from the old walls, they could never tread on earthly ground any more than we, approaching from the side of modern realism, can overleap the gulf between our domain and theirs. Yet, if we seek to disenchant ourselves, it may readily be done. Crossing the bridge on which we stand, and passing a little farther on, we come to the entrance of the castle, abutting on the highway, and hospitably open at certain hours to all curious pilgrims who choose to disburse half a crown or so toward the support of the earl's domestics. The sight of that long series of historic rooms, full of such splendor and rarities as a great English family necessarily gathers about itself in its hereditary abode, and in the lapse of ages, is well worth the money, or ten times as much, if indeed the value of the spectacle could be reckoned in money's-worth. But after the attendant has hurried you from end to end of the edifice, repeating a guide-book by rote, and exorcising each successive hall of its poetic glamour and witchcraft by the mere tone in which he talks about it, you will make the doleful discovery that Warwick Castle has ceased to be a dream. It is better, methinks, to linger on the bridge, gazing at Caesar's Tower and Guy's Tower, in the dim English sunshine above, and in the placid Avon below, and still keep them as thoughts in your own mind, than climb to their summits, or touch even a stone of their actual substance. They will have all the more reality for you, as stalwart relics of immemorial time, if you are reverent enough to leave them in the intangible sanctity of a poetic vision.

From the bridge over the Avon, the road passes in front of the castle-gate, and soon enters the principal street of Warwick, a little beyond St. John's School-House, already described. Chester itself, most antique of English towns, can hardly show quainter architectural shapes than many of the buildings that border this street. They are mostly of the timber-and-plaster kind, with bowed and decrepit ridge-poles, and a whole chronology of various patchwork in their walls; their low-browed doorways open upon a sunken floor; their projecting stories peep, as it were, over one another's shoulders, and rise into a multiplicity of peaked gables; they have curious windows, breaking out irregularly all over the house, some even in the roof, set in their own little peaks, opening lattice-wise, and furnished with twenty small panes of lozenge-shaped glass. The architecture of these edifices (a visible oaken framework, showing the whole skeleton of the house, — as if a man's bones should be arranged on his outside, and his flesh seen through the interstices) is often imitated by modern builders, and with sufficiently picturesque effect. The objection is, that such houses, like all imitations of by-gone styles, have an air of affectation; they do not seem to be built in earnest; they are no better than playthings, or overgrown baby-houses, in which nobody should be expected to encounter the serious realities of either birth or death. Besides, originating nothing, we leave no fashions for another age to copy, when we ourselves shall have grown antique.

Old as it looks, all this portion of Warwick has over-brimmed, as it were, from the original settlement, being outside of the ancient wall. The street soon runs under an arched gateway, with a church or some other venerable structure above it, and admits us into the heart of town. At one of my first visits, I witnessed a military display. A regiment of Warwickshire militia, probably commanded by the Earl, was going though its drill in the market-place; and on the collar of one of the officers was embroidered the Bear and Ragged Staff, which has been the cognizance of the Warwick earldom from time immemorial. The soldiers were sturdy young men, with the simple, stolid, yet kindly, faces of English rustics, looking exceedingly well in a body, but slouching into a yeoman-like carriage and appearance the moment they were dismissed from drill. Squads of them were distributed everywhere about the streets, and sentinels were posted at various points; and I saw a sergeant, with a great key in his hand (big enough to have been the key of the castle's main entrance when the gate was thickest and heaviest) apparently setting a guard. Thus, centuries after feudal times are past, we find warriors still gathering under the old castle-walls, and commanded by a feudal lord, just as in the days of the King-Maker, who, no doubt, often mustered his retainers in the same market-place where I beheld this modern regiment.

The interior of the town wears a less old-fashioned aspect than the suburbs through which we approach it; and the High Street has shops with modern plate glass, and buildings with stuccoed fronts, exhibiting as few projections to hang a thought or sentiment upon as if an architect of to-day had planned them. And, indeed, so far as their surface goes, they are perhaps new enough to stand unabashed in an American street; but behind these renovated faces, with their monotonous lack of expression, there is probably the substance of the same old town that wore a Gothic exterior in the Middle Ages. The street is an emblem of England itself. What seems new in it is chiefly a skilful and fortunate adaptation of what such a people as ourselves would destroy. The new things are based and supported on sturdy old things, and derive a massive strength from their deep and immemorial foundations, though with such limitations and impediments as only an Englishman could endure. But he likes to feel the weight of all the past upon his back; and, moreover, the antiquity that overburdens him has taken root in his being, and has grown to be rather a hump than a pack, so that there is no getting rid of it without tearing his whole structure to pieces. In my judgment, as he appears to be sufficiently comfortable under the mouldy accretion, he had better stumble on with it as long as he can. He presents a spectacle which is by no means without its charm for a disinterested and unencumbered observer.

When the old edifice, or the antiquated custom or institution, appears in its pristine form, without any attempt at intermarrying it with modern fashions, an American cannot but admire the picturesque effect produced by the sudden cropping up of an apparently dead-and-buried state of society into the actual present, of which he is himself a part. We need not go far in Warwick without encountering an instance of the kind. Proceeding westward through the town, we find ourselves confronted by a huge mass of natural rock, hewn into something like architectural shape, and penetrated by a vaulted passage, which may well have been one of King Cymbeline's original gateways; and on the top of the rock, over the archway, sits a small old church, communicating with an ancient edifice, or assemblage of edifices, that look down from a similar elevation on the side of the street. A range of trees half hides the latter establishment from the sun. It presents a curious and venerable specimen of the timber-and-plaster style of building, in which some of the finest old houses in England are constructed: the front projects into porticos and vestibules, and rises into many gables, some in a row, and other crowning semi-detached portions of the structure; the windows mostly open on hinges, but show a delightful irregularity of shape and position; a multiplicity of chimneys break through the roof at their own will, or, at least, without any settled purpose of the architect. The whole affair looks very old, — so old indeed that the front bulges forth, as if the timber frame-work were a little weary, at last, of standing erect so long; but the state of repair is so perfect, and there is such an indescribable aspect of continuous vitality within the system of this aged house, that you feel confident that there may be safe shelter yet, and perhaps for centuries to come, under its time-honored roof. And on a bench, sluggishly enjoying the sunshine, and looking into the street of Warwick as from a life apart, a few old men are generally to be seen, wrapped in long cloaks, on which you may detect the glistening of a silver badge representing the Bear and Ragged Staff. These decorated worthies are some of the twelve brethren of Leicester's Hospital, — a community which subsists to-day under the identical modes that were established for it in the reign of Queen Elizabeth, and of course retains many features of a social life that has vanished almost everywhere else.

The edifice itself dates from a much older period than the charitable institution of which it is now the home. It was the seat of a religious fraternity far back in the Middle Ages, and continued so till Henry VIII. turned all the priesthood of England out of doors, and put the most unscrupulous of his favorites into their vacant abodes. In many instances, the old monks had chosen the sites of their domiciles so well, and built them on such a broad system of beauty and convenience, that their lay-occupants found it easy to convert them into stately and comfortable homes; and as such they still exist, with something of the antique reverence lingering about them. The structure now before us seems to have been first granted to Sir Nicholas Lestrange, who perhaps intended, like other men, to establish his household gods in the niches whence he had thrown down the images of saints, and to lay his hearth where an altar had stood. But there was probably a natural reluctance in those days (when Catholicism, so lately repudiated, must needs have retained an influence over all but the most obdurate characters) to bring one's hopes of domestic prosperity and a fortunate lineage into direct hostility with the awful claims of the ancient religion. At all events, there is still a superstitious idea, betwixt a fantasy and a belief, that the possession of former Church-property has drawn a curse along with it, not only among the posterity of those to whom it was originally granted, but wherever it has subsequently been transferred, even if honestly bought and paid for. There are families, now inhabiting some of the beautiful old abbeys, who appear to indulge a species of pride in recording the strange deaths and ugly shapes of misfortune that have occurred among their predecessors, and may be supposed likely to dog their own pathway down the ages of futurity. Whether Sir Nicholas Lestrange, in the beef-eating days of Old Harry and Elizabeth, was a nervous man, and subject to apprehensions of this kind, I cannot tell; but it is certain that he speedily rid himself of the spoils of the Church, and that, within twenty years afterwards, the edifice became the property of the famous Dudley, Earl of Leicester, brother of the Earl of Warwick. He devoted the ancient religious precinct to a charitable use, endowing it with an ample revenue, and making it the perpetual home of twelve poor, honest, and war-broken soldiers, mostly his own retainers, and natives either of Warwickshire or Gloucestershire. These veterans, or others wonderfully like them, still occupy their monkish dormitories, and haunt the time-darkened corridors and galleries of the hospital, leading a life of old-fashioned comfort, wearing the old-fashioned cloaks, and burnishing the identical silver badges which the Earl of Leicester gave to the original twelve. He is said to have been a bad man in his day; but he has succeeded in prolonging one good deed into what was to him a distant future.

On the projecting story, over the arched entrance, there is the date, 1571, and several coats-of-arms, either the Earl's or those of his kindred, and immediately above the doorway a stone sculpture of the Bear and Ragged Staff.

Passing through the arch, we find ourselves in a quadrangle, or enclosed court, such as always formed the central part of a great family residence in Queen Elizabeth's time, and earlier. There can hardly be a more perfect specimen of such an establishment than Leicester's Hospital. The quadrangle is a sort of sky-roofed hall, to which there is convenient access from all parts of the house. The four inner fronts, with their high, steep roofs and sharp gables, look into it from antique windows, and through open corridors and galleries along the sides; and there seems to be a richer display of architectural devices and ornaments, quainter carvings in oak, and more fantastic shapes of the timber framework, than on the side toward the street.   On the wall opposite the arched entrance are the following inscriptions, comprising such moral rules, I presume, as were deemed most essential for the daily observance of the community: "Honor all Men" — "Fear God" — "Honor the King" — "Love the Brotherhood"; and again, as if this latter injunction needed emphasis and repetition among a household of aged people soured with the hard fortune of their previous lives, — "Be kindly affectioned one to another." One sentence, over a door communicating with the Master's side of the house, is addressed to that dignitary, — "He that ruleth over men must be just."   All these are charactered in old English letters, and form part of the elaborate ornamentation of the house.   Everywhere — on the walls, over windows and doors, and at all points where there is room to place them — appear escutcheons of arms, cognizances, and crests, emblazoned in their proper colors, and illuminating the ancient quadrangle with their splendor.   One of these devices is a large image of a porcupine on an heraldic wreath, being the crest of the Lords de Lisle.   But especially is the cognizance of the Bear and Ragged Staff repeated over and over, and over again and again, in a great variety of attitudes, — at full-length and half-length, in paint and in oaken sculpture, in bas-relief and rounded image.   The founder of the hospital was certainly disposed to reckon his own beneficence as among the hereditary glories of his race; and had he lived and died a half-century earlier, he would have kept up an old Catholic custom, by enjoining the twelve bedesmen to pray for the welfare of his soul.

At my first visit, some of the brethren were seated on the bench outside of the edifice, looking down into the street; but they did not vouchsafe me a word, and seemed so estranged from modern life, so enveloped in antique customs and old-fashioned cloaks, that to converse with them would have been like shouting across the gulf between our age and Queen Elizabeth's. So I passed into the quadrangle, and found it quite solitary, except that a plain and neat old woman happened to be crossing it, with an aspect of business and carefulness that bespoke her a woman of this world, and not merely a shadow of the past. Asking her if I could come in, she answered very readily and civilly that I might, and said that I was free to look about me, hinting a hope, however, that I would not open the private doors of the brotherhood, as some visitors were in the habit of doing. Under her guidance, I went into what was formerly the great hall of the establishment, where King James I. had once been feasted by an Earl of Warwick, as is commemorated by an inscription on the cobwebbed and dingy wall. It is a very spacious and barn-like apartment, with a brick floor, and a vaulted roof, the rafters of which are oaken beams, wonderfully carved, but hardly visible in the duskiness that broods aloft. The hall may have made a splendid appearance, when it was decorated with rich tapestry, and illuminated with chandeliers, cressets, and torches glistening upon silver dishes, where King James sat at supper among his brilliantly dressed nobles; but it has come to base uses in these latter days, — being improved, in Yankee phrase, as a brewery and wash-room, and as a cellar for the brethren's separate allotments of coal.

The old lady here left me to myself, and I returned into the quadrangle. It was very quiet, very handsome, in its own obsolete style, and must be an exceedingly comfortable place for the old people to lounge in, when the inclement winds render it inexpedient to walk abroad. There are shrubs against the wall, on one side; and on another is a cloistered walk, adorned with stags' heads and antlers, and running beneath a covered gallery, up to which ascends a balustraded staircase. In the portion of the edifice opposite the entrance-arch are the apartments of the Master; and looking into the window (as the old woman, at no request of mine, had specially informed me that I might), I saw a low, but vastly comfortable parlor, very handsomely furnished, and altogether a luxurious place. It had a fireplace with an immense arch, the antique breadth of which extended almost from wall to wall of the room, though now fitted up in such a way, that the modern coal-grate looked very diminutive in the midst. Gazing into this pleasant interior, it seemed to me, that, among these venerable surroundings, availing himself of whatever was good in former things, and eking out their imperfection with the results of modern ingenuity, the Master might lead a not unenviable life. On the cloistered side of the quadrangle, where the dark oak panels made the enclosed space dusky, I beheld a curtained window reddened by a great blaze from within, and heard the bubbling and squeaking of something — doubtless very nice and succulent — that was being cooked at the kitchen-fire. I think, indeed, that a whiff or two of the savory fragrance reached my nostrils; at all events, the impression grew upon me that Leicester's Hospital is one of the jolliest old domiciles in England.

I was about to depart, when another old woman, very plainly dressed, but fat, comfortable, and with a cheerful twinkle in her eyes, came in through the arch, and looked curiously at me. This repeated apparition of the gentle sex (though by no means under its loveliest guise) had still an agreeable effect in modifying my ideas of an institution which I had supposed to be of a stern and monastic character. She asked whether I wished to see the hospital, and said that the porter, whose office it was to attend to visitors, was dead, and would be buried that very day, so that the whole establishment could not conveniently be shown me. She kindly invited me, however, to visit the apartment occupied by her husband and herself; so I followed her up the antique staircase, along the gallery, and into a small, oak-panelled parlor, where sat an old man in a long blue garment, who arose and saluted me with much courtesy. He seemed a very quiet person, and yet had a look of travel and adventure, and gray experience, such as I could have fancied in a palmer of ancient times, who might likewise have worn a similar costume. The little room was carpeted and neatly furnished; a portrait of its occupant was hanging on the wall; and on a table were two swords crossed, — one, probably, his own battle-weapon, and the other, which I drew half out of the scabbard, had an inscription on the blade, purporting that it had been taken from the field of Waterloo. My kind old hostess was anxious to exhibit all the particulars of their housekeeping, and led me into the bedroom, which was in the nicest order, with a snow-white quilt upon the bed; and in a little intervening room was a washing and bathing apparatus; a convenience (judging from the personal aspect and atmosphere of such parties) seldom to be met with in the humbler ranks of British life.

The old soldier and his wife both seemed glad of somebody to talk with; but the good woman availed herself of the privilege far more copiously than the veteran himself, insomuch that he felt it expedient to give her an occasional nudge with his elbow in her well-padded ribs. "Don't you be so talkative!" quoth he; and, indeed, he could hardly find space for a word, and quite as little after his admonition as before. Her nimble tongue ran over the whole system of life in the hospital. The brethren, she said, had a yearly stipend (the amount of which she did not mention), and such decent lodgings as I saw, and some other advantages, free; and, instead of being pestered with a great many rules, and made to dine together at a great table, they could manage their little household matters as they liked, buying their own dinners, and having them cooked in the general kitchen, and eating them snugly in their own parlors. "And," added she, rightly deeming this the crowning privilege, "with the Master's permission, they can have their wives to take care of them; and no harm comes of it; and what more can an old man desire?" It was evident enough that the good dame found herself in what she considered very rich clover, and, moreover, had plenty of small occupations to keep her from getting rusty and dull; but the veteran impressed me as deriving far less enjoyment from the monotonous ease, without fear of change or hope of improvement, that had followed upon thirty years of peril and vicissitude. I fancied, too, that, while pleased with the novelty of a stranger's visit, he was still a little shy of becoming a spectacle for the stranger's curiosity; for, if he chose to be morbid about the matter, the establishment was but an almshouse, in spite of its old-fashioned magnificence, and his fine blue cloak only a pauper's garment with a silver badge on it that perhaps galled his shoulder. In truth, the badge and the peculiar garb, though quite in accordance with the manners of the Earl of Leicester's age, are repugnant to modern prejudices, and might fitly and humanely be abolished.

A year or two afterwards I paid another visit to the hospital, and found a new porter established in office, and already capable of talking like a guide-book about the history, antiquities, and present condition of the charity. He informed me that the twelve brethren are selected from among old soldiers of good character, whose other resources must not exceed an income of five pounds; thus excluding all commissioned officers, whose half-pay would of course be more than that amount. They receive from the hospital an annuity of eighty pounds each, besides their apartments, a garment of fine blue cloth, an annual abundance of ale, and a privilege at the kitchen-fire; so that, considering the class from which they are taken, they may well reckon themselves among the fortunate of the earth. Furthermore, they are invested with political rights, acquiring a vote for member of Parliament in virtue either of their income or brotherhood. On the other hand, as regards their personal freedom or conduct, they are subject to a supervision which the Master of the hospital might render extremely annoying, were he so inclined; but the military restraint under which they have spent the active portion of their lives makes it easier for them to endure the domestic discipline here imposed upon their age. The porter bore his testimony (whatever were its value)to their being as contented and happy as such a set of old people could possibly be, and affirmed that they spent much time in burnishing their silver badges, and were as proud of them as a nobleman of his star. These badges, by the by, except one that was stolen and replaced in Queen Anne's time, are the very same that decorated the original twelve brethren.

I have seldom met with a better guide than my friend the porter. He appeared to take a genuine interest in the peculiarities of the establishment, and yet had an existence apart from them, so that he could the better estimate what those peculiarities were. To be sure, his knowledge and observation were confined to external things, but, so far, had a sufficiently extensive scope. He led me up the staircase and exhibited portions of the timber framework of the edifice that are reckoned to be eight or nine hundred years old, and are still neither worm-eaten nor decayed; and traced out what had been a great hall in the days of the Catholic fraternity, though its area is now filled up with the apartments of the twelve brethren; and pointed to ornaments of sculptured oak, done in an ancient religious style of art, but hardly visible amid the vaulted dimness of the roof. Thence we went to the chapel — the Gothic church which I noted several pages back — surmounting the gateway that stretches half across the street. Here the brethren attend daily prayer, and have each a prayer-book of the finest paper, with a fair, large type for their old eyes. The interior of the chapel is very plain, with a picture of no merit for an altar-piece, and a single old pane of painted glass in the great eastern window, representing, — no saint, nor angel, as is customary in such cases, — but that grim sinner, the Earl of Leicester. Nevertheless, amid so many tangible proofs of his human sympathy, one comes to doubt whether the Earl could have been such a hardened reprobate, after all.

We ascended the tower of the chapel, and looked down between its battlements into the street, a hundred feet below us; while clambering half-way up were foxglove-flowers, weeds, small shrubs, and tufts of grass, that had rooted themselves into the roughnesses of the stone foundation. Far around us lay a rich and lovely English landscape, with many a church-spire and noble country-seat, and several objects of high historic interest. Edge Hill, where the Puritans defeated Charles I., is in sight on the edge of the horizon, and much nearer stands the house where Cromwell lodged on the night before the battle. Right under our eyes, and half enveloping the town with high-shouldering wall, so that all the closely compacted streets seemed but a precinct of the estate, was the Earl of Warwick's delightful park, a wide extent of sunny lawns, interspersed with broad contiguities of forest-shade. Some of the cedars of Lebanon were there, — a growth of trees in which the Warwick family take an hereditary pride. The two highest towers of the castle heave themselves up out of a mass of foliage, and look down in a lordly manner upon the plebeian roofs of the town, a part of which are slate-covered (these are the modern houses), and a part are coated with old red tiles, denoting the more ancient edifices. A hundred and sixty or seventy years ago, a great fire destroyed a considerable portion of the town, and doubtless annihilated many structures of a remote antiquity; at least, there was a possibility of very old houses in the long past of Warwick, which King Cymbeline is said to have founded in the year ONE of the Christian era!

And this historic fact or poetic fiction, whichever it may be, brings to mind a more indestructible reality than anything else that has occurred within the present field of our vision; though this includes the scene of Guy of Warwick's legendary exploits, and some of those of the Round Table, to say nothing of the Battle of Edge Hill. For perhaps it was in the landscape now under our eyes that Posthumus wandered with the King's daughter, the sweet, chaste, faithful, and courageous Imogen, the tenderest and womanliest woman that Shakespeare ever made immortal in the world. The silver Avon, which we see flowing so quietly by the gray castle, may have held their images in its bosom.

The day, though it began brightly, had long been overcast, and the clouds now spat down a few spiteful drops upon us, besides that the east-wind was very chill; so we descended the winding tower-stair, and went next into the garden, one side of which is shut in by almost the only remaining portion of the old city-wall. A part of the garden-ground is devoted to grass and shrubbery, and permeated by gravel-walks, in the centre of one of which is a beautiful stone vase of Egyptian sculpture, that formerly stood on the top of a Nilometer, or graduated pillar for measuring the rise and fall of the river Nile. On the pedestal is a Latin inscription by Dr. Parr, who (his vicarage of Hatton being so close at hand) was probably often the Master's guest, and smoked his interminable pipe along these garden-walks. Of the vegetable-garden, which lies adjacent, the lion's share is appropriated to the Master, and twelve small, separate patches to the individual brethren, who cultivate them at their own judgment and by their own labor; and their beans and cauliflowers have a better flavor, I doubt not, than if they had received them directly from the dead hand of the Earl of Leicester, like the rest of their food. In the farther part of the garden is an arbor for the old men's pleasure and convenience, and I should like well to sit down among them there, and find out what is really the bitter and the sweet of such a sort of life. As for the old gentlemen themselves, they put me queerly in mind of the Salem Custom House, and the venerable personages whom I found so quietly at anchor there.

The Master's residence, forming one entire side of the quadrangle, fronts on the garden, and wears an aspect at once stately and homely. It can hardly have undergone any perceptible change within three centuries; but the garden, into which its old windows look has probably put off a great many eccentricities and quaintnesses, in the way of cunningly clipped shrubbery, since the gardener of Queen Elizabeth's reign threw down his rusty shears and took his departure. The present Master's name is Harris; he is a descendant of the founder's family, a gentleman of independent fortune, and a clergyman of the Established Church, as the regulations of the hospital require him to be. I know not what are his official emoluments; but, according to all English precedent, an ancient charitable fund is certain to be held directly for the behoof of those who administer it, and perhaps incidentally, in a moderate way, for the nominal beneficiaries; and, in the case before us, the twelve brethren being so comfortably provided for, the Master is likely to be at least as comfortable as all the twelve together. Yet I ought not, even in a distant land, to fling an idle gibe against a gentleman of whom I really know nothing, except that the people under his charge bear all possible tokens of being tended and cared for as sedulously as if each of them sat by a warm fireside of his own, with a daughter bustling round the hearth to make ready his porridge and his titbits. It is delightful to think of the good life which a suitable man, in the Master's position, has an opportunity to lead, — linked to time-honored customs, welded in with an ancient system, never dreaming of radical change, and bringing all the mellowness and richness of the past down into these railway-days, which do not compel him or his community to move a whit quicker than of yore. Everybody can appreciate the advantages of going ahead; it might be well, sometimes, to think whether there is not a word or two to be said in favor of standing still or going to sleep.

From the garden we went into the kitchen, where the fire was burning hospitably, and diffused a genial warmth far and wide, together with the fragrance of some old English roast-beef, which, I think, must at that moment have been done nearly to a turn. The kitchen is a lofty, spacious, and noble room, partitioned off round the fireplace, by a sort of semicircular oaken screen, or rather, an arrangement of heavy and high-backed settles, with an ever-open entrance between them, on either side of which is the omnipresent image of the Bear and Ragged Staff, three feet high, and excellently carved in oak, now black with time and unctuous kitchen-smoke. The ponderous mantel-piece, likewise of carved oak, towers high towards the dusky ceiling, and extends its mighty breadth to take in a vast area of hearth, the arch of the fireplace being positively so immense that I could compare it to nothing but the city gateway. Above its cavernous opening were crossed two ancient halberds, the weapons, possibly, of soldiers who had fought under Leicester in the Low Countries; and elsewhere on the walls were displayed several muskets, which some of the present inmates of the hospital may have levelled against the French. Another ornament of the mantel-piece was a square of silken needlework or embroidery, faded nearly white, but dimly representing the wearisome Bear and Ragged Staff, which we should hardly look twice at, only that it was wrought by the fair fingers of poor Amy Robsart, and beautifully framed in oak from Kenilworth Castle, at the expense of a Mr. Conner, a countryman of our own. Certainly, no Englishman would be capable of this little bit of enthusiasm. Finally, the kitchen-firelight glistens on a splendid display of copper flagons, all of generous capacity, and one of them about as big as a half-barrel; the smaller vessels contain the customary allowance of ale, and the larger one is filled with that foaming liquor on four festive occasions of the year, and emptied amain by the jolly brotherhood. I should be glad to see them do it; but it would be an exploit fitter for Queen Elizabeth's age than these degenerate times.

The kitchen is the social hall of the twelve brethren. In the daytime, they bring their little messes to be cooked here, and eat them in their own parlors; but after a certain hour, the great hearth is cleared and swept, and the old men assemble round its blaze, each with his tankard and his pipe, and hold high converse through the evening. If the Master be a fit man for his office, methinks he will sometimes sit down sociably among them; for there is an elbow-chair by the fireside which it would not demean his dignity to fill, since it was occupied by King James at the great festival of nearly three centuries ago. A sip of the ale and a whiff of the tobacco-pipe would put him in friendly relations with his venerable household; and then we can fancy him instructing them by pithy apo-

thegms and religious texts, which were first uttered here by
some Catholic priest and have impregnated the atmosphere
ever since. If a joke goes round, it shall be of an elder coinage
than Joe Miller's, as old as Lord Bacon's collection, or as the
jest-book that Master Slender asked for when he lacked small-
talk for sweet Anne Page. No news shall be spoken of, later
than the drifting ashore, on the northern coast, of some stern-
post or figure-head, a barnacled fragment of one of the great
galleons of the Spanish Armada. What a tremor would pass
through the antique group, if a damp newspaper should suddenly be spread to dry before the fire! They would feel as if
either that printed sheet or they themselves must be an unreal-
ity. What a mysterious awe, if the shriek of the railway-train,
as it reaches the Warwick station, should ever so faintly invade
their ears! Movement of any kind seems inconsistent with
the stability of such an institution. Nevertheless, I trust that
the ages will carry it along with them; because it is such a
pleasant kind of dream for an American to find his way thither,
and behold a piece of the sixteenth century set into our prosaic
times, and then to depart, and think of its arched doorway as
a spell-guarded entrance which will never be accessible or visible to him any more.

Not far from the market-place of Warwick stands the great
church of St. Mary's: a vast edifice, indeed, and almost worthy
to be a cathedral. People who pretend to skill in such matters
say that it is in a poor style of architecture, though designed (or,
at least, extensively restored) by Sir Christopher Wren; but I
thought it very striking, with its wide, high, and elaborate
windows, its tall towers, its immense length, and (for it was
long before I outgrew this Americanism, the love of an old
thing merely for the sake of its age) the tinge of gray antiquity
over the whole. Once, while I stood gazing up at the tower,
the clock struck twelve with a very deep intonation, and immediately some chimes began to play, and kept up their
resounding music for five minutes, as measured by the hand
upon the dial. It was a very delightful harmony, as airy as

the notes of birds, and seemed a not unbecoming freak of half-sportive fancy in the huge, ancient, and solemn church; although I have seen an old-fashioned parlor-clock that did precisely the same thing, in its small way.

The great attraction of this edifice is the Beauchamp (or, as the English, who delight in vulgarizing their fine old Norman names, call it, the Beechum) Chapel, where the Earls of Warwick and their kindred have been buried, from four hundred years back till within a recent period. It is a stately and very elaborate chapel, with a large window of ancient painted glass, as perfectly preserved as any that I remember seeing in England, and remarkably vivid in its colors. Here are several monuments with marble figures recumbent upon them, representing the Earls in their knightly armor, and their dames in the ruffs and court-finery of their day, looking hardly stiffer in stone than they must needs have been in their starched linen and embroidery. The renowned Earl of Leicester of Queen Elizabeth's time, the benefactor of the hospital, reclines at full length on the tablet of one of these tombs, side by side with his Countess, — not Amy Robsart, but a lady who (unless I have confused the story with some other mouldy scandal) is said to have avenged poor Amy's murder by poisoning the Earl himself. Be that as it may, both figures, and especially the Earl, look like the very types of ancient Honor and Conjugal Faith. In consideration of his long-enduring kindness to the twelve brethren, I cannot consent to believe him as wicked as he is usually depicted; and it seems a marvel, now that so many well-established historical verdicts have been reversed, why some enterprising writer does not make out Leicester to have been the pattern nobleman of his age.

In the centre of the chapel is the magnificent memorial of its founder, Richard Beauchamp, Earl of Warwick in the time of Henry VI. On a richly ornamented altar-tomb of gray marble lies the bronze figure of a knight in gilded armor, most admirably executed: for the sculptors of those days had wonderful skill in their own style, and could make so lifelike an

image of a warrior, in brass or marble, that, if a trumpet were
sounded over his tomb, you would expect him to start up and
handle his sword. The Earl whom we now speak of, however,
has slept soundly in spite of a more serious disturbance than
any blast of a trumpet, unless it were the final one. Some
centuries after his death, the floor of the chapel fell down and
broke open the stone coffin in which he was buried; and among
the fragments appeared the anciently entombed Earl of Warwick, with the color scarcely faded out of his cheeks, his eyes
a little sunken, but in other respects looking as natural as if
he had died yesterday. But exposure to the atmosphere appeared to begin and finish the long-delayed process of decay
in a moment, causing him to vanish like a bubble; so that,
almost before there had been time to wonder at him, there
was nothing left of the stalwart Earl save his hair. This sole
relic the ladies of Warwick made prize of, and braided it into
rings and brooches for their own adornment; and thus, with
a chapel and a ponderous tomb built on purpose to protect
his remains, this great nobleman could not help being brought
untimely to the light of day, nor even keep his lovelocks on
his skull after he had so long done with love. There seems
to be a fatality that disturbs people in their sepulchres, when
they have been over-careful to render them magnificent and
impregnable, — as witness the builders of the Pyramids, and
Hadrian, Augustus, and the Scipios, and most other personages
whose mausoleums have been conspicuous enough to attract
the violator; and as for dead men's hair, I have seen a lock of
King Edward the Fourth's, of a reddish-brown color, which
perhaps was once twisted round the delicate forefinger of Mistress Shore.

The direct lineage of the renowned characters that lie buried
in this splendid chapel has long been extinct. The earldom
is now held by the Grevilles, descendants of the Lord Brooke
who was slain in the Parliamentary War; and they have recently
(that is to say, within a century) built a burial-vault on the
other side of the church, calculated (as the sexton assured me,

with a nod as if he were pleased) to afford suitable and respectful accommodation to as many as fourscore coffins. Thank Heaven, the old man did not call them "CASKETS"! — a vile modern phrase, which compels a person of sense and good taste to shrink more disgustfully than ever before from the idea of being buried at all. But as regards those eighty coffins, only sixteen have as yet been contributed; and it may be a question with some minds, not merely whether the Grevilles will hold the earldom of Warwick until the full number shall be made up, but whether earldoms and all manner of lordships will not have faded out of England long before those many generations shall have passed from the castle to the vault. I hope not. A titled and landed aristocracy, if anywise an evil and an encumbrance, is so only to the nation which is doomed to bear it on its shoulders; and an American, whose sole relation to it is to admire its picturesque effect upon society, ought to be the last man to quarrel with what affords him so much gratuitous enjoyment. Nevertheless, conservative as England is, and though I scarce ever found an Englishman who seemed really to desire change, there was continually a dull sound in my ears as if the old foundations of things were crumbling away. Some time or other, — by no irreverent effort of violence, but, rather, in spite of all pious efforts to uphold a heterogeneous pile of institutions that will have outlasted their vitality, — at some unexpected moment, there must come a terrible crash. The sole reason why I should desire it to happen in my day is, that I might be there to see! But the ruin of my own country is, perhaps, all that I am destined to witness; and that immense catastrophe (though I am strong in the faith that there is a national lifetime of a thousand years in us yet) would serve any man well enough as his final spectacle on earth.

If the visitor is inclined to carry away any little memorial of Warwick, he had better go to an Old Curiosity Shop in the High Street, where there is a vast quantity of obsolete gewgaws, great and small, and many of them so pretty and ingenious

that you wonder how they came to be thrown aside and forgotten. As regards its minor tastes, the world changes, but
does not improve; it appears to me, indeed, that there have
been epochs of far more exquisite fancy than the present one,
in matters of personal ornament, and such delicate trifles as
we put upon a drawing-room table, a mantel-piece, or a what-
not. The shop in question is near the East Gate, but is hardly
to be found without careful search, being denoted only by the
name of "REDFERN," painted not very conspicuously in the
top-light of the door. Immediately on entering, we find ourselves among a confusion of old rubbish and valuables, ancient
armor, historic portraits, ebony cabinets inlaid with pearl, tall,
ghostly clocks, hideous old china, dim looking-glasses in frames
of tarnished magnificence, — a thousand objects of strange
aspect, and others that almost frighten you by their likeness
in unlikeness to things now in use. It is impossible to give
an idea of the variety of articles, so thickly strewn about that
we can scarcely move without overthrowing some great curiosity with a crash, or sweeping away some small one hitched to
our sleeves. Three stories of the entire house are crowded in
like manner. The collection even as we see it exposed to view,
must have been got together at great cost; but the real treasures
of the establishment lie in secret repositories, whence they
are not likely to be drawn forth at an ordinary summons;
though, if a gentleman with a competently long purse should
call for them, I doubt not that the signet-ring of Joseph's
friend Pharaoh, or the Duke of Alva's leading staff, or the
dagger that killed the Duke of Buckingham (all of which I
have seen), or any other almost incredible thing, might make
its appearance. Gold snuff-boxes, antique gems, jewelled goblets, Venetian wine-glasses (which burst when poison is poured
into them, and therefore must not be used for modern wine-
drinking), jasper-handled knives, painted Sêvres teacups, — in
short, there are all sorts of things that a virtuoso ransacks the
world to discover.

It would be easier to spend a hundred pounds in Mr. Redfern's shop than to keep the money in one's pocket; but, for my part, I contented myself with buying a little old spoon of silver-gilt, and fantastically shaped, and got it at all the more reasonable rate because there happened to be no legend attached to it. I could supply any deficiency of that kind at much less expense than regilding the spoon!

Recollections of a Gifted Woman

[Shakespeare Country]

FROM Leamington to Stratford-on-Avon the distance is eight
or nine miles, over a road that seemed to me most beautiful.
Not that I can recall any memorable peculiarities; for the
country, most of the way, is a succession of the gentlest swells
and subsidences, affording wide and far glimpses of champaign
scenery here and there, and sinking almost to a dead level as
we draw near Stratford. Any landscape in New England,
even the tamest, has a more striking outline, and, besides,
would have its blue eyes open in those lakelets that we encounter almost from mile to mile at home, but of which the
Old Country is utterly destitute; or it would smile in our faces
through the medium of the wayside brooks that vanish under
a low stone arch on one side of the road, and sparkle out again
on the other. Neither of these pretty features is often to be
found in an English scene. The charm of the latter consists
in the rich verdure of the fields, in the stately wayside trees
and carefully kept plantations of wood, and in the old and
high cultivation that has humanized the very sods by mingling
so much of man's toil and care among them. To an American
there is a kind of sanctity even in an English turnip-field,
when he thinks how long that small square of ground has
been known and recognized as a possession, transmitted from

father to son, trodden often by memorable feet, and utterly redeemed from savagery by old acquaintanceship with civilized eyes.   The wildest things in England are more than half tame. The trees, for instance, whether in hedge-row, park, or what they call forest, have nothing wild about them.   They are never ragged; there is a certain decorous restraint in the freest outspread of their branches, though they spread wider than any self-nurturing tree; they are tall, vigorous, bulky, with a look of age-long life, and a promise of more years to come, all of which will bring them into closer kindred with the race of man.   Somebody or other has known them from the sapling upward; and if they endure long enough, they grow to be traditionally observed and honored, and connected with the fortunes of old families, till, like Tennyson's Talking Oak, they babble with a thousand leafy tongues to ears that can understand them.

An American tree, however, if it could grow in fair competition with an English one of similar species, would probably be the more picturesque object of the two.   The Warwickshire elm has not so beautiful a shape as those that overhang our village street; and as for the redoubtable English oak, there is a certain John Bullism in its figure, a compact rotundity of foliage, a lack of irregular and various outline, that make it look wonderfully like a gigantic cauliflower.   Its leaf, too, is much smaller than that of most varieties of American oak; nor do I mean to doubt that the latter, with free leave to grow, reverent care and cultivation, and immunity from the axe, would live out its centuries as sturdily as its English brother, and prove far the nobler and more majestic specimen of a tree at the end of them.   Still, however one's Yankee patriotism may struggle against the admission, it must be owned that the trees and other objects of an English landscape take hold of the observer by numberless minute tendrils, as it were, which, look as closely as we choose, we never find in an American scene.   The parasitic growth is so luxuriant, that the trunk of the tree, so gray and dry in our climate, is better worth observing than the boughs and foliage; a verdant mossiness coats it all over; so that it looks almost as green as the leaves; and often, moreover, the stately stem is clustered about, high upward, with creeping and twining shrubs, the ivy, and sometimes the mistletoe, close-clinging friends, nurtured by the moisture and never too fervid sunshine, and supporting themselves by the old tree's abundant strength. We call it a parasitical vegetation; but, if the phrase imply any reproach, it is unkind to bestow it on this beautiful affection and relationship which exist in England between one order of plants and another: the strong tree being always ready to give support to the trailing shrub, lift it to the sun, and feed it out of its own heart, if it crave such food; and the shrub, on its part, repaying its foster-father with an ample luxuriance of beauty, and adding Corinthian grace to the tree's lofty strength. No bitter winter nips these tender little sympathies, no hot sun burns the life out of them; and therefore they outlast the longevity of the oak, and, if the woodman permitted, would bury it in a green grave, when all is over.

Should there be nothing else along the road to look at, an English hedge might well suffice to occupy the eyes, and, to a depth beyond what he would suppose, the heart of an American. We often set out hedges in our own soil, but might as well set out figs or pineapples and expect to gather fruit of them. Something grows, to be sure, which we choose to call a hedge; but it lacks the dense, luxuriant variety of vegetation that is accumulated into the English original, in which a botanist would find a thousand shrubs and gracious herbs that the hedgemaker never thought of planting there. Among them, growing wild, are many of the kindred blossoms of the very flowers which our pilgrim fathers brought from England, for the sake of their simple beauty and homelike associations, and which we have ever since been cultivating in gardens. There is not a softer trait to be found in the character of those stern men than that they should have been sensible of these flower-roots clinging among the fibres of their rugged hearts, and have felt the necessity of bringing them over sea and making them hereditary in the new land, instead of trusting to what rarer beauty the wilderness might have in store for them.

Or, if the roadside has no hedge, the ugliest stone fence (such as, in America, would keep itself bare and unsympathizing till the end of time) is sure to be covered with the small handiwork of Nature; that careful mother lets nothing go naked there, and if she cannot provide clothing, gives at least embroidery. No sooner is the fence built than she adopts and adorns it as a part of her original plan, treating the hard, uncomely construction as if it had all along been a favorite idea of her own. A little sprig of ivy may be seen creeping up the side of the low wall and clinging fast with its many feet to the rough surface; a tuft of grass roots itself between two of the stones, where a pinch or two of wayside dust has been moistened into nutritious soil for it; a small bunch of fern grows in another crevice; a deep, soft, verdant moss spreads itself along the top, and over all the available inequalities of the fence; and where nothing else will grow, lichens stick tenaciously to the bare stones, and variegate the monotonous gray with hues of yellow and red. Finally, a great deal of shrubbery clusters along the base of the stone wall, and takes away the hardness of its outline; and in due time, as the upshot of these apparently aimless or sportive touches, we recognize that the beneficent Creator of all things, working through his hand-maiden whom we call Nature, has designed to mingle a charm of divine gracefulness even with so earthly an institution as a boundary fence. The clown who wrought at it little dreamed what fellow-laborer he had.

The English should send us photographs of portions of the trunks of trees, the tangled and various products of a hedge, and a square foot of an old wall. They can hardly send anything else so characteristic. Their artists, especially of the later school, sometimes toil to depict such subjects, but are apt to stiffen the lithe tendrils in the process. The poets

succeed better, with Tennyson at their head, and often produce
ravishing effects by dint of a tender minuteness of touch, to
which the genius of the soil and climate artfully impels them:
for, as regards grandeur, there are loftier scenes in many countries than the best that England can show; but, for the picturesqueness of the smallest object that lies under its gentle gloom
and sunshine, there is no scenery like it anywhere.

In the foregoing paragraphs I have strayed away to a long
distance from the road to Stratford-on-Avon; for I remember
no such stone fences as I have been speaking of in Warwickshire, nor elsewhere in England, except among the Lakes, or
in Yorkshire, and the rough and hilly countries to the north
of it.   Hedges there were along my road, however, and broad,
level fields, rustic hamlets, and cottages of ancient date, —
from the roof of one of which the occupant was tearing away
the thatch, and showing what an accumulation of dust, dirt,
mouldiness, roots of weeds, families of mice, swallows'-nests,
and hordes of insects had been deposited there since that old
straw was new.   Estimating its antiquity from these tokens,
Shakespeare himself, in one of his morning rambles out of
his native town, might have seen the thatch laid on; at all
events, the cottage-walls were old enough to have known him
as a guest.   A few modern villas were also to be seen, and
perhaps there were mansions of old gentility at no great distance, but hidden among trees; for it is a point of English
pride that such houses seldom allow themselves to be visible
from the high-road.   In short, I recollect nothing specially remarkable along the way, nor in the immediate approach to
Stratford; and yet the picture of that June morning has a glory
in my memory, owing chiefly, I believe, to the charm of the
English summer-weather, the really good days of which are the
most delightful that mortal man can ever hope to be favored
with.   Such a genial warmth!   A little too warm, it might
be, yet only to such a degree as to assure an American (a
certainty to which he seldom attains till attempered to the
customary austerity of an English summer-day) that he was

quite warm enough.   And after all, there was an unconquerable freshness in the atmosphere, which every little movement of a breeze shook over me like a dash of the ocean-spray.   Such days need bring us no other happiness than their own light and temperature.   No doubt, I could not have enjoyed it so exquisitely, except that there must be still latent in us, Western wanderers (even after an absence of two centuries and more), an adaptation to the English climate which makes us sensible of a motherly kindness in its scantiest sunshine, and overflows us with delight at its more lavish smiles.

The spire of Shakespeare's church — the Church of the Holy Trinity — begins to show itself among the trees at a little distance from Stratford.   Next we see the shabby old dwellings, intermixed with mean-looking houses of modern date; and the streets being quite level, you are struck and surprised by nothing so much as the tameness of the general scene, as if Shakespeare's genius were vivid enough to have wrought pictorial splendors in the town where he was born.   Here and there, however, a queer edifice meets your eye, endowed with the individuality that belongs only to the domestic architecture of times gone by; the house seems to have grown out of some odd quality in its inhabitant, as a sea-shell is moulded from within by the character of its inmate; and having been built in a strange fashion, generations ago, it has ever since been growing stranger and quainter, as old humorists are apt to do. Here, too (as so often impressed me in decayed English towns), there appeared to be a greater abundance of aged people wearing small-clothes and leaning on sticks than you could assemble on our side of the water by sounding a trumpet and proclaiming a reward for the most venerable.   I tried to account for this phenomenon by several theories: as, for example, that our new towns are unwholesome for age and kill it off unseasonably; or that our old men have a subtile sense of fitness, and die of their own accord rather than live in an unseemly contrast with youth and novelty: but the secret may be, after all, that hair-dyes, false teeth, modern arts of dress,

and contrivances of a skin-deep youthfulness, have not crept
into these antiquated English towns, and so people grow old
without the weary necessity of seeming younger than they are.

After wandering through two or three streets, I found my
way to Shakespeare's birthplace, which is almost a smaller and
humbler house than any description can prepare the visitor to
expect; so inevitably does an august inhabitant make his abode
palatial to our imaginations, receiving his guests, indeed, in a
castle in the air, until we unwisely insist on meeting him
among the sordid lanes and alleys of lower earth.   The portion
of the edifice with which Shakespeare had anything to do is
hardly large enough, in the basement, to contain the butcher's
stall that one of his descendants kept, and that still remains
there, windowless, with the cleaver-cuts in its hacked counter,
which projects into the street under a little penthouse-roof, as
if waiting for a new occupant.

The upper half of the door was open, and, on my rapping
at it, a young person in black made her appearance and admitted me; she was not a menial, but remarkably genteel (an
American characteristic) for an English girl, and was probably
the daughter of the old gentlewoman who takes care of the
house.   This lower room has a pavement of gray slabs of stone,
which may have been rudely squared when the house was new,
but are now all cracked, broken, and disarranged in a most
unaccountable way.   One does not see how any ordinary usage,
for whatever length of time, should have so smashed these
heavy stones; it is as if an earthquake had burst up through the
floor, which afterwards had been imperfectly trodden down
again.   The room is whitewashed and very clean, but wofully
shabby and dingy, coarsely built, and such as the most poetical
imagination would find it difficult to idealize.   In the rear of
this apartment is the kitchen, a still smaller room, of a similar
rude aspect; it has a great, rough fireplace, with space for a
large family under the blackened opening of the chimney, and
an immense passageway for the smoke, through which Shakespeare may have seen the blue sky by day and the stars glim-

mering down at him by night.   It is now a dreary spot where
the long-extinguished embers used to be.   A glowing fire, even
if it covered only a quarter part of the hearth, might still do
much towards making the old kitchen cheerful.   But we get
a depressing idea of the stifled, poor, sombre kind of life that
could have been lived in such a dwelling, where this room
seems to have been the gathering-place of the family, with no
breadth or scope, no good retirement, but old and young
huddling together cheek by jowl.   What a hardy plant was
Shakespeare's genius, how fatal its development, since it could
not be blighted in such an atmosphere!   It only brought human nature the closer to him, and put more unctuous earth
about his roots.

Thence I was ushered up stairs to the room in which Shakespeare is supposed to have been born: though, if you peep too
curiously into the matter, you may find the shadow of an ugly
doubt on this, as well as most other points of his mysterious
life.   It is the chamber over the butcher's shop, and is lighted
by one broad window containing a great many small, irregular
panes of glass.   The floor is made of planks, very rudely hewn,
and fitting together with little neatness; the naked beams and
rafters, at the sides of the room and overhead, bear the original
marks of the builder's broad-axe, with no evidence of an attempt to smooth off the job.   Again we have to reconcile
ourselves to the smallness of the space enclosed by these illustrious walls, — a circumstance more difficult to accept, as regards
places that we have heard, read, thought, and dreamed much
about, than any other disenchanting particular of a mistaken
ideal.   A few paces — perhaps seven or eight — take us from
end to end of it.   So low it is, that I could easily touch the
ceiling, and might have done so without a tiptoe-stretch, had
it been a good deal higher; and this humility of the chamber
has tempted a vast multitude of people to write their names
overhead in pencil.   Every inch of the side-walls, even into
the obscurest nooks and corners, is covered with a similar
record; all the windowpanes, moreover, are scrawled with

diamond signatures, among which is said to be that of Walter Scott; but so many persons have sought to immortalize themselves in close vicinity to his name, that I really could not trace him out.   Methinks it is strange that people do not strive to forget their forlorn little identities, in such situations, instead of thrusting them forward into the dazzle of a great renown, where, if noticed, they cannot but be deemed impertinent.

This room, and the entire house, so far as I saw it, are whitewashed and exceedingly clean; nor is there the aged, musty smell with which old Chester first made me acquainted, and which goes far to cure an American of his excessive predilection for antique residences.   An old lady, who took charge of me upstairs, had the manners and aspect of a gentlewoman, and talked with somewhat formidable knowledge and appreciative intelligence about Shakespeare.   Arranged on a table and in chairs were various prints, views of houses and scenes connected with Shakespeare's memory, together with editions of his works and local publications about his home and haunts, from the sale of which this respectable lady perhaps realizes a handsome profit.   At any rate, I bought a good many of them, conceiving that it might be the civilest way of requiting her for her instructive conversation and the trouble she took in showing me the house.   It cost me a pang (not a curmudgeonly, but a gentlemanly one) to offer a downright fee to the ladylike girl who had admitted me; but I swallowed my delicate scruples with some little difficulty, and she digested hers, so far as I could observe, with no difficulty at all.   In fact, nobody need fear to hold out half a crown to any person with whom he has occasion to speak a word in England.

I should consider it unfair to quit Shakespeare's house without the frank acknowledgment that I was conscious of not the slighest emotion while viewing it, nor any quickening of the imagination.   This has often happened to me in my visits to memorable places.   Whatever pretty and apposite reflections I may have made upon the subject had either occurred to me before I ever saw Stratford, or have been elaborated since.   It is pleasant, nevertheless, to think that I have seen the place; and I believe that I can form a more sensible and vivid idea of Shakespeare as a flesh-and-blood individual now that I have stood on the kitchen-hearth and in the birth-chamber; but I am not quite certain that this power of realization is altogether desirable in reference to a great poet.   The Shakespeare whom I met there took various guises, but had not his laurel on.   He was successively the roguish boy, — the youthful deer-stealer, — the comrade of players, — the too familiar friend of Davenant's mother, — the careful, thrifty, thriven man of property who came back from London to lend money on bond, and occupy the best house in Stratford, — the mellow, red-nosed, autumnal boon-companion of John a' Combe, — and finally (or else the Stratford gossips belied him), the victim of convivial habits, who met his death by tumbling into a ditch on his way home from a drinking-bout, and left his second-best bed to his poor wife.

I feel, as sensibly as the reader can, what horrible impiety it is to remember these things, be they true or false.   In either case, they ought to vanish out of sight on the distant ocean-line of the past, leaving a pure, white memory, even as a sail, though perhaps darkened with many stains, looks snowy white on the far horizon.   But I draw a moral from these unworthy reminiscences and this embodiment of the poet, as suggested by some of the grimy actualities of his life. It is for the high interests of the world not to insist upon finding out that its greatest men are, in a certain lower sense, very much the same kind of men as the rest of us, and often a little worse; because a common mind cannot properly digest such a discovery, nor ever know the true proportion of the great man's good and evil, nor how small a part of him it was that touched our muddy or dusty earth.   Thence comes moral bewilderment, and even intellectual loss, in regard to what is best of him. When Shakespeare invoked a curse on the man who should stir his bones, he perhaps meant the larger share of it for him

or them who should pry into his perishing earthliness, the
defects or even the merits of the character that he wore in
Stratford, when he had left mankind so much to muse upon
that was imperishable and divine. Heaven keep me from incurring any part of the anathema in requital for the irreverent
sentences above written! . . .

This has been too sad a story.* To lighten the recollection
of it, I will think of my stroll homeward past Charlecote Park,
where I beheld the most stately elms, singly, in clumps, and
in groves, scattered all about in the sunniest, shadiest, sleepiest
fashion; so that I could not but believe in lengthened, loitering, drowsy enjoyment which these trees must have in their
existence.   Diffused over slow-paced centuries, it need not be
keen nor bubble into thrills and ecstasies, like the momentary
delights of short-lived human beings.   They were civilized
trees, known to man, and befriended by him for ages past.
There is an indescribable difference — as I believe I have
heretofore endeavored to express — between the tamed, but by
no means effete (on the contrary, the richer and more luxuriant), nature of England, and the rude, shaggy, barbarous nature
which offers us its racier companionship in America.   No less
a change has been wrought among the wildest creatures that
inhabit what the English call their forests.   By and by, among
those refined and venerable trees, I saw a large herd of deer,
mostly reclining, but some standing in picturesque groups,
while the stags threw their large antlers aloft, as if they had
been taught to make themselves tributary to the scenic effect.
Some were running fleetly about, vanishing from light into
shadow and glancing forth again, with here and there a little
fawn careering at its mother's heels.   These deer are almost
in the same relation to the wild, natural state of their kind
that the trees of an English park hold to the rugged growth of
an American forest.   They have held a certain intercourse
with man for immemorial years; and, most probably, the stag

*[An account of Delia Bacon's insanity.]

that Shakespeare killed was one of the progenitors of this very herd, and may himself have been a partly civilized and humanized deer, though in a less degree than these remote posterity. They are a little wilder than sheep, but they do not snuff the air at the approach of human beings, nor evince much alarm at their pretty close proximity; although if you continue to advance, they toss their heads and take to their heels in a kind of mimic terror, or something akin to feminine skittishness, with a dim remembrance or tradition, as it were, of their having come of a wild stock. They have so long been fed and protected by man, that they must have lost many of their native instincts, and, I suppose, could not live comfortably through even an English winter without human help. One is sensible of a gentle scorn at them for such dependency, but feels none the less kindly disposed towards the half-domesticated race; and it may have been his observation of these tamer characteristics in the Charlecote herd that suggested to Shakespeare the tender and pitiful description of a wounded stag, in "As You Like It."

At a distance of some hundreds of yards from Charlecote Hall, and almost hidden by the trees between it and the roadside, is an old brick archway and porter's lodge. In connection with this entrance there appears to have been a wall and an ancient moat, the latter of which is still visible, a shallow, grassy scoop along the base of an embankment of the lawn. About fifty yards within the gateway stands the house, forming three sides of a square, with three gables in a row on the front, and on each of the two wings; and there are several towers and turrets at the angles, together with projecting windows, antique balconies, and other quaint ornaments suitable to the half-Gothic taste in which the edifice was built. Over the gateway is the Lucy coat of arms, emblazoned in its proper colors. The mansion dates from the early days of Elizabeth, and probably looked very much the same as now when Shakespeare was brought before Sir Thomas Lucy for outrages among his deer.   The impression is not that of gray antiquity, but of stable and time-honored gentility, still as vital as ever.

It is a most delightful place.   All about the house and domain there is a perfection of comfort and domestic taste, an amplitude of convenience, which could have been brought about only by the slow ingenuity and labor of many successive generations, intent upon adding all possible improvement to the home where years gone by and years to come give a sort of permanence to the intangible present.   An American is sometimes tempted to fancy that only by this long process can real homes be produced.   One man's lifetime is not enough for the accomplishment of such a work of art and nature, almost the greatest merely temporary one that is confided to him; too little, at any rate, — yet perhaps too long when he is discouraged by the idea that he must make his house warm and delightful for a miscellaneous race of successors, of whom the one thing certain is, that his own grandchildren will not be among them.   Such repinings as are here suggested, however, come only from the fact, that, bred in English habits of thought, as most of us are, we have not yet modified our instincts to the necessities of our new forms of life.   A lodging in a wigwam or under a tent has really as many advantages, when we come to know them, as a home beneath the roof-tree of Charlecote Hall.   But, alas! our philosophers have not yet taught us what is best, nor have our poets sung us what is beautifullest, in the kind of life that we must lead; and therefore we still read the old English wisdom, and harp upon the ancient strings.   And thence it happens, that, when we look at a time-honored hall, it seems more possible for men who inherit such a home, than for ourselves, to lead noble and graceful lives, quietly doing good and lovely things as their daily work, and achieving deeds of simple greatness when circumstances require them.   I sometimes apprehend that our institutions may perish before we shall have discovered the most precious of the possibilities which they involve.

Lichfield and Uttoxeter

AFTER my first visit to Leamington Spa, I went by an indirect route to Lichfield, and put up at the Black Swan. Had I known where to find it, I would much rather have established myself at the inn formerly kept by the worthy Mr. Boniface, so famous for his ale in Farquhar's time. The Black Swan is an oldfashioned hotel, its street-front being penetrated by an arched passage, in either side of which is an entrance-door to the different parts of the house, and through which, and over the large stones of its pavement, all vehicles and horsemen rumble and clatter into an enclosed court-yard, with a thunderous uproar among the contiguous rooms and chambers. I appeared to be the only guest of the spacious establishment, but may have had a few fellow-lodgers hidden in their separate parlors, and utterly eschewing that community of interests which is the characteristic feature of life in an American hotel. At any rate, I had the great, dull, dingy, and dreary coffeeroom, with its heavy old mahogany chairs and tables, all to myself, and not a soul to exchange a word with, except the waiter, who, like most of his class in England, had evidently left his conversational abilities uncultivated. No former practice of solitary living, nor habits of reticence, nor well-tested self-dependence for occupation of mind and amusement, can

quite avail, as I now proved, to dissipate the ponderous gloom
of an English coffee-room under such circumstances as these,
with no book at hand save the county-directory, nor any newspaper but a torn local journal of five days ago.   So I buried
myself, betimes, in a huge heap of ancient feathers (there is
no other kind of bed in these old inns), let my head sink into
an unsubstantial pillow, and slept a stifled sleep, infested with
such a fragmentary confusion of dreams that I took them to
be a medley, compounded of the night-troubles of all my
predecessors in that same unrestful couch.   And when I awoke,
the musty odor of a by-gone century was in my nostrils, — a
faint, elusive smell, of which I never had any conception before
crossing the Atlantic.

In the morning, after a mutton-chop and a cup of chiccory
in the dusky coffee-room, I went forth and bewildered myself a
little while among the crooked streets, in quest of one or two
objects that had chiefly attracted me to the spot.   The city is of
very ancient date, and its name in the old Saxon tongue has a
dismal import that would apply well, in these days and forever
henceforward, to many an unhappy locality in our native land.
Lichfield signifies "The Field of the Dead Bodies," — an epithet, however, which the town did not assume in remembrance
of a battle, but which probably sprung up by a natural process,
like a sprig of rue or other funereal weed, out of the graves
of two princely brothers, sons of a pagan king of Mercia, who
were converted by St. Chad, and afterwards martyred for their
Christian faith.   Nevertheless, I was but little interested in
the legends of the remote antiquity of Lichfield, being drawn
thither partly to see its beautiful cathedral, and still more, I
believe, because it was the birthplace of Dr. Johnson, with
whose sturdy English character I became acquainted, at a very
early period in my life, through the good offices of Mr. Boswell.
In truth, he seems as familiar to my recollection, and almost
as vivid in his personal aspect to my mind's eye, as the kindly
figure of my own grandfather.   It is only a solitary child, —
left much to such wild modes of culture as he chooses for him-

self while yet ignorant what culture means, standing on tiptoe to pull down books from no very lofty shelf, and then shutting himself up, as it were, between the leaves, going astray through the volume at his own pleasure, and comprehending it rather by his sensibilities and affections than his intellect, — that child is the only student that ever gets the sort of intimacy which I am now thinking of, with a literary personage. I do not remember, indeed, ever caring much about any of the stalwart Doctor's grandiloquent productions, except his two stern and masculine poems, "London," and "The Vanity of Human Wishes;" it was as a man, a talker, and a humorist, that I knew and loved him, appreciating many of his qualities perhaps more thoroughly than I do now, though never seeking to put my instinctive perception of his character into language.

Beyond all question, I might have had a wiser friend than he. The atmosphere in which alone he breathed was dense; his awful dread of death showed how much muddy imperfection was to be cleansed out of him, before he could be capable of spiritual existence; he meddled only with the surface of life, and never cared to penetrate further than to ploughshare depth; his very sense and sagacity were but a one-eyed clear-sightedness. I laughed at him, sometimes, standing beside his knee. And yet, considering that my native propensities were towards Fairy Land, and also how much yeast is generally mixed up with the mental sustenance of a New-Englander, it may not have been altogether amiss, in those childish and boy-ish days, to keep pace with this heavy-footed traveller, and feed on the gross diet that he carried in his knapsack. It is wholesome food even now. And, then, how English! Many of the latent sympathies that enabled me to enjoy the Old Country so well, and that so readily amalgamated themselves with the American ideas that seemed most adverse to them, may have been derived from, or fostered and kept alive by, the great English moralist. Never was a descriptive epithet more nicely appropriate than that! Dr. Johnson's morality was as English an article as a beefsteak.

The city of Lichfield (only the cathedral-towns are called cities in England) stands on an ascending site. It has not so many old gabled houses as Coventry, for example, but still enough to gratify an American appetite for the antiquities of domestic architecture. The people, too, have an old-fashioned way with them, and stare at the passing visitor, as if the railway had not yet quite accustomed them to the novelty of strange faces moving along their ancient sidewalks. The old women whom I met, in several instances, dropt me a courtesy; and as they were of decent and comfortable exterior, and kept quietly on their way without pause or further greeting, it certainly was not allowable to interpret their little act of respect as a modest method of asking for sixpence; so that I had the pleasure of considering it a remnant of the reverential and hospitable manners of elder times, when the rare presence of a stranger might be deemed worth a general acknowledgment. Positively, coming from such humble sources, I took it all the more as a welcome on behalf of the inhabitants, and would not have exchanged it for an invitation from the mayor and magistrates to a public dinner. Yet I wish, merely for the experiment's sake, that I could have emboldened myself to hold out the aforesaid sixpence to at least one of the old ladies....

I know not what rank the Cathedral of Lichfield holds among its sister edifices in England, as a piece of magnificent architecture. Except that of Chester (the grim and simple nave of which stands yet unrivalled in my memory), and one or two small ones in North Wales, hardly worthy of the name of cathedrals, it was the first that I had seen. To my uninstructed vision, it seemed the object best worth gazing at in the whole world; and now, after beholding a great many more, I remember it with less prodigal admiration only because others are as magnificent as itself. The traces remaining in my memory represent it as airy rather than massive. A multitude of beautiful shapes appeared to be comprehended within its single outline; it was a kind of kaleidoscopic mystery so rich a variety of aspects did it assume from each altered point of view, through the presentation of a different face, and the rearrangement of its peaks and pinnacles and the three battlemented towers, with the spires that shot heavenward from all three, but one loftier than its fellows. Thus it impressed you, at every change, as a newly created structure of the passing moment, in which yet you lovingly recognized the half-vanished structure of the instant before, and felt, moreover, a joyful faith in the indestructible existence of all this cloudlike vicissitude. A Gothic cathedral is surely the most wonderful work which mortal man has yet achieved, so vast, so intricate, and so profoundly simple, with such strange, delightful recesses in its grand figure, so difficult to comprehend within one idea, and yet all so consonant that it ultimately draws the beholder and his universe into its harmony. It is the only thing in the world that is vast enough and rich enough.

Not that I felt, or was worthy to feel, an unmingled enjoyment in gazing at this wonder. I could not elevate myself to its spiritual height, any more than I could have climbed from the ground to the summit of one of its pinnacles. Ascending but a little way, I continually fell back and lay in a kind of despair, conscious that a flood of uncomprehended beauty was pouring down upon me, of which I could appropriate only the minutest portion. After a hundred years, incalculably as my higher sympathies might be invigorated by so divine an employment, I should still be a gazer from below and at an awful distance, as yet remotely excluded from the interior mystery. But it was something gained, even to have that painful sense of my own limitations, and that half-smothered yearning to soar beyond them. The cathedral showed me how earthly I was, but yet whispered deeply of immortality. After all, this was probably the best lesson that it could bestow, and, taking it as thoroughly as possible home to my heart, I was fain to be content. If the truth must be told, my ill-trained enthusiasm soon flagged, and I began to lose the vision of a spiritual or ideal edifice behind the time-worn and weather-stained front of the actual structure. Whenever

that is the case, it is most reverential to look another way;
but the mood disposes one to minute investigation, and I
took advantage of it to examine the intricate and multitudinous adornment that was lavished on the exterior wall of
this great church.   Everywhere, there were empty niches where
statues had been thrown down, and here and there a statue
still lingered in its niche; and over the chief entrance, and
extending across the whole breadth of the building, was a
row of angels, sainted personages, martyrs, and kings, sculptured in reddish stone.   Being much corroded by the moist
English atmosphere, during four or five hundred winters that
they had stood there, these benign and majestic figures per-
versely put me in mind of the appearance of a sugar image,
after a child has been holding it in his mouth.   The venerable infant Time has evidently found them sweet morsels.

Inside of the Minster there is a long and lofty nave, transepts
of the same height, and side-aisles and chapels, dim nooks of
holiness, where in Catholic times the lamps were continually
burning before the richly decorated shrines of saints.   In the
audacity of my ignorance, as I humbly acknowledge it to have
been, I criticised this great interior as too much broken into
compartments, and shorn of half its rightful impressiveness
by the interposition of a screen betwixt the nave and chancel.
It did not spread itself in breadth, but ascended to the roof
in lofty narrowness.   One large body of worshippers might
have knelt down in the nave, others in each of the transepts,
and smaller ones in the side-aisles, besides an indefinite number of esoteric enthusiasts in the mysterious sanctities beyond
the screen.   Thus it seemed to typify the exclusiveness of sects,
rather than the world-wide hospitality of genuine religion.
I had imagined a cathedral with a scope more vast.   These
Gothic aisles, with their groined arches overhead, supported
by clustered pillars in long vistas up and down, were venerable and magnificent, but included too much of the twilight
of that monkish gloom out of which they grew.   It is no
matter whether I ever came to a more satisfactory appreciation

of this kind of architecture; the only value of my strictures being to show the folly of looking at noble objects in the wrong mood, and the absurdity of a new visitant pretending to hold any opinion whatever on such subjects, instead of surrendering himself to the old builder's influence with child-like simplicity.

A great deal of white marble decorates the old stone-work of the aisles, in the shape of altars, obelisks, sarcophagi, and busts. Most of these memorials are commemorative of people locally distinguished, especially the deans and canons of the Cathedral, with their relatives and families; and I found but two monuments of personages whom I had ever heard of, — one being Gilbert Walmesley and the other Lady Mary Wortley Montagu, a literary acquaintance of my boyhood. It was really pleasant to meet her there; for after a friend has lain in the grave far into the second century, she would be unreasonable to require any melancholy emotions in a chance interview at her tombstone. It adds a rich charm to sacred edifices, this time-honored custom of burial in churches, after a few years, at least, when the mortal remains have turned to dust beneath the pavement, and the quaint devices and inscriptions still speak to you above. The statues, that stood or reclined in several recesses of the Cathedral, had a kind of life, and I regarded them with an odd sort of deference, as if they were privileged denizens of the precinct. It was singular, too, how the memorial of the latest buried person, the man whose features were familiar in the streets of Lichfield only yesterday, seemed precisely as much at home here as his mediaeval predecessors. Henceforward he belonged to the Cathedral like one of its original pillars. Methought this impression in my fancy might be the shadow of a spiritual fact. The dying melt into the great multitude of the Departed as quietly as a drop of water into the ocean, and, it may be, are conscious of no unfamiliarity with their new circumstances, but immediately become aware of an insufferable strangeness in the world which they have quitted. Death has not taken them away, but brought them home.

The vicissitudes and mischances of sublunary affairs, however, have not ceased to attend upon these marble inhabitants; for I saw the upper fragment of a sculptured lady, in a very old-fashioned garb, the lower half of whom had doubtless been demolished by Cromwell's soldiers when they took the Minster by storm. And there lies the remnant of this devout lady on her slab, ever since the outrage, as for centuries before, with a countenance of divine serenity, and her hands clasped in prayer, symbolizing a depth of religious faith which no earthly turmoil or calamity could disturb. Another piece of sculpture (apparently a favorite subject in the Middle Ages, for I have seen several like it in other cathedrals) was a reclining skeleton, as faithfully representing an open-work of bones as could well be expected in a solid block of marble, and at a period, moreover, when the mysteries of the human frame were rather to be guessed at than revealed. Whatever the anatomical defects of his production, the old sculptor had succeeded in making it ghastly beyond measure. How much mischief has been wrought upon us by this invariable gloom of the Gothic imagination; flinging itself like a death-scented pall over our conceptions of the future state, smothering our hopes, hiding our sky, and inducing dismal efforts to raise the harvest of immortality out of what is most opposite to it, — the grave!

The cathedral service is performed twice every day: at ten o'clock and at four. When I first entered, the choristers (young and old, but mostly, I think, boys, with voices inexpressibly sweet and clear, and as fresh as bird-notes) were just winding up their harmonious labors, and soon came thronging through a side-door from the chancel into the nave. They were all dressed in long white robes, and looked like a peculiar order of beings, created on purpose to hover between the roof and pavement of that dim, consecrated edifice, and illuminate it with divine melodies, reposing themselves, mean-

while, on the heavy grandeur of the organ-tones like cherubs
on a golden cloud. All at once, however, one of the cherubic
multitude pulled off his white gown, thus transforming himself before my very eyes into a commonplace youth of the day,
in modern frock coat and trousers of a decidedly provincial
cut. This absurd little incident, I verily believe, had a sinister
effect in putting me at odds with the proper influences of the
Cathedral, nor could I quite recover a suitable frame of mind
during my stay there. But, emerging into the open air, I
began to be sensible that I had left a magnificent interior
behind me, and I have never quite lost the perception and
enjoyment of it in these intervening years.

A large space in the immediate neighborhood of the Cathedral is called the Close, and comprises beautifully kept lawns
and a shadowy walk bordered by the dwellings of the ecclesiastical dignitaries of the diocese. All this row of episcopal,
canonical, and clerical residences has an air of the deepest
quiet, repose, and well-protected though not inaccessible seclusion. They seemed capable of including everything that a
saint could desire, and a great many more things than most
of us sinners generally succeed in acquiring. Their most
marked feature is a dignified comfort, looking as if no disturbance or vulgar intrusiveness could ever cross their thres-
holds, encroach upon their ornamented lawns, or straggle into
the beautiful gardens that surround them with flower-beds
and rich clumps of shrubbery. The episcopal palace is a
stately mansion of stone, built somewhat in the Italian style,
and bearing on its front the figures 1687, as the date of its
erection. A large edifice of brick, which, if I remember, stood
next to the palace, I took to be the residence of the second
dignitary of the Cathedral; and, in that case, it must have
been the youthful home of Addison, whose father was Dean
of Lichfield. I tried to fancy his figure on the delightful walk
that extends in front of those priestly abodes, from which
and the interior lawns it is separated by an open-work iron
fence, lined with rich old shrubbery, and overarched by a

minster-aisle of venerable trees. This path is haunted by the shades of famous personages who have formerly trodden it. Johnson must have been familiar with it, both as a boy, and in his subsequent visits to Lichfield, an illustrious old man. Miss Seward, connected with so many literary reminiscences, lived in one of the adjacent houses. Tradition says that it was a favorite spot of Major André, who used to pace to and fro under these trees, waiting, perhaps, to catch a last angel-glimpse of Honoria Sneyd, before he crossed the ocean to encounter his dismal doom from an American court-martial. David Garrick, no doubt, scampered along the path in his boyish days, and, if he was an early student of the drama, must often have thought of those two airy characters of the "Beaux' Stratagem," Archer and Aimwell, who, on this very ground, after attending service at the Cathedral, contrive to make acquaintance with the ladies of the comedy. These creatures of mere fiction have as positive a substance now as the sturdy old figure of Johnson himself. They live, while realities have died. The shadowy walk still glistens with their gold-embroidered memories.

Seeking for Johnson's birthplace, I found it in St. Mary's Square, which is not so much a square as the mere widening of a street. The house is tall and thin, of three stories, with a square front and a roof rising steep and high. On a side-view, the building looks as if it had been cut in two in the midst, there being no slope of the roof on that side. A ladder slanted against the wall, and a painter was giving a livelier hue to the plaster. In a corner-room of the basement, where old Michael Johnson may be supposed to have sold books, is now what we should call a dry-goods store, or, according to the English phrase, a mercer's and haberdasher's shop. The house has a private entrance on a cross-street, the door being accessible by several much-worn stone steps, which are bordered by an iron balustrade. I set my foot on the steps and laid my hand on the balustrade, where Johnson's hand and foot must many a time have been, and ascending to the door,

I knocked once, and again, and again, and got no admittance. Going round to the shop-entrance, I tried to open it, but found it as fast bolted as the gate of Paradise. It is mortifying to be so balked in one's little enthusiasms; but looking round in quest of somebody to make inquiries of, I was a good deal consoled by the sight of Dr. Johnson himself, who happened, just at that moment, to be sitting at his ease nearly in the middle of St. Mary's Square, with his face turned towards his father's house.

Of course, it being almost fourscore years since the Doctor laid aside his weary bulk of flesh, together with the ponderous melancholy that had so long weighed him down, the intelligent reader will at once comprehend that he was marble in his substance, and seated in a marble chair, on an elevated stone pedestal. In short, it was a statue, sculptured by Lucas, and placed here in 1838, at the expense of Dr. Law, the reverend chancellor of the diocese.

The figure is colossal (though perhaps not much more so than the mountainous Doctor himself) and looks down upon the spectator from its pedestal of ten or twelve feet high, with a broad and heavy benignity of aspect, very like in feature to Sir Joshua Reynolds's portrait of Johnson, but calmer and sweeter in expression. Several big books are piled up beneath his chair, and, if I mistake not, he holds a volume in his hand, thus blinking forth at the world out of his learned abstraction, owl-like, yet benevolent at heart. The statue is immensely massive, a vast ponderosity of stone, not finely spiritualized, nor, indeed, fully humanized, but rather resembling a great stone-bowlder than a man. You must look with the eyes of faith and sympathy, or, possibly, you might lose the human being altogether, and find only a big stone within your mental grasp. On the pedestal are three bas-reliefs. In the first, Johnson is represented as hardly more than a baby, bestriding an old man's shoulders, resting his chin on the bald head, which he embraces with his little arms, and listening earnestly to the High-Church eloquence of Dr. Sacheverell.

In the second tablet, he is seen riding to school on the shoulders of two of his comrades, while another boy supports him in the rear.

The third bas-relief possesses, to my mind, a great deal of pathos, to which my appreciative faculty is probably the more alive, because I have always been profoundly impressed by the incident here commemorated, and long ago tried to tell it for the behoof of childish readers. It shows Johnson in the market-place of Uttoxeter, doing penance for an act of disobedience to his father, committed fifty years before. He stands bareheaded, a venerable figure, and a countenance extremely sad and woe-begone, with the wind and rain driving hard against him, and thus helping to suggest to the spectator the gloom of his inward state. Some market-people and children gaze awe-stricken into his face, and an aged man and woman, with clasped and uplifted hand, seem to be praying for him. These latter personages (whose introduction by the artist is none the less effective, because, in queer proximity, there are some commodities of market-day in the shape of living ducks and dead poultry) I interpreted to represent the spirits of Johnson's father and mother, lending what aid they could to lighten his half-century's burden of remorse.

I had never heard of the above-described piece of sculpture before; it appears to have no reputation as a work of art, nor am I at all positive that it deserves any. For me, however, it did as much as sculpture could, under the circumstances, even if the artist of the Libyan Sibyl had wrought it, by reviving my interest in the sturdy old Englishman, and particularly by freshening my perception of a wonderful beauty and pathetic tenderness in the incident of the penance. So, the next day, I left Lichfield for Uttoxeter, on one of the few purely sentimental pilgrimages that I ever undertook, to see the very spot where Johnson had stood. Boswell, I think, speaks of the town (its name is pronounced Yuteoxeter) as being about nine miles off from Lichfield, but the county-map would indicate a greater distance; and by rail, passing from one line to another, it is as much as eighteen miles. I have always had an idea of old Michael Johnson sending his literary merchandise by carrier's wagon, journeying to Uttoxeter afoot on market-day morning, selling books through the busy hours, and returning to Lichfield at night. This could not possibly have been the case.

Arriving at the Uttoxeter station, the first objects that I saw, with a green field or two between them and me, were the tower and gray steeple of a church, rising among red-tiled roofs and a few scattered trees. A very short walk takes you from the station up into the town. It had been my previous impression that the market-place of Uttoxeter lay immediately roundabout the church; and, if I remember the narrative aright, Johnson, or Boswell in his behalf, describes his father's book-stall as standing in the market-place, close beside the sacred edifice. It is impossible for me to say what changes may have occurred in the topography of the town, during almost a century and a half since Michael Johnson retired from business, and ninety years, at least, since his son's penance was performed. But the church has now merely a street of ordinary width passing around it, while the market-place, though near at hand, neither forms a part of it nor is really contiguous, nor would its throng and bustle be apt to overflow their boundaries and surge against the churchyard and the old gray tower. Nevertheless, a walk of a minute or two brings a person from the centre of the market-place to the church door; and Michael Johnson might very conveniently have located his stall and laid out his literary ware in the corner at the tower's base; better there, indeed, than in the busy centre of an agricultural market. But the picturesque arrangement and full impressiveness of the story absolutely require that Johnson shall not have done his penance in a corner, ever so little retired, but shall have been the very nucleus of the crowd, — the midmost man of the market-place, — a central image of Memory and Remorse, contrasting with and overpowering the petty materialism around him. He himself, having the force to throw vitality and truth into what persons differently constituted might reckon a mere external ceremony, and an absurd one, could not have failed to see this necessity. I am resolved, therefore, that the true site of Dr. Johnson's penance was in the middle of the market-place.

That important portion of the town is a rather spacious and irregularly shaped vacuity, surrounded by houses and shops, some of them old, with red-tiled roofs, others wearing a pretence of newness, but probably as old in their inner substance as the rest. The people of Uttoxeter seemed very idle in the warm summer-day, and were scattered in little groups along the sidewalks, leisurely chatting with one another, and often turning about to take a deliberate stare at my humble self; insomuch that I felt as if my genuine sympathy for the illustrious penitent, and my many reflections about him, must have imbued me with some of his own singularity of mien. If their great-grandfathers were such redoubtable starers in the Doctor's day, his penance was no light one. This curiosity indicates a paucity of visitors to the little town, except for market purposes, and I question if Uttoxeter ever saw an American before. The only other thing that greatly impressed me was the abundance of public houses, one at every step or two: Red Lions, White Harts, Bulls' Heads, Mitres, Cross Keys, and I know not what besides. These are probably for the accommodation of the farmers and peasantry of the neighborhood on marketday, and content themselves with a very meagre business on other days of the week. At any rate, I was the only guest in Uttoxeter at the period of my visit, and had but an infinitesimal portion of patronage to distribute among such a multitude of inns. The reader, however, will possibly be scandalized to learn what was the first, and, indeed, the only important affair that I attended to, after coming so far to indulge a solemn and high emotion, and standing now on the very spot where my pious errand should have been consummated. I stepped into one of the rustic hostleries and got my dinner, — bacon and greens, some mutton-chops, juicier and more delectable than all America could serve up at the President's table, and a gooseberry pudding; a sufficient meal for six yeomen, and good enough for a prince, besides a pitcher of foaming ale, the whole at the pitiful small charge of eighteen-pence!

Dr. Johnson would have forgiven me, for nobody had a heartier faith in beef and mutton than himself. And as regards my lack of sentiment in eating my dinner, — it was the wisest thing I had done that day. A sensible man had better not let himself be betrayed into these attempts to realize the things which he has dreamed about, and which, when they cease to be purely ideal in his mind, will have lost the truest of their truth, the loftiest and profoundest part of their power over his sympathies. Facts, as we really find them, whatever poetry they may involve, are covered with a stony excrescence of prose, resembling the crust on a beautiful sea-shell, and they never show their most delicate and divinest colors until we shall have dissolved away their grosser actualities by steeping them long in a powerful menstruum of thought. And seeking to actualize them again, we do but renew the crust. If this were otherwise, — if the moral sublimity of a great fact depended in any degree on its garb of external circumstances, things which change and decay, — it could not itself be immortal and ubiquitous, and only a brief point of time and a little neighborhood would be spiritually nourished by its grandeur and beauty.

Such were a few of the reflections which I mingled with my ale, as I remember to have seen an old quaffer of that excellent liquor stir up his cup with a sprig of some bitter and fragrant herb. Meanwhile I found myself still haunted by a desire to get a definite result out of my visit to Uttoxeter. The hospitable inn was called the Nag's Head, and, standing beside the market-place, was as likely as any other to have entertained old Michael Johnson in the days when he used to come hither to sell books. He, perhaps, had dined on bacon and greens, and drunk his ale, and smoked his pipe, in the very room where I now sat, which was a low, ancient room, certainly much older than Queen Anne's time, with a red-brick floor, and a white-washed ceiling, traversed by bare, rough beams, the whole in the rudest fashion, but extremely neat. Neither did it lack ornament, the walls being hung with colored engravings of prize oxen and other pretty prints, and the mantel-piece adorned with earthen-ware figures of shepherdesses in the Arcadian taste of long ago. Michael Johnson's eyes might have rested on that self-same earthen image, to examine which more closely I had just crossed the brick pavement of the room. And, sitting down again, still as I sipped my ale, I glanced through the open window into the sunny market-place, and wished that I could honestly fix on one spot rather than another, as likely to have been the holy site where Johnson stood to do his penance.

How strange and stupid it is that tradition should not have marked and kept in mind the very place! How shameful (nothing less than that) that there should be no local memorial of this incident, as beautiful and touching a passage as can be cited out of any human life! No inscription of it, almost as sacred as a verse of Scripture on the wall of the church! No statue of the venerable and illustrious penitent in the market-place to throw a wholesome awe over its earthliness, its frauds and petty wrongs, of which the benumbed fingers of conscience can make no record, its selfish competition of each man with his brother or his neighbor, its traffic of soul-substance for a little worldly gain! Such a statue, if the piety of the people did not raise it, might almost have been expected to grow up out of the pavement of its own accord on the spot that had been watered by the rain that dripped from Johnson's garments, mingled with his remorseful tears.

Long after my visit to Uttoxeter, I was told that there were individuals in the town who could have shown me the exact, indubitable spot where Johnson performed his penance. I was assured, moreover, that sufficient interest was felt in the subject to have induced certain local discussions as to the expediency of erecting a memorial. With all deference to my polite informant, I surmise that there is a mistake, and decline, without further and precise evidence, giving credit to either of the above statements. The inhabitants know nothing, as a matter of general interest, about the penance, and care nothing for the scene of it. If the clergyman of the parish, for example, had ever heard of it, would he not have used the theme time and again, wherewith to work tenderly and profoundly on the souls committed to his charge? If parents were familiar with it, would they not teach it to their young ones at the fireside, both to insure reverence to their own gray hairs, and to protect the children from such unavailing regrets as Johnson bore upon his heart for fifty years? If the site were ascertained, would not the pavement thereabouts be worn with reverential footsteps? Would not every town-born child be able to direct the pilgrim thither? While waiting at the station, before my departure, I asked a boy who stood near me, — an intelligent and gentlemanly lad twelve or thirteen years old, whom I should take to be a clergyman's son, — I asked him if he had ever heard the story of Dr. Johnson, how he stood an hour doing penance near that church, the spire of which rose before us. The boy stared and answered, —

"No!"

"Were you born in Uttoxeter?"

"Yes."

I inquired if no circumstance such as I had mentioned was known or talked about among the inhabitants.

"No," said the boy; "not that I ever heard of."

Just think of the absurd little town, knowing nothing of the only memorable incident which ever happened within its boundaries since the old Britons built it, this sad and lovely story, which consecrates the spot (for I found it holy to my contemplation, again, as soon as it lay behind me) in the heart of a stranger from three thousand miles over the sea! It but confirms what I have been saying that sublime and beautiful facts are best understood when etherealized by distance.

Pilgrimage to Old Boston

WE set out at a little past eleven, and made our first stage to Manchester. We were by this time sufficiently Anglicized to reckon the morning a bright and sunny one; although the May sunshine was mingled with water, as it were, and distempered with a very bitter east-wind.

Lancashire is a dreary county (all, at least, except its hilly portions), and I have never passed through it without wishing myself anywhere but in that particular spot where I then happened to be. A few places along our route were historically interesting; as, for example, Bolton, which was the scene of many remarkable events in the Parliamentary War, and in the market-square of which one of the Earls of Derby was beheaded. We saw, along the wayside, the never-failing green fields, hedges, and other monotonous features of an ordinary English landscape. There were little factory villages, too, or larger towns, with their tall chimneys, and their pennons of black smoke, their ugliness of brick-work, and their heaps of refuse matter from the furnace, which seems to be the only kind of stuff which Nature cannot take back to herself and resolve into the elements, when man has thrown it aside. These hillocks of waste and effete mineral always disfigure the neighborhood of iron-mongering towns, and, even after a considerable antiquity, are hardly made decent with a little grass.

At a quarter to two we left Manchester by the Sheffield and Lincoln Railway. The scenery grew rather better than that through which we had hitherto passed, though still by no means very striking; for (except in the show-districts, such as the Lake country, or Derbyshire) English scenery is not particularly well worth looking at, considered as a spectacle or a picture. It has a real, homely charm of its own, no doubt; and the rich verdure, and the thorough finish added by human art, are perhaps as attractive to an American eye as any stronger feature could be. Our journey, however, between Manchester and Sheffield was not through a rich tract of country, but along a valley walled in by bleak, ridgy hills extending straight as a rampart, and across black moorlands with here and there a plantation of trees. Sometimes there were long and gradual ascents, bleak, windy, and desolate, conveying the very impression which the reader gets from many passages of Miss Brontë's novels, and still more from those of her two sisters. Old stone or brick farm-houses, and, once in a while, an old church-tower, were visible; but these are almost too common objects to be noticed in an English landscape.

On a railway, I suspect, what little we do see of the country is seen quite amiss, because it was never intended to be looked at from any point of view in that straight line; so that it is like looking at the wrong side of a piece of tapestry. The old highways and foot-paths were as natural as brooks and rivulets, and adapted themselves by an inevitable impulse to the physiognomy of the country; and, furthermore, every object within view of them had some subtile reference to their curves and undulations; but the line of a railway is perfectly artificial, and puts all precedent things at sixes-and-sevens. At any rate, be the cause what it may, there is seldom anything worth seeing within the scope of a railway traveller's eye; and if there were, it requires an alert marksman to take a flying shot at the picturesque.

At one of the stations (it was near a village of ancient aspect, nestling round a church, on a wide Yorkshire moor) I saw a tall old lady in black, who seemed to have just alighted from the train. She caught my attention by a singular movement of the head, not once only, but continually repeated, and at regular intervals, as if she were making a stern and solemn protest against some action that developed itself before her eyes, and were foreboding terrible disaster, if it should be persisted in. Of course, it was nothing more than a paralytic or nervous affection; yet one might fancy that it had its origin in some unspeakable wrong, perpetrated half a lifetime ago in this old gentlewoman's presence, either against herself or somebody whom she loved still better. Her features had a wonderful sternness, which, I presume, was caused by her habitual effort to compose and keep them quiet, and thereby counteract the tendency to paralytic movement. The slow, regular, and inexorable character of the motion — her look of force and self-control, which had the appearance of rendering it voluntary, while yet it was so fateful — have stamped this poor lady's face and gesture into my memory; so that, some dark day or other, I am afraid she will reproduce herself in a dismal romance.

The train stopped a minute or two, to allow the tickets to be taken, just before entering the Sheffield station, and thence I had a glimpse of the famous town of razors and penknives, enveloped in a cloud of its own diffusing. My impressions of it are extremely vague and misty, — or rather, smoky: for Sheffield seems to me smokier than Manchester, Liverpool, or Birmingham, — smokier than all England besides, unless Newcastle be the exception. It might have been Pluto's own metropolis, shrouded in sulphurous vapor; and, indeed, our approach to it had been by the Valley of the Shadow of Death, through a tunnel three miles in length, quite traversing the breadth and depth of a mountainous hill.

After passing Sheffield, the scenery became softer, gentler, yet more picturesque. At one point we saw what I believe to be the utmost northern verge of Sherwood Forest, — not consisting, however, of thousand-year oaks, extant from Robin Hood's days, but of young and thriving plantations, which will require a century or two of slow English growth to give them much breadth of shade. Earl Fitzwilliam's property lies in this neighborhood, and probably his castle was hidden among some soft depth of foliage not far off. Farther onward the country grew quite level around us, whereby I judged that we must now be in Lincolnshire; and shortly after six o'clock we caught the first glimpse of the cathedral towers, though they loomed scarcely huge enough for our preconceived idea of them. But, as we drew nearer, the great edifice began to assert itself, making us acknowledge it to be larger than our receptivity could take in.

At the railway-station we found no cab (it being an unknown vehicle in Lincoln), but only an omnibus belonging to the Saracen's Head, which the driver recommended as the best hotel in the city, and took us thither accordingly. It received us hospitably, and looked comfortable enough; though, like the hotels of most old English towns, it had a musty fragrance of antiquity, such as I have smelt in a seldom-opened London church where the broad-aisle is paved with tombstones. The house was of an ancient fashion, the entrance into its interior court-yard being through an arch, in the side of which is the door of the hotel. There are long corridors, an intricate arrangement of passages, and up-and-down meandering of staircases, amid which it would be no marvel to encounter some forgotten guest who had gone astray a hundred years ago, and was still seeking for his bedroom while the rest of his generation were in their graves. There is no exaggerating the confusion of mind that seizes upon a stranger in the bewildering geography of a great old-fashioned English inn.

This hotel stands in the principal street of Lincoln, and within a very short distance of one of the ancient city-gates, which is arched across the public way, with a smaller arch for foot-passengers on either side; the whole, a gray, time-gnawn, ponderous, shadowy structure, through the dark vista of which you look into the Middle Ages. The street is narrow, and retains many antique peculiarities; though, unquestionably, English domestic architecture has lost its most impressive features, in the course of the last century. In this respect, there are finer old towns than Lincoln: Chester, for instance, and Shrewsbury, — which last is unusually rich in those quaint and stately edifices where the gentry of the shire used to make their winter abodes, in a provincial metropolis. Almost everywhere, nowadays, there is a monotony of modern brick or stuccoed fronts, hiding houses that are older than ever, but obliterating the picturesque antiquity of the street.

Between seven and eight o'clock (it being still broad daylight in these long English days) we set out to pay a preliminary visit to the exterior of the Cathedral. Passing through the Stone Bow, as the city gate close by is called, we ascended a street which grew steeper and narrower as we advanced, till at last it got to be the steepest street I ever climbed, — so steep that any carriage, if left to itself, would rattle downward much faster than it could possibly be drawn up. Being almost the only hill in Lincolnshire, the inhabitants seem disposed to make the most of it. The houses on each side had no very remarkable aspect, except one with a stone portal and carved ornaments, which is now a dwelling-place for poverty-stricken people, but may have been an aristocratic abode in the days of the Norman kings, to whom its style of architecture dates back. This is called the Jewess's House, having been inhabited by a woman of that faith who was hanged six hundred years ago.

And still the street grew steeper and steeper. Certainly, the Bishop and clergy of Lincoln ought not to be fat men, but of very spirtual, saint-like, almost angelic habit, if it be a frequent part of their ecclesiastical duty to climb this hill; for it is a real penance, and was probably performed as such, and groaned over accordingly, in monkish times. Formerly, on the day of his installation, the Bishop used to ascend the hill barefoot, and was doubtless cheered and invigorated by looking upward to the grandeur that was to console him for the humility of his approach. We, likewise, were beckoned onward by glimpses of the cathedral towers; and, finally, attaining an open square on the summit, we saw an old Gothic gateway to the left hand, and another to the right. The latter had apparently been a part of the exterior defences of the Cathedral, at a time when the edifice was fortified. The west front rose behind. We passed through one of the side-arches of the Gothic portal, and found ourselves in the Cathedral Close, a wide, level space, where the great Minster had fair room to sit, looking down on the ancient structures that surround it, all of which, in former days, were the habitations of its dignitaries and officers. Some of them are still occupied as such, though others are in too neglected and dilapidated a state to seem worthy of so splendid an establishment. Unless it be Salisbury Close, however (which is incomparably rich as regards the old residences that belong to it), I remember no more comfortably picturesque precincts round any other cathedral. But, in truth, almost every cathedral close, in turn, has seemed to me the loveliest, cosiest, safest, least wind-shaken, most decorous, and most enjoyable shelter that ever the thrift and selfishness of mortal man contrived for himelf. How delightful, to combine all this with the service of the temple!

Lincoln Cathedral is built of a yellowish brownstone, which appears either to have been largely restored, or else does not assume the hoary, crumbly surface that gives such a venerable aspect to most of the ancient churches and castles in England. In many parts, the recent restorations are quite evident; but other, and much the larger portions, can scarcely have been touched for centuries: for there are still the gargoyles, perfect, or with broken noses, as the case may be, but showing that variety and fertility of grotesque extravagance which no modern imitation can effect. There are innumerable niches, too, up the whole height of the towers, above and around the entrance, and all over the walls: most of them empty, but a few containing the lamentable remnants of headless saints and

angels. It is singular what a native animosity lives in the
human heart against carved images, insomuch that, whether
they represent Christian saint or Pagan deity, all unsophisti-
cated men seize the first safe opportunity to knock off their
heads! In spite of all dilapidations, however, the effect of
the west front of the Cathedral is still exceedingly rich, being
covered from massive base to airy summit with the minutest
details of sculpture and carving: at least, it was so once; and
even now the spiritual impression of its beauty remains so
strong, that we have to look twice to see that much of it has
been obliterated. I have seen a cherry-stone carved all over
by a monk, so minutely that it must have cost him half a lifetime of labor; and this cathedral-front seems to have been
elaborated in a monkish spirit, like that cherry-stone. Not
that the result is in the least petty, but miraculously grand,
and all the more so for the faithful beauty of the smallest
details. . . .

We now went home to the Saracen's Head; and as the
weather was very unpropitious, and it sprinkled a little now
and then, I would gladly have felt myself released from further
thraldom to the Cathedral. But it had taken possession of me,
and would not let me be at rest; so at length I found myself
compelled to climb the hill again between daylight and dusk.
A mist was now hovering about the upper height of the great
central tower, so as to dim and half obliterate its battlements
and pinnacles, even while I stood in the close beneath it. It
was the most impressive view that I had had. The whole
lower part of the structure was seen with perfect distinctness;
but at the very summit the mist was so dense as to form an
actual cloud, as well defined as ever I saw resting on a moun-
tain-top. Really and literally, here was a "cloud-capt tower."

The entire Cathedral, too, transfigured itself into a richer
beauty and more imposing majesty than ever. The longer I
looked, the better I loved it. Its exterior is certainly far more
beautiful than that of York Minster; and its finer effect is due,
I think, to the many peaks in which the structure ascends, and

to the pinnacles which, as it were, repeat and reëcho them into the sky. York Cathedral is comparatively square and angular in its general effect; but in this at Lincoln there is a continual mystery of variety, so that at every glance you are aware of a change, and a disclosure of something new, yet working an harmonious development of what you have heretofore seen. The west front is unspeakably grand, and may be read over and over again forever, and still show undetected meanings, like a great, broad page of marvellous writing in black-letter, — so many sculptured ornaments there are, blossoming out before your eyes, and gray statues that have grown there since you looked last, and empty niches, and a hundred airy canopies beneath which carved images used to be, and where they will show themselves again, if you gaze long enough. — But I will not say another word about the Cathedral.

We spent the rest of the day within the sombre precincts of the Saracen's Head, reading yesterday's "Times," "The Guide-Book of Lincoln," and "The Directory of the Eastern Counties." Dismal as the weather was, the street beneath our window was enlivened with a great bustle and turmoil of people all the evening, because it was Saturday night, and they had accomplished their week's toil, received their wages, and were making their small purchases against Sunday, and enjoying themselves as well as they knew how. A band of music passed to and fro several times, with the rain-drops falling into the mouth of the brazen trumpet and pattering on the bass-drum; a spirit-shop, opposite the hotel, had a vast run of custom; and a coffee-dealer, in the open air, found occasional vent for his commodity, in spite of the cold water that dripped into the cups. The whole breadth of the street, between the Stone Bow and the bridge across the Witham, was thronged to overflowing, and humming with human life.

Observing in the Guide-Book that a steamer runs on the river Witham between Lincoln and Boston, I inquired of the waiter, and learned that she was to start on Monday at ten o'clock. Thinking it might be an interesting trip, and a pleasant variation of our customary mode of travel, we determined to make the voyage. . . .

At last, in mid-afternoon, we beheld the tall tower of Saint Botolph's Church (three hundred feet high, the same elevation as the tallest tower of Lincoln Cathedral) looming in the distance. At about half past four we reached Boston (which name has been shortened, in the course of ages, by the quick and slovenly English pronunciation, from Botolph's town), and were taken by a cab to the Peacock, in the market-place. It was the best hotel in town, though a poor one enough; and we were shown into a small, stifled parlor, dingy, musty, and scented with stale tobacco-smoke, — tobacco-smoke two days old, for the waiter assured us that the room had not more recently been fumigated. An exceedingly grim waiter he was, apparently a genuine descendant of the old Puritans of this English Boston, and quite as sour as those who people the daughter-city in New England. Our parlor had the one recommendation of looking into the market-place, and affording a sidelong glimpse of the tall spire and noble old church.

In my first ramble about the town, chance led me to the river-side, at that quarter where the port is situated. Here were long buildings of an old-fashioned aspect, seemingly warehouses, with windows in the high, steep roofs. The Custom House found ample accommodation within an ordinary dwelling-house. Two or three large schooners were moored along the river's brink, which had here a stone margin; another large and handsome schooner was evidently just finished, rigged and equipped for her first voyage; the rudiments of another were on the stocks, in a ship-yard bordering on the river. Still another, while I was looking on, came up the stream, and lowered her mainsail, from a foreign voyage. An old man on the bank hailed her and inquired about her cargo; but the Lincolnshire people have such a queer way of talking English that I could not understand the reply. Farther down the river, I saw a brig, approaching rapidly under sail. The whole scene made an odd impression of bustle, and sluggishness, and decay, and a remnant of wholesome life; and I could not but contrast it with the mighty and populous activity of our own Boston, which was once the feeble infant of this old English town, — the latter, perhaps, almost stationary ever since that day, as if the birth of such an offspring had taken away its own principle of growth. I thought of Long Wharf, and Faneuil Hall, and Washington Street, and the Great Elm, and the State House, and exulted lustily, — but yet began to feel at home in this good old town, for its very name's sake, as I never had before felt, in England.

The next morning we came out in the early sunshine (the sun must have been shining nearly four hours, however, for it was after eight o'clock), and strolled about the streets, like people who had a right to be there. The market-place of Boston is an irregular square, into one end of which the chancel of the church slightly projects. The gates of the church-yard were open and free to all passengers, and the common footway of the towns-people seems to lie to and fro across it. It is paved, according to English custom, with flat tombstones; and there are also raised or altar tombs, some of which have armorial bearings on them. One clergyman has caused himself and his wife to be buried right in the middle of the stone-bordered path that traverses the churchyard; so that not an individual of the thousands who pass along this public way can help trampling over him or her. The scene, nevertheless, was very cheerful in the morning sun: people going about their business in the day's primal freshness, which was just as fresh here as in younger villages; children with milk-pails loitering over the burial-stones; school-boys playing leap-frog with the altar-tombs; the simple old town preparing itself for the day, which would be like myriads of other days that had passed over it, but yet would be worth living through. And down on the churchyard, where were buried many generations whom it remembered in their time, looked the stately tower of Saint Botolph; and it was good to see and think of such an age-long giant intermarrying the present epoch with a distant

past, and getting quite imbued with human nature by being
so immemorially connected with men's familiar knowledge and
homely interests.   It is a noble tower; and the jackdaws, evidently have pleasant homes in their hereditary nests among
its topmost windows, and live delightful lives, flitting and cawing about its pinnacles and flying buttresses.   I should almost
like to be a jackdaw myself, for the sake of living up there.

In front of the church, not more than twenty yards off, and
with a low brick wall between, flows the river Witham.   On
the hither bank a fisherman was washing his boat; and another
skiff, with her sail lazily half twisted, lay on the opposite strand.
The stream at this point is about of such width, that, if the
tall tower were to tumble over flat on its face, its top-stone
might perhaps reach to the middle of the channel.   On the
farther shore there is a line of antique-looking houses, with
roofs of red tile, and windows opening out of them, — some
of these dwellings being so ancient that the Reverend Mr.
Cotton, subsequently our first Boston minister, must have seen
them with his own bodily eyes when he used to issue from the
front-portal after service.   Indeed, there must be very many
houses here, and even some streets, that bear much the aspect
that they did when the Puritan divine paced solemnly among
them.

In our rambles about town, we went into a bookseller's shop
to inquire if he had any description of Boston for sale.   He
offered me (or, rather, produced for inspection, not supposing
that I would buy it) a quarto history of the town, published
by subscription, nearly forty years ago.   The bookseller showed
himself a well-informed and affable man, and a local antiquary, to whom a party of inquisitive strangers were a godsend.
He had met with several Americans, who, at various times,
had come on pilgrimages to this place, and he had been in
correspondence with others.   Happening to have heard the
name of one member of our party, he showed us great courtesy
and kindness, and invited us into his inner domicile, where,
as he modestly intimated, he kept a few articles which it might

interest us to see. So we went with him through the shop, up stairs, into the private part of his establishment; and, really, it was one of the rarest adventures I ever met with, to stumble upon this treasure of a man, with his treasury of antiquities and curiosities, veiled behind the unostentatious front of a bookseller's shop, in a very moderate line of village business. The two up-stair rooms into which he introduced us were so crowded with inestimable articles, that we were almost afraid to stir for fear of breaking some fragile thing that had been accumulating value for unknown centuries.

The apartment was hung round with pictures and old engravings, many of which were extremely rare. Premising that he was going to show us something very curious, Mr. Porter went into the next room and returned with a counterpane of fine linen, elaborately embroidered with silk, which so profusely covered the linen that the general effect was as if the main texture were silken. It was stained and seemed very old, and had an ancient fragrance. It was wrought all over with birds and flowers in a most delicate style of needlework, and among other devices, more than once repeated, was the cipher, M. S., — being the initials of one of the most unhappy names that ever a woman bore. This quilt was embroidered by the hands of Mary Queen of Scots, during her imprisonment at Fotheringay Castle; and having evidently been a work of years, she had doubtless shed many tears over it, and wrought many doleful thoughts and abortive schemes into its texture, along with the birds and flowers. As a counterpart to this most precious relic, our friend produced some of the handiwork of a former Queen of Otaheite, presented by her to Captain Cook; it was a bag, cunningly made of some delicate vegetable stuff, and ornamented with feathers. Next, he brought out a green silk waistcoat of very antique fashion, trimmed about the edges and pocket-holes with a rich and delicate embroidery of gold and silver. This (as the possessor of the treasure proved, by tracing its pedigree till it came into his hands) was once the vestment of Queen Elizabeth's Lord Burleigh; but that great statesman must have been a person of very moderate girth in the chest and waist; for the garment was hardly more than a comfortable fit for a boy of eleven, the smallest American of our party, who tried on the gorgeous waistcoat.   Then, Mr. Porter produced some curiously engraved drinking-glasses, with a view of Saint Botolph's steeple on one of them, and other Boston edifices, public or domestic, on the remaining two, very admirably done.   These crystal goblets had been a present, long ago, to an old master of the Free School from his pupils; and it is very rarely, I imagine, that a retired schoolmaster can exhibit such trophies of gratitude and affection, won from the victims of his birch rod.

Our kind friend kept bringing out one unexpected and wholly unexpectable thing after another, as if he were a magician, and had only to fling a private signal into the air, and some attendant imp would hand forth any strange relic he might choose to ask for.   He was especially rich in drawings by the Old Masters, producing two or three, of exquisite delicacy, by Raphael, one by Salvator, a head by Rembrandt, and others, in chalk or pen-and-ink, by Giordano, Benvenuto Cellini, and hands almost as famous; and besides what were shown us, there seemed to be an endless supply of art-treasures in reserve.   On the wall hung a crayon-portrait of Sterne, never engraved, representing him as a rather young man, blooming, and not uncomely; it was the worldly face of a man fond of pleasure, but without that ugly, keen, sarcastic, odd expression that we see in his only engraved portrait.   The picture is an original, and must needs be very valuable; and we wish it might be prefixed to some new and worthier biography of a writer whose character the world has always treated with singular harshness, considering how much it owes him. There was likewise a crayon-portrait of Sterne's wife, looking so haughty and unamiable, that the wonder is, not that he ultimately left her, but how he ever contrived to live a week with such an awful woman.

After looking at these, and a great many more things than

I can remember, above stairs, we went down to a parlor, where this wonderful bookseller opened an old cabinet, containing numberless drawers, and looking just fit to be the repository of such knickknacks as were stored up in it. He appeared to possess more treasures than he himself knew of, or knew where to find; but, rummaging here and there, he brought forth things new and old: rose-nobles, Victorian crowns, gold angels, double sovereigns of George IV., two-guinea pieces of George II.; a marriage-medal of the first Napoleon, only forty-five of which were ever struck off, and of which even the British Museum does not contain a specimen like this, in gold; a brass medal, three or four inches in diameter, of a Roman emperor; together with buckles, bracelets, amulets, and I know not what besides. There was a green silk tassel from the fringe of Queen Mary's bed at Holyrood Palace. There were illuminated missals, antique Latin Bibles, and (what may seem of especial interest to the historian) a Secret-Book of Queen Elizabeth, in manuscript, written, for aught I know, by her own hand. On examination, however, it proved to contain, not secrets of state, but recipes for dishes, drinks, medicines, washes, and all such matters of housewifery, the toilet, and domestic quackery, among which we were horrified by the title of one of the nostrums, "How to kill a Fellow quickly"! We never doubted that bloody Queen Bess might often have had occasion for such a recipe, but wondered at her frankness, and at her attending to these anomalous necessities in such a methodical way. The truth is, we had read amiss, and the Queen had spelt amiss: the word was "Fellon," — a sort of whitlow,* — not "Fellow."

Our hospitable friend now made us drink a glass of wine, as old and genuine as the curiosities of his cabinet; and, while sipping it, we ungratefully tried to excite his envy, by telling him various things, interesting to an antiquary and virtuoso, which we had seen in the course of our travels about England.

---

*[A sore on fingers or toes.]

We spoke, for instance, of a missal bound in solid gold and set around with jewels, but of such intrinsic value as no setting could enhance, for it was exquisitely illuminated, throughout, by the hand of Raphael himself.   We mentioned a little silver case which once contained a portion of the heart of Louis XIV. nicely done up in spices, but, to the owner's horror and astonishment, Dean Buckland popped the kingly morsel into his mouth, and swallowed it.   We told about the black-letter prayer-book of King Charles the Martyr, used by him upon the scaffold, taking which into our hands, it opened of itself at the Communion Service; and there, on the left-hand page, appeared a spot about as large as a sixpence, of a yellowish or brownish hue: a drop of the king's blood had fallen there.

Mr. Porter now accompanied us to the church, but first leading us to a vacant spot of ground where old John Cotton's vicarage had stood till a very short time since.   According to our friend's description, it was a humble habitation, of the cottage order, built of brick, with a thatched roof.   The site is now rudely fenced in, and cultivated as a vegetable garden. In the right-hand aisle of the church there is an ancient chapel, which, at the time of our visit, was in process of restoration, and was to be dedicated to Mr. Cotton, whom these English people consider as the founder of our American Boston.   It would contain a painted memorial-window, in honor of the old Puritan minister.   A festival in commemoration of the event was to take place in the ensuing July, to which I had myself received an invitation, but I knew too well the pains and penalties incurred by an invited guest at public festivals in England to accept it.   It ought to be recorded (and it seems to have made a very kindly impression of our kinsfolk here) that five hundred pounds had been contributed by persons in the United States, principally in Boston, towards the cost of the memorial-window, and the repair and restoration of the chapel.

After we emerged from the chapel, Mr. Porter approached us with the vicar, to whom he kindly introduced us, and then took his leave. May a stranger's benediction rest upon him! He is a most pleasant man; rather, I imagine, a virtuoso than an antiquary; for he seemed to value the Queen of Otaheite's bag as highly as Queen Mary's embroidered quilt, and to have an omnivorous appetite for everything strange and rare. Would that we could fill up his shelves and drawers (if there are any vacant spaces left) with the choicest trifles that have dropped out of Time's carpet-bag, or give him the carpet-bag itself, to take out what he will!

The vicar looked about thirty years old, a gentleman, evidently assured of his position (as clergymen of the Established Church invariably are), comfortable and well-to-do, a scholar and a Christian, and fit to be a bishop, knowing how to make the most of life without prejudice to the life to come. I was glad to see such a model English priest so suitably accommodated with an old English church. He kindly and courteously did the honors, showing us quite round the interior, giving us all the information that we required, and then leaving us to the quiet enjoyment of what we came to see.

The interior of St. Botolph's is very fine and satisfactory, as stately, almost, as a cathedral, and has been repaired — so far as repairs were necessary — in a chaste and noble style. The great eastern window is of modern painted glass, but is the richest, mellowest, and tenderest modern window that I have ever seen: the art of painting these glowing transparencies in pristine perfection being one that the world has lost. The vast, clear space of the interior church delighted me. There was no screen, — nothing between the vestibule and the altar to break the long vista; even the organ stood aside, — though it by and by made us aware of its presence by a melodious roar. Around the walls there were old engraved brasses, and a stone coffin, and an alabaster knight of Saint John, and an alabaster lady, each recumbent at full length, as large as life, and in perfect preservation, except for a slight modern touch at the tips of their noses. In the chancel we saw a great deal of oaken work, quaintly and admirably carved, especially about the seats formerly appropriated to the monks, which were so contrived as to tumble down with a tremendous crash if the occupant happened to fall asleep.

We now essayed to climb into the upper regions. Up we went, winding and still winding round the circular stairs, till we came to the gallery beneath the stone roof of the tower, whence we could look down and see the raised Font, and my Talma lying on one of the steps, and looking about as big as a pocket-handkerchief. Then up again, up, up, up, through a yet smaller staircase, till we emerged into another stone gallery, above the jackdaws, and far above the roof beneath which we had before made a halt. Then up another flight, which led us into a pinnacle of the temple, but not the highest; so, retracing our steps, we took the right turret this time, and emerged into the loftiest lantern, where we saw level Lincolnshire, far and near, though with a haze on the distant horizon. There were dusty roads, a river, and canals, converging towards Boston, which — a congregation of red-tiled roofs — lay beneath our feet, with pygmy people creeping about its narrow streets. We were three hundred feet aloft, and the pinnacle on which we stood is a landmark forty miles at sea.

Content, and weary of our elevation, we descended the corkscrew stairs and left the church; the last object that we noticed in the interior being a bird, which appeared to be at home there, and responded with its cheerful notes to the swell of the organ. Pausing on the church-steps, we observed that there were formerly two statues, one on each side of the doorway; the canopies still remaining and the pedestals being about a yard from the ground. Some of Mr. Cotton's Puritan parishioners are probably responsible for the disappearance of these stone saints. This doorway at the base of the tower is now much dilapidated, but must once have been very rich and of a peculiar fashion. It opens its arch through a great square tablet of stone, reared against the front of the tower. On most of the projections, whether on the tower or about the body of the church, there are gargoyles of genuine Gothic grotesqueness, — fiends, beasts, angels, and combinations of all three; and where portions of the edifice are restored, the modern sculptors have tried to imitate these wild fantasies, but with very poor success. Extravagance and absurdity have still their law, and should pay as rigid obedience to it as the primmest things on earth.

In our further rambles about Boston, we crossed the river by a bridge, and observed that the larger part of the town seems to lie on that side of its navigable stream. The crooked streets and narrow lanes reminded me much of Hanover Street, Ann Street, and other portions of the North End of our American Boston, as I remember that picturesque region in my boyish days. It is not unreasonable to suppose that the local habits and recollections of the first settlers may have had some influence on the physical character of the streets and houses in the New England metropolis; at any rate, here is a similar intricacy of bewildering lanes, and numbers of old peaked and projecting-storied dwellings, such as I used to see there. It is singular what a home-feeling and sense of kindred I derived from this hereditary connection and fancied physiognomical resemblance between the old town and its well-grown daughter, and how reluctant I was, after chill years of banishment, to leave this hospitable place, on that account. Moreover, it recalled some of the features of another American town, my own dear native place, when I saw the seafaring people leaning against posts, and sitting on planks, under the lee of warehouses, — or lolling on longboats, drawn up high and dry, as sailors and old wharf-rats are accustomed to do, in seaports of little business. In other respects, the English town is more village-like than either of the American ones. The women and budding girls chat together at their doors, and exchange merry greetings with young men; children chase one another in the summer twilight; schoolboys sail little boats on the river, or play at marbles across the flat tombstones in the churchyard; and ancient men, in breeches and long waistcoats, wander slowly about the streets, with a certain familiarity of deportment, as if each one were everybody's grandfather. I have frequently observed, in old English towns, that Old Age comes forth more cheerfully and genially into the sunshine than among ourselves, where the rush, stir, bustle, and irreverent energy of youth are so preponderant, that the poor, forlorn grandsires begin to doubt whether they have a right to breathe in such a world any longer, and so hide their silvery heads in solitude. Speaking of old men, I am reminded of the scholars of the Boston Charity School, who walk about in antique, long-skirted blue coats, and knee-breeches, and with bands at their necks, — perfect and grotesque pictures of the costume of three centuries ago.

On the morning of our departure, I looked from the parlor-window of the Peacock into the market-place, and beheld its irregular square already well covered with booths, and more in process of being put up, by stretching tattered sail-cloth on poles. It was market-day. The dealers were arranging their commodities, consisting chiefly of vegetables, the great bulk of which seemed to be cabbages. Later in the forenoon there was a much greater variety of merchandise: basket-work, both for fancy and use; twig-brooms, beehives, oranges, rustic attire; all sorts of things, in short, that are commonly sold at a rural fair. I heard the lowing of cattle, too, and the bleating of sheep, and found that there was a market for cows, oxen, and pigs, in another part of the town. A crowd of towns-people and Lincolnshire yeomen elbowed one another in the square; Mr. Punch was speaking in one corner, and a vagabond juggler tried to find space for his exhibition in another: so that my final glimpse of Boston was calculated to leave a livelier impression than my former ones. Meanwhile the tower of Saint Botolph's looked benignantly down; and I fancied it was bidding me farewell, as it did Mr. Cotton, two or three hundred years ago, and telling me to describe its venerable height, and the town beneath it, to the people of the American city, who are partly akin, if not to the living inhabitants of Old Boston, yet to some of the dust that lies in its churchyard.

One thing more. They have a Bunker Hill in the vicinity of their town; and (what could hardly be expected of an English community) seem proud to think that their neighborhood has given name to our first and most widely celebrated and best remembered battle-field.

Near Oxford

ON a fine morning in September we set out on an excursion to Blenheim, — the sculptor and myself being seated on the box of our four-horse carriage, two more of the party in the dicky, and the others less agreeably accommodated inside. We had no coachman, but two postilions in short scarlet jackets and leather breeches with top-boots, each astride of a horse; so that, all the way along, when not otherwise attracted, we had the interesting spectacle of their up-and-down bobbing in the saddle. It was a sunny and beautiful day, a specimen of the perfect English weather, just warm enough for comfort, — indeed, a little too warm, perhaps, in the noontide sun, — yet retaining a mere spice or suspicion of austerity, which made it all the more enjoyable. . . .

After driving a good way, we came to a battlemented tower and adjoining house, which used to be the residence of the Ranger of Woodstock Park, who held charge of the property for the King before the Duke of Marlborough possessed it. The keeper opened the door for us, and in the entrance-hall we found various things that had to do with the chase and woodland sports. We mounted the staircase, through several stories, up to the top of the tower, whence there was a view of the spires of Oxford, and of points much farther off, — very indistinctly seen, however, as is usually the case with the misty distances of England. Returning to the ground-floor, we were ushered into the room in which died Wilmot, the wicked Earl of Rochester, who was Ranger of the Park in Charles II.'s time. It is a low and bare little room, with a window in front, and a smaller one behind; and in the contiguous entrance-room there are the remains of an old bedstead, beneath the canopy of which, perhaps, Rochester may have made the penitent end that Bishop Burnet attributes to him. I hardly know what it is, in this poor fellow's character, which affects us with greater tenderness on his behalf than for all the other profligates of his day, who seem to have been neither better nor worse than himself. I rather suspect that he had a human heart which never quite died out of him, and the warmth of which is still faintly perceptible amid the dissolute trash which he left behind.

Methinks, if such good fortune ever befell a bookish man, I should choose this lodge for my own residence, with the topmost room of the tower for a study, and all the seclusion of cultivated wildness beneath to ramble in. There being no such possibility, we drove on, catching glimpses of the palace in new points of view, and by and by came to Rosamond's Well. The particular tradition that connects Fair Rosamond with it is not now in my memory; but if Rosamond ever lived and loved, and ever had her abode in the maze of Woodstock, it may well be believed that she and Henry sometimes sat beside this spring. It gushes out from a bank, through some old stone-work, and dashes its little cascade (about as abundant as one might turn out of a large pitcher) into a pool, whence it steals away towards the lake, which is not far removed. The water is exceedingly cold, and as pure as the legendary Rosamond was not, and is fancied to possess medicinal virtues, like springs at which saints have quenched their thirst. There were two or three old women and some children in attendance with tumblers, which they present to visitors, full of the consecrated water; but most of us filled the tumblers for ourselves, and drank.

Thence we drove to the Triumphal Pillar which was erected in honor of the Great Duke, and on the summit of which he stands, in a Roman garb, holding a winged figure of Victory in his hand, as an ordinary man might hold a bird. The column is I know not how many feet high, but lofty enough, at any rate, to elevate Marlborough far above the rest of the world, and to be visible a long way off; and it is so placed in reference to other objects, that, wherever the hero wandered about his grounds, and especially as he issued from his mansion, he must inevitably have been reminded of his glory. In truth, until I came to Blenheim, I never had so positive and material an idea of what Fame really is — of what the admiration of his country can do for a successful warrior — as I carry away with me and shall always retain. Unless he had the moral force of a thousand men together, his egotism (beholding himself everywhere, imbuing the entire soil, growing in the woods, rippling and gleaming in the water, and pervading the very air with his greatness) must have been swollen within him like the liver of a Strasburg goose. On the huge tablets inlaid into the pedestal of the column, the entire Act of Parliament, bestowing Blenheim on the Duke of Marlborough and his posterity, is engraved in deep letters, painted black on the marble ground. The pillar stands exactly a mile from the principal front of the palace, in a straight line with the precise centre of its entrance-hall; so that, as already said, it was the Duke's principal object of contemplation.

We now proceeded to the palace-gate, which is a great pillared archway, of wonderful loftiness and state, giving admittance into a spacious quadrangle. A stout, elderly, and rather surly footman in livery appeared at the entrance, and took possession of whatever canes, umbrellas, and parasols he could get hold of, in order to claim sixpence on our departure. This had a somewhat ludicrous effect. There is much public outcry against the meanness of the present Duke in his arrangements for the admission of visitors (chiefly, of course, his native countrymen) to view the magnificent palace which their forefathers bestowed upon his own.   In many cases, it seems hard that a private abode should be exposed to the intrusion of the public merely because the proprietor has inherited or created a splendor which attracts general curiosity; insomuch that his home loses its sanctity and seclusion for the very reason that it is better than other men's houses.   But in the case of Blenheim, the public have certainly an equitable claim to admission, both because the fame of its first inhabitant is a national possession, and because the mansion was a national gift, one of the purposes of which was to be a token of gratitude and glory to the English people themselves.   If a man chooses to be illustrious, he is very likely to incur some little inconveniences himself, and entail them on his posterity.   Nevertheless, his present Grace of Marlborough absolutely ignores the public claim above suggested, and (with a thrift of which even the hero of Blenheim himself did not set the example) sells tickets admitting six persons at ten shillings; if only one person enters the gate, he must pay for six; and if there are seven in company, two tickets are required to admit them.   The attendants, who meet you everywhere in the park and palace, expect fees on their own private account, — their noble master pocketing the ten shillings.   But, to be sure, the visitor gets his money's worth, since it buys him the right to speak just as freely of the Duke of Marlborough as if he were the keeper of the Cremorne Gardens.[1] . . .

One whole wing of the palace is occupied by the library, a most noble room, with a vast perspective length from end to end.   Its atmosphere is brighter and more cheerful than that of most libraries: a wonderful contrast to the old college-li-

---

[1] The above was written two or three years ago, or more; and the Duke of that day has since transmitted his coronet to his successor, who, we understand, has adopted much more liberal arrangements. There is seldom anything to criticise or complain of, as regards the facility of obtaining admission to interesting private houses in England.

braries of Oxford, and perhaps less sombre and suggestive of thoughtfulness than any large library ought to be; inasmuch as so many studious brains as have left their deposit on the shelves cannot have conspired without producing a very serious and ponderous result. Both walls and ceiling are white, and there are elaborate doorways and fireplaces of white marble. The floor is of oak, so highly polished that our feet slipped upon it as if it had been New England ice. At one end of the room stands a statue of Queen Anne in her royal robes, which are so admirably designed and exquisitely wrought that the spectator certainly gets a strong conception of her royal dignity; while the face of the statue, fleshy and feeble, doubtless conveys a suitable idea of her personal character. The marble of this work, long as it has stood there, is as white as snow just fallen, and must have required most faithful and religious care to keep it so. As for the volumes of the library, they are wired within the cases, and turn their gilded backs upon the visitor, keeping their treasures of wit and wisdom just as intangible as if still in the unwrought mines of human thought.

I remember nothing else in the palace, except the chapel, to which we were conducted last, and where we saw a splendid monument to the first Duke and Duchess, sculptured by Rysbrach, at the cost, it is said, of forty thousand pounds. The design includes the statues of the deceased dignitaries, and various allegorical flourishes, fantasies, and confusions; and beneath sleep the great Duke and his proud wife, their veritable bones and dust, and probably all the Marlboroughs that have since died. It is not quite a comfortable idea, that these mouldy ancestors still inhabit, after their fashion, the house where their successors spend the passing day; but the adulation lavished upon the hero of Blenheim could not have been consummated, unless the palace of his lifetime had become likewise a stately mausoleum over his remains, — and such we felt it all to be, after gazing at his tomb.

The next business was to see the private gardens. An old Scotch under-gardener admitted us and led the way, and seemed to have a fair prospect of earning the fee all by himself; but by and by another respectable Scotchman made his appearance and took us in charge, proving to be the head-gardener in person. He was extremely intelligent and agreeable, talking both scientifically and lovingly about trees and plants, of which there is every variety capable of English cultivation. Positively, the Garden of Eden cannot have been more beautiful than this private garden of Blenheim. It contains three hundred acres, and by the artful circumlocution of the paths, and the undulations, and the skilfully interposed clumps of trees, is made to appear limitless. The sylvan delights of a whole country are compressed into this space, as whole fields of Persian roses go to the concoction of an ounce of precious attar. The world within that garden-fence is not the same weary and dusty world with which we outside mortals are conversant; it is a finer, lovelier, more harmonious Nature; and the Great Mother lends herself kindly to the gardener's will, knowing that he will make evident the half-obliterated traits of her pristine and ideal beauty, and allow her to take all the credit and praise to herself. I doubt whether there is ever any winter within that precinct, — any clouds, except the fleecy ones of summer. The sunshine that I saw there rests upon my recollection of it as if it were eternal. The lawns and glades are like the memory of places where one has wandered when first in love.

What a good and happy life might be spent in a paradise like this! And yet, at that very moment, the besotted Duke (ah! I have let out a secret which I meant to keep to myself; but the ten shillings must pay for all) was in that very garden (for the guide told us so, and cautioned our young people not to be too uproarious), and, if in a condition for arithmetic, was thinking of nothing nobler than how many ten-shilling tickets had that day been sold. Republican as I am, I should still love to think that noblemen lead noble lives, and that all this stately and beautiful environment may serve to elevate them a little way above the rest of us. If it fail to do so, the disgrace falls equally upon the whole race of mortals as on themselves; because it proves that no more favorable conditions of existence would eradicate our vices and weaknesses.   How sad, if this be so!   Even a herd of swine, eating the acorns under those magnificent oaks of Blenheim, would be cleanlier and of better habits than ordinary swine. . . .

We next stopped at Stanton Harcourt, where we were received at the parsonage with a hospitality which we should take delight in describing, if it were allowable to make public acknowledgment of the private and personal kindnesses which we never failed to find ready for our needs.   An American in an English house will soon adopt the opinion that the English are the very kindest people on earth, and will retain that idea as long, at least, as he remains on the inner side of the threshold.   Their magnetism is of a kind that repels strongly while you keep beyond a certain limit, but attracts as forcibly if you get within the magic line.

It was at this place, if I remember right, that I heard a gentleman ask a friend of mine whether he was the author of "The Red Letter A"; and, after some consideration (for he did not seem to recognize his own book, at first, under this improved title), our countryman responded, doubtfully, that he believed so.   The gentleman proceeded to inquire whether our friend had spent much time in America, — evidently thinking that he must have been caught young, and have had a tincture of English breeding, at least, if not birth, to speak the language so tolerably, and appear so much like other people. This insular narrowness is exceedingly queer, and of very frequent occurrence, and is quite as much a characteristic of men of education and culture as of clowns.

Stanton Harcourt is a very curious old place.   It was formerly the seat of the ancient family of Harcourt, which now has its principal abode at Nuneham Courtney, a few miles off. The parsonage is a relic of the family mansion, or castle, other portions of which are close at hand; for, across the garden, rise two gray towers, both of them picturesquely venerable, and interesting for more than their antiquity.   One of these towers, in its entire capacity, from height to depth, consituted the kitchen of the ancient castle, and is still used for domestic purposes, although it has not, nor ever had, a chimney; or, we might rather say, it is itself one vast chimney, with a hearth of thirty feet square, and a flue and aperture of the same size. There are two huge fireplaces within, and the interior walls of the tower are blackened with the smoke that for centuries used to gush forth from them, and climb upward, seeking an exit through some wide air-holes in the conical roof, full seventy feet above.   These lofty openings were capable of being so arranged, with reference to the wind, that the cooks are said to have been seldom troubled by the smoke; and here, no doubt, they were accustomed to roast oxen whole, with as little fuss and ado as a modern cook would roast a fowl.   The inside of the tower is very dim and sombre (being nothing but rough stone walls, lighted only from the apertures above mentioned), and has still a pungent odor of smoke and soot, the reminiscence of the fires and feasts of generations that have passed away.   Methinks the extremest range of domestic economy lies between an American cooking-stove and the ancient kitchen, seventy dizzy feet in height and all one fireplace, of Stanton Harcourt.

Now — the place being without a parallel in England, and therefore necessarily beyond the experience of an American — it is somewhat remarkable, that, while we stood gazing at this kitchen, I was haunted and perplexed by an idea that somewhere or other I had seen just this strange spectacle before. The height, the blackness, the dismal void, before my eyes, seemed as familiar as the decorous neatness of my grandmother's kitchen; only my unaccountable memory of the scene was lighted up with an image of lurid fires blazing all round the dim interior circuit of the tower.   I had never before had so pertinacious an attack, as I could not but suppose it, of that odd state of mind wherein we fitfully and teasingly remember some previous scene or incident, of which the one now passing appears to be but the echo and reduplication. Though the explanation of the mystery did not for some time occur to me, I may as well conclude the matter here. In a letter of Pope's, addressed to the Duke of Buckingham, there is an account of Stanton Harcourt (as I now find, although the name is not mentioned), where he resided while translating a part of the "Iliad." It is one of the most admirable pieces of description in the language, — playful and picturesque, with fine touches of humorous pathos, — and conveys as perfect a picture as ever was drawn of a decayed English country-house; and among other rooms, most of which have since crumbled down and disappeared, he dashes off the grim aspect of this kitchen, — which, moreover, he peoples with witches, engaging Satan himself as head-cook, who stirs the infernal caldrons that seethe and bubble over the fires. This letter, and others relative to his abode here, were very familiar to my earlier reading, and, remaining still fresh at the bottom of my memory, caused the weird and ghostly sensation that came over me on beholding the real spectacle that had formerly been made so vivid to my imagination.

Our next visit was to the church, which stands close by, and is quite as ancient as the remnants of the castle. In a chapel or side-aisle, dedicated to the Harcourts, are found some very interesting family monuments, — and among them, recumbent on a tombstone, the figure of an armed knight of the Lancastrian party, who was slain in the Wars of the Roses. His features, dress, and armor are painted in colors, still wonderfully fresh, and there still blushes the symbol of the Red Rose, denoting the faction for which he fought and died. His head rests on a marble or alabaster helmet; and on the tomb lies the veritable helmet, it is to be presumed, which he wore in battle, — a ponderous iron case, with the visor complete, and remnants of the gilding that once covered it. The crest is a large peacock, not of metal, but of wood. Very possibly, this helmet was but an heraldic adornment of his tomb; and, indeed, it seems strange that it has not been stolen before now, especially in Cromwell's time, when knightly tombs were little respected, and when armor was in request. However, it is needless to dispute with the dead knight about the identity of his iron pot, and we may as well allow it to be the very same that so often gave him the headache in his lifetime. Leaning against the wall, at the foot of the tomb, is the shaft of a spear, with a woefully tattered and utterly faded banner appended to it, — the knightly banner beneath which he marshalled his followers in the field. As it was absolutely falling to pieces, I tore off one little bit, no longer than a finger-nail, and put it into my waistcoat-pocket; but seeking it subsequently, it was not to be found. . . .

I mentioned that there were two towers remaining of the old castle: the one containing the kitchen we have already visited; the other, still more interesting, is next to be described. It is some seventy feet high, gray and reverend, but in excellent repair, though I could not perceive that anything had been done to renovate it. The basement story was once the family chapel, and is, of course, still a consecrated spot. At one corner of the tower is a circular turret, within which a narrow staircase, with worn steps of stone, winds round and round as it climbs upward, giving access to a chamber on each floor, and finally emerging on the battlemented roof. Ascending this turret-stair, and arriving at the third story, we entered a chamber, not large, though occupying the whole area of the tower, and lighted by a window on each side. It was wainscoted from floor to ceiling with dark oak, and had a little fireplace in one of the corners. The window-panes were small and set in lead. The curiosity of this room is, that it was once the residence of Pope, and that he here wrote a considerable part of the translation of Homer, and likewise, no doubt, the admirable letters to which I have referred above. The room once contained a record by himself, scratched with a diamond on one of the window-panes (since removed for safe-keeping to Nuneham Courtney, where it was shown me), purporting that he had here finished the fifth book of the "Iliad" on such a day.

A poet has a fragrance about him, such as no other human being is gifted withal; it is indestructible, and clings for evermore to everything that he has touched. I was not impressed, at Blenheim, with any sense that the mighty Duke still haunted the palace that was created for him; but here, after a century and a half, we are still conscious of the presence of that decrepit little figure of Queen Anne's time, although he was merely a casual guest in the old tower, during one or two summer months. However brief the time and slight the connection, his spirit cannot be exorcised so long as the tower stands. In my mind, moreover, Pope, or any other person with an available claim, is right in adhering to the spot, dead or alive; for I never saw a chamber that I should like better to inhabit, — so comfortably small, in such a safe and inaccessible seclusion, and with a varied landscape from each window. One of them looks upon the church, close at hand, and down into the green churchyard, extending almost to the foot of the tower; the others have views wide and far, over a gently undulating tract of country. If desirous of a loftier elevation, about a dozen more steps of the turret-stair will bring the occupant to the summit of the tower, — where Pope used to come, no doubt, in the summer evenings, and peep — poor little shrimp that he was! — through the embrasures of the battlement.

From Stanton Harcourt we drove — I forget how far — to a point where a boat was waiting for us upon the Thames, or some other stream; for I am ashamed to confess my ignorance of the precise geographical whereabout. . . .

At three o'clock or thereabouts (or sooner or later, — for I took little heed of time, and only wished that these delightful wanderings might last forever) we reached Folly Bridge, at Oxford. Here we took possession of a spacious barge, with a house in it, and a comfortable dining-room or drawing-room within the house, and a level roof, on which we could sit at ease, or dance if so inclined. These barges are common at Oxford, — some very splendid ones being owned by the students of the different colleges, or by clubs. They are drawn by horses, like canal-boats; and a horse being attached to our own barge, he trotted off at a reasonable pace, and we slipped through the water behind him, with a gentle and pleasant motion, which, save for the constant vicissitude of cultivated scenery, was like no motion at all. It was life without the trouble of living; nothing was ever more quietly agreeable. In this happy state of mind and body we gazed at Christ Church meadows, as we passed, and at the receding spires and towers of Oxford, and on a good deal of pleasant variety along the banks: young men rowing or fishing; troops of naked boys bathing, as if this were Arcadia, in the simplicity of the Golden Age; country-houses, cottages, water-side inns, all with something fresh about them, as not being sprinkled with the dust of the highway. We were a large party now; for a number of additional guests had joined us at Folly Bridge, and we comprised poets, novelists, scholars, sculptors, painters, architects, men and women of renown, dear friends, genial, outspoken, open-hearted Englishmen, — all voyaging onward together, like the wise ones of Gotham in a bowl. I remember not a single annoyance, except, indeed, that a swarm of wasps came aboard of us and alighted on the head of one of our young gentlemen, attracted by the scent of the pomatum which he had been rubbing into his hair. He was the only victim, and his small trouble the one little flaw in our day's felicity, to put us in mind that we were mortal.

Meanwhile a table had been laid in the interior of our barge, and spread with cold ham, cold fowl, cold pigeon-pie, cold beef, and other substantial cheer, such as the English love, and Yankees too, — besides tarts, and cakes, and pears, and plums, — not forgetting, of course, a goodly provision of port, sherry, and champagne, and bitter ale, which is like mother's milk to an Englishman, and soon grows equally acceptable to his American cousin. By the time these matters had been properly attended to, we had arrived at that part of the Thames which passes by Nuneham Courtney, a fine estate belonging to the Harcourts, and the present residence of the family. Here we landed, and, climbing a steep slope from the river-side, paused a moment or two to look at an architectural object, called the Carfax, the purport of which I do not well understand. Thence we proceeded onward, through the loveliest park and woodland scenery I ever saw, and under as beautiful a declining sunshine as heaven ever shed over earth, to the stately mansion-house. . . .

And now I take leave of Oxford without even an attempt to describe it, — there being no literary faculty, attainable or conceivable by me, which can avail to put it adequately, or even tolerably, upon paper. It must remain its own sole expression; and those whose sad fortune it may be never to behold it have no better resource than to dream about gray, weather-stained, ivy-grown edifices, wrought with quaint Gothic ornament, and standing around grassy quadrangles, where cloistered walks have echoed to the quiet footsteps of twenty generations,— lawns and gardens of luxurious repose, shadowed with canopies of foliage, and lit up with sunny glimpses through archways of great boughs, —spires, towers, and turrets, each with its history and legend, — dimly magnificent chapels, with painted windows of rare beauty and brilliantly diversified hues, creating an atmosphere of richest gloom, — vast college-halls, high-windowed, oaken-panelled, and hung round with portraits of the men, in every age, whom the University has nurtured to be illustrious, — long vistas of alcoved libraries, where the wisdom and learned folly of all time is shelved, — kitchens (we throw in this feature by way of ballast, and because it would not be English Oxford without its beef and beer), with huge fireplaces, capable of roasting a hundred joints at once, — and cavernous cellars, where rows of piled-up hogsheads seethe and fume with that mighty malt-liquor which is the true milk of Alma Mater: make all these things vivid in your dream, and you will never know nor believe how inadequate is the result to represent even the merest outside of Oxford. . . .

Some of the Haunts of Burns

... MOSS GIEL is not more than a mile from Mauchline, and the road extends over a high ridge of land, with a view of far hills and green slopes on either side. Just before we reached the farm, the driver stopped to point out a hawthorn, growing by the wayside, which he said was Burns's "Lousie Thorn"; and I devoutly plucked a branch, although I have really forgotten where or how this illustrious shrub has been celebrated. We then turned into a rude gateway, and almost immediately came to the farm-house of Moss Giel, standing some fifty yards removed from the highroad, behind a tall hedge of hawthorn, and considerably overshadowed by trees. The house is a whitewashed stone cottage, like thousands of others in England and Scotland, with a thatched roof, on which grass and weeds have intruded a picturesque, though alien growth. There is a door and one window in front, besides another little window that peeps out among the thatch. Close by the cottage, and extending back at right angles from it, so as to enclose the farm-yard, are two other buildings of the same size, shape, and general appearance as the house: any one of the three looks just as fit for a human habitation as the two others, and all three look still more suitable for donkey-stables and pigsties. As we drove into the farm-yard, bounded on three sides by these three hovels, a large dog began to bark at us; and some women and children made their appearance, but seemed to demur about admitting us, because the master and mistress were very religious people, and had not yet come back from the Sacrament at Mauchline.

However, it would not do to be turned back from the very threshold of Robert Burns; and as the women seemed to be merely straggling visitors, and nobody, at all events, had a right to send us away, we went into the back door, and, turning to the right, entered a kitchen. It showed a deplorable lack of housewifely neatness, and in it there were three or four children, one of whom, a girl eight or nine years old, held a baby in her arms. She proved to be the daughter of the people of the house, and gave us what leave she could to look about us. Thence we stepped across the narrow mid-passage of the cottage into the only other apartment below stairs, a sitting-room, where we found a young man eating bread and cheese. He informed us that he did not live there, and had only called in to refresh himself on his way home from church. This room, like the kitchen, was a noticeably poor one, and, besides being all that the cottage had to show for a parlor, it was a sleeping-apartment, having two beds, which might be curtained off, on occasion. The young man allowed us liberty (so far as in him lay) to go up stairs. Up we crept, accordingly; and a few steps brought us to the top of the staircase, over the kitchen, where we found the wretchedest little sleeping-chamber in the world, with a sloping roof under the thatch, and two beds spread upon the bare floor. This, most probably, was Burn's chamber; or, perhaps, it may have been that of his mother's servant-maid; and, in either case, this rude floor, at one time or another, must have creaked beneath the poet's midnight tread. On the opposite side of the passage was the door of another attic-chamber, opening which, I saw a considerable number of cheeses on the floor.

The whole house was pervaded with a frowzy smell, and also a dunghill odor; and it is not easy to understand how the atmosphere of such a dwelling can be any more agreeable or salubrious morally than it appeared to be physically. No virgin, surely, could keep a holy awe about her while stowed higgledy-piggledy with coarse-natured rustics into this narrowness and filth. Such a habitation is calculated to make beasts of men and women; and it indicates a degree of barbarism which I did not imagine to exist in Scotland, that a tiller of broad fields, like the farmer of Mauchline, should have his abode in a pigsty. It is sad to think of anybody — not to say a poet, but any human being — sleeping, eating, thinking, praying, and spending all his home-life in this miserable hovel; but, methinks, I never in the least knew how to estimate the miracle of Burns's genius, nor his heroic merit for being no worse man, until I thus learned the squalid hindrances amid which he developed himself. Space, a free atmosphere, and cleanliness have a vast deal to do with the possibilities of human virtue....

From Moss Giel we drove through a variety of pleasant scenes, some of which were familiar to us by their connection with Burns....

The road from Ayr passes Alloway Kirk, and crosses the Doon by a modern bridge, without swerving much from a straight line. To reach the old bridge, it appears to have made a bend, shortly after passing the kirk, and then to have turned sharply towards the river. The new bridge is within a minute's walk of the monument; and we went thither, and leaned over its parapet to admire the beautiful Doon, flowing wildly and sweetly between its deep and wooded banks. I never saw a lovelier scene; although this might have been even lovelier if a kindly sun had shone upon it. The ivy-grown, ancient bridge, with its high arch, through which we had a picture of the river and the green banks beyond, was absolutely the most picturesque object, in a quiet and gentle way, that ever blessed my eyes. Bonny Doon, with its wooded banks, and the boughs dipping into the water! The memory of them, at this moment, affects me like the song of birds, and Burns crooning some verses, simple and wild, in accordance with their native melody.

It was impossible to depart without crossing the very bridge of Tam's adventure; so we went thither, over a now disused portion of the road, and, standing on the centre of the arch, gathered some ivy-leaves from that sacred spot. This done, we returned as speedily as might be to Ayr, whence, taking the rail, we soon beheld Ailsa Craig rising like a pyramid out of the sea. Drawing nearer to Glasgow, Ben Lomond hove in sight, with a dome-like summit, supported by a shoulder on each side. But a man is better than a mountain; and we had been holding intercourse, if not with the reality, at least with the stalwart ghost of one of Earth's memorable sons, amid the scenes where he lived and sung. We shall appreciate him better as a poet, hereafter; for there is no writer whose life, as a man, has so much to do with his fame, and throws such a necessary light upon whatever he has produced. Henceforth, there will be a personal warmth for us in everything that he wrote; and, like his countrymen, we shall know him in a kind of personal way, as if we had shaken hands with him, and felt the thrill of his actual voice.

A London Suburb

ONE of our English summers looks, in the retrospect, as if it had been patched with more frequent sunshine than the sky of England ordinarily affords; but I believe that it may be only a moral effect, — a "light that never was on sea nor land," — caused by our having found a particularly delightful abode in the neighborhood of London. In order to enjoy it, however, I was compelled to solve the problem of living in two places at once, — an impossibility which I so far accomplished as to vanish, at frequent intervals, out of men's sight and knowledge on one side of England, and take my place in a circle of familiar faces on the other, so quietly that I seemed to have been there all along. It was the easier to get accustomed to our new residence, because it was not only rich in all the material properties of a home, but had also the home-like atmosphere, the household element, which is of too intangible a character to be let even with the most thoroughly furnished lodging-house. A friend had given us his suburban residence, with all its conveniences, elegances, and snuggeries, — its drawing rooms and library, still warm and bright with the recollection of the genial presences that we had known there, — its closets, chambers, kitchen, and even its wine-cellar, if we could have availed ourselves of so dear and delicate a trust, — its lawn and cosey garden-nooks, and whatever else makes up the multitudinous idea of an English home, — he had transferred it all to us, pilgrims and dusty wayfarers, that we might rest and take our ease during his summer's absence on the Continent. We had long been dwelling in tents, as it were, and morally shivering by hearths which, heap the bituminous coal upon them as we might, no blaze could render cheerful. I remember, to this day, the dreary feeling with which I sat by our first English fireside, and watched the chill and rainy twilight of an autumn day darkening down upon the garden; while the portrait of the preceding occupant of the house (evidently a most unamiable personage in his lifetime) scowled inhospitably from above the mantel-piece, as if indignant that an American should try to make himself at home there. Possibly it may appease his sulky shade to know that I quitted his abode as much a stranger as I entered it. But now, at last, we were in a genuine British home, where refined and warmhearted people had just been living their daily life, and had left us a summer's inheritance of slowly ripened days, such as a stranger's hasty opportunities so seldom permit him to enjoy.

Within so trifling a distance of the central spot of all the world (which, as Americans have at present no centre of their own, we may allow to be somewhere in the vicinity, we will say, of St. Paul's Cathedral), it might have seemed natural that I should be tossed about by the turbulence of the vast London whirlpool. But I had drifted into a still eddy, where conflicting movements made a repose, and, wearied with a good deal of uncongenial activity, I found the quiet of my temporary haven more attractive than anything that the great town could offer. I already knew London well; that is to say, I had long ago satisfied (so far as it was capable of satisfaction) that mysterious yearning — the magnetism of millions of hearts operating upon one — which impels every man's individuality to mingle itself with the immensest mass of human life within his scope. Day after day, at an earlier period, I had trodden the thronged thoroughfares, the broad, lonely squares, the lanes, alleys, and strange labyrinthine courts, the parks, the gardens and enclosures of ancient studious societies, so retired and silent amid the city uproar, the markets, the foggy streets along the river-side, the bridges, — I had sought all parts of the metropolis, in short, with an unweariable and indiscriminating curiosity; until few of the native inhabitants, I fancy, had turned so many of its corners as myself. These aimless wanderings (in which my prime purpose and achievement were to lose my way, and so to find it the more surely) had brought me, at one time or another, to the sight and actual presence of almost all the objects and renowned localities that I had read about, and which had made London the dream-city of my youth. I had found it better than my dream; for there is nothing else in life comparable (in that species of enjoyment, I mean) to the thick, heavy, oppressive, sombre delight which an American is sensible of, hardly knowing whether to call it a pleasure or a pain, in the atmosphere of London. The result was, that I acquired a home-feeling there, as nowhere else in the world, — though afterwards I came to have a somewhat similar sentiment in regard to Rome; and as long as either of those two great cities shall exist, the cities of the Past and of the Present, a man's native soil may crumble beneath his feet without leaving him altogether homeless upon earth.

Thus, having once fully yielded to its influence, I was in a manner free of the city, and could approach or keep away from it as I pleased. Hence it happened, that, living within a quarter of an hour's rush of the London Bridge Terminus, I was oftener tempted to spend a whole summer-day in our garden than to seek anything new or old, wonderful or commonplace, beyond its precincts. It was a delightful garden, of no great extent, but comprising a good many facilities for repose and enjoyment, such as arbors and garden-seats, shrubbery, flower-beds, rose-bushes in a profusion of bloom, pinks, poppies, geraniums, sweet-peas, and a variety of other scarlet, yellow, blue, and purple blossoms, which I did not trouble myself to recognize individually, yet had always a vague sense

of their beauty about me.   The dim sky of England has a most
happy effect on the coloring of flowers, blending richness with
delicacy in the same texture; but in this garden, as everywhere
else, the exuberance of English verdure had a greater charm
than any tropical splendor or diversity of hue.   The hunger
for natural beauty might be satisfied with grass and green
leaves forever.   Conscious of the triumph of England in this
respect, and loyally anxious for the credit of my own country,
it gratified me to observe what trouble and pains the English
gardeners are fain to throw away in producing a few sour
plums and abortive pears and apples, — as, for example, in
this very garden, where a row of unhappy trees were spread
out perfectly flat against a brick wall, looking as if impaled
alive, or crucified, with a cruel and unattainable purpose of
compelling them to produce rich fruit by torture.   For my
part, I never ate an English fruit, raised in the open air, that
could compare in flavor with a Yankee turnip.

The garden included that prime feature of English domestic
scenery, a lawn.   It had been levelled, carefully shorn, and
converted into a bowling-green, on which we sometimes essayed
to practice the time-honored game of bowls, most unskilfully,
yet not without a perception that it involves a very pleasant
mixture of exercise and ease, as is the case with most of the
old English pastimes.   Our little domain was shut in by the
house on one side, and in other directions by a hedge-fence
and a brick wall, which last was concealed or softened by shrubbery and the impaled fruit-trees already mentioned.   Over all
the outer region, beyond our immediate precincts, there was
an abundance of foliage, tossed aloft from the near or distant
trees with which that agreeable suburb is adorned.   The effect
was wonderfully sylvan and rural, insomuch that we might
have fancied ourselves in the depths of a wooded seclusion;
only that, at brief intervals, we could hear the galloping sweep
of a railway-train passing within a quarter of a mile, and its
discordant screech, moderated by a little farther distance, as it
reached the Blackheath Station.   That harsh, rough sound,

seeking me out so inevitably, was the voice of the great world summoning me forth. I know not whether I was the more pained or pleased to be thus constantly put in mind of the neighborhood of London; for, on the one hand, my conscience stung me a little for reading a book, or playing with children in the grass, when there were so many better things for an enlightened traveller to do, — while, at the same time, it gave a deeper delight to my luxurious idleness, to contrast it with the turmoil which I escaped. On the whole, however, I do not repent of a single wasted hour, and only wish that I could have spent twice as many in the same way; for the impression on my memory is, that I was as happy in that hospitable garden as the English summer-day was long.

One chief condition of my enjoyment was the weather. Italy has nothing like it, nor America. There never was such weather except in England, where, in requital of a vast amount of horrible east-wind between February and June, and a brown October and black November, and a wet, chill, sunless winter, there are a few weeks of incomparable summer, scattered through July and August, and the earlier portion of September, small in quantity, but exquisite enough to atone for the whole year's atmospherical delinquencies. After all, the prevalent sombreness may have brought out those sunny intervals in such high relief, that I see them, in my recollection, brighter than they really were: a little light makes a glory for people who live habitually in a gray gloom. The English, however, do not seem to know how enjoyable the momentary gleams of their summer are; they call it broiling weather, and hurry to the seaside with red, perspiring faces, in a state of combustion and deliquescence; and I have observed that even their cattle have similar susceptibilities, seeking the deepest shade, or standing midleg deep in pools and streams to cool themselves, at temperatures which our own cows would deem little more than barely comfortable. To myself, after the summer heats of my native land had somewhat effervesced out of my blood and memory, it was the weather of Paradise itself. It might

be a little too warm; but it was that modest and inestimable
superabundance which constitutes a bounty of Providence, instead of just a niggardly enough.   During my first year in
England, residing in perhaps the most ungenial part of the
kingdom, I could never be quite comfortable without a fire on
the hearth; in the second twelvemonth, beginning to get ac-
climatized, I became sensible of an austere friendliness, shy,
but sometimes almost tender, in the veiled, shadowy, seldom
smiling summer; and in the succeeding years, — whether that
I had renewed my fibre with English beef and replenished my
blood with English ale, or whatever were the cause, — I grew
content with winter and especially in love with summer, desir-
ing little more for happiness than merely to breathe and bask.
At the midsummer which we are now speaking of, I must needs
confess that the noontide sun came down more fervently than
I found altogether tolerable; so that I was fain to shift my
position with the shadow of the shrubbery, making myself the
movable index of a sundial that reckoned up the hours of an
almost interminable day.

For each day seemed endless, though never wearisome.   As
far as your actual experience is concerned, the English summer-
day has positively no beginning and no end.   When you awake,
at any reasonable hour, the sun is already shining through the
curtains; you live through unnumbered hours of Sabbath quietude, with a calm variety of incident softly etched upon their
tranquil lapse; and at length you become conscious that it is
bedtime again, while there is still enough daylight in the sky
to make the pages of your book distinctly legible.   Night, if
there be any such season, hangs down a transparent veil
through which the by-gone day beholds its successor; or, if not
quite true of the latitude of London, it may be soberly affirmed
of the more nothern parts of the island, that To-morrow is born
before its Yesterday is dead.   They exist together in the golden
twilight, where the decrepit old day dimly discerns the face
of the ominous infant; and you, though a mere mortal, may
simultaneously touch them both with one finger of recollection

and another of prophecy. I cared not how long the day might be, nor how many of them. I had earned this repose by a long course of irksome toil and perturbation, and could have been content never to stray out of the limits of that suburban villa and its garden. If I lacked anything beyond, it would have satisfied me well enough to dream about it, instead of struggling for its actual possession. At least, this was the feeling of the moment; although the transitory, flitting, and irresponsible character of my life there was perhaps the most enjoyable element of all, as allowing me much of the comfort of house and home, without any sense of their weight upon my back. The nomadic life has great advantages, if we can find tents ready pitched for us at every stage.

So much for the interior of our abode, — a spot of deepest quiet, within reach of the intensest activity. But, even when we stepped beyond our own gate, we were not shocked with any immediate presence of the great world. We were dwelling in one of those oases that have grown up (in comparatively recent years, I believe) on the wide waste of Blackheath, which otherwise offers a vast extent of unoccupied ground in singular proximity to the metropolis. As a general thing, the proprietorship of the soil seems to exist in everybody and nobody; but exclusive rights have been obtained, here and there, chiefly by men whose daily concerns link them with London, so that you find their villas or boxes standing along village streets which have often more of an American aspect than the elder English settlements. The scene is semi-rural. Ornamental trees overshadow the sidewalks, and grassy margins border the wheel-tracks. The houses, to be sure, have certain points of difference from those of an American village, bearing tokens of architectural design, though seldom of individual taste; and, as far as possible, they stand aloof from the street, and separated each from its neighbor by hedge or fence, in accordance with the careful exclusiveness of the English character, which impels the occupant, moreover, to cover the front of his dwelling with as much concealment of shrubbery as his limits will allow.

Through the interstices, you catch glimpses of well-kept lawns, generally ornamented with flowers, and with what the English call rock-work, being heaps of ivy-grown stones and fossils, designed for romantic effect in a small way. Two or three of such village streets as are here described take a collective name, — as, for instance, Blackheath Park, — and constitute a kind of community of residents, with gateways, kept by a policeman, and a semi-privacy, stepping beyond which, you find yourself on the breezy heath.

On this great, bare, dreary common I often went astray, as I afterwards did on the Campagna of Rome, and drew the air (tainted with London smoke though it might be) into my lungs by deep inspirations, with a strange and unexpected sense of desert freedom. The misty atmosphere helps you to fancy a remoteness that perhaps does not quite exist. During the little time that it lasts, the solitude is as impressive as that of a Western prairie or forest; but soon the railway shriek, a mile or two away, insists upon informing you of your whereabout; or you recognize in the distance some landmark that you may have known, — an insulated villa, perhaps, with its garden-wall around it, or the rudimental street of a new settlement which is sprouting on this otherwise barren soil. Half a century ago, the most frequent token of man's beneficent contiguity might have been a gibbet, and the creak, like a tavern sign, of a murderer swinging to and fro in irons. Blackheath, with its highwaymen and footpads, was dangerous in those days; and even now, for aught I know, the Western prairie may still compare favorably with it as a safe region to go astray in. When I was acquainted with Blackheath, the ingenious device of garroting had recently come into fashion; and I can remember, while crossing those waste places at midnight, and hearing footsteps behind me, to have been sensibly encouraged by also hearing, not far off, the clinking hoof-tramp of one of the horse-patrols who do regular duty there. About sunset, or a little later, was the time when the broad and somewhat desolate peculiarity of the heath seemed to me to put on its utmost impressiveness. At that hour, finding myself on elevated ground, I once had a view of immense London, four or five miles off, with the vast Dome in the midst, and the towers of the two Houses of Parliament rising up into the smoky canopy, the thinner substance of which obscured a mass of things, and hovered about the objects that were most distinctly visible, — a glorious and sombre picture, dusky, awful, but irresistibly attractive, like a young man's dream of the great world, foretelling at that distance a grandeur never to be fully realized.

While I lived in that neighborhood, the tents of two or three sets of cricket-players were constantly pitched on Blackheath, and matches were going forward that seemed to involve the honor and credit of communities or counties, exciting an interest in everybody but myself, who cared not what part of England might glorify itself at the expense of another. It is necessary to be born an Englishman, I believe, in order to enjoy this great national game; at any rate, as a spectacle for an outside observer, I found it lazy, lingering, tedious, and utterly devoid of pictorial effects. Choice of other amusements was at hand. Butts for archery were established, and bows and arrows were to be let, at so many shots for a penny, — there being abundance of space for a farther flight-shot than any modern archer can lend to his shaft. Then there was an absurd game of throwing a stick at crockery-ware, which I have witnessed a hundred times, and personally engaged in once or twice, without ever having the satisfaction to see a bit of broken crockery. In other spots you found donkeys for children to ride, and ponies of a very meek and patient spirit, on which the Cockney pleasure-seekers of both sexes rode races and made wonderful displays of horsemanship. By way of refreshment there was gingerbread (but, as a true patriot, I must pronounce it greatly inferior to our native dainty), and ginger-beer, and probably stancher liquor among the booth-keeper's hidden stores. The frequent railway-trains, as well as the numerous steamers to Greenwich, have made the vacant portions of Blackheath a play-ground and breathing-place for the London-

ers, readily and very cheaply accessible; so that, in view of this
broader use and enjoyment, I a little grudged the tracts that
have been filched away, so to speak, and individualized by
thriving citizens.   One sort of visitors especially interested me:
they were schools of little boys or girls, under the guardianship
of their instructors, — charity schools, as I often surmised from
their aspect, collected among dark alleys and squalid courts;
and hither they were brought to spend a summer afternoon,
these pale little progeny of the sunless nooks of London, who
had never known that the sky was any broader than that narrow and vapory strip above their native lane.   I fancied that
they took but a doubtful pleasure, being half affrighted at the
wide, empty space overhead and round about them, finding the
air too little medicated with smoke, soot, and graveyard ex-
halations, to be breathed with comfort, and feeling shelterless
and lost because grimy London, their slatternly and disreputable mother, had suffered them to stray out of her arms.

Passing among these holiday people, we come to one of the
gateways of Greenwich Park, opening through an old brick
wall.   It admits us from the bare heath into a scene of antique
cultivation and woodland ornament, traversed in all directions
by avenues of trees, many of which bear tokens of a venerable
age.   These broad and well-kept pathways rise and decline
over the elevations, and along the bases of gentle hills, which
diversify the whole surface of the Park.   The loftiest and most
abrupt of them (though but of very moderate height) is one
of the earth's noted summits, and may hold up its head with
Mont Blanc and Chimborazo, as being the site of Greenwich
Observatory, where, if all nations will consent to say so, the
longitude of our great globe begins.   I used to regulate my
watch by the broad dial-plate against the Observatory wall,
and felt it pleasant to be standing at the very centre of Time
and Space.

There are lovelier parks than this in the neighborhood of
London, richer scenes of greensward and cultivated trees; and
Kensington, especially, in a summer afternoon, has seemed to

me as delightful as any place can or ought to be, in a world which, some time or other, we must quit. But Greenwich, too, is beautiful, — a spot where the art of man has conspired with Nature, as if he and the great mother had taken counsel together how to make a pleasant scene, and the longest liver of the two had faithfully carried out their mutual design. It has, likewise, an additional charm of its own, because, to all appearance, it is the people's property and play-ground in a much more genuine way than the aristocratic resorts in closer vicinity to the metropolis. It affords one of the instances in which the monarch's property is actually the people's, and shows how much more natural is their relation to the sovereign than to the nobility, which pretends to hold the intervening space between the two: for a nobleman makes a paradise only for himself, and fills it with his own pomp and pride; whereas the people are sooner or later the legitimate inheritors of whatever beauty kings and queens create, as now of Greenwich Park. On Sundays, when the sun shone, and even on those grim and sombre days when, if it do not actually rain, the English persist in calling it fine weather, it was too good to see how sturdily the plebeians trod under their own oaks, and what fulness of simple enjoyment they evidently found there. They were the people, — not the populace, — specimens of a class whose Sunday clothes are a distinct kind of garb from their week-day ones; and this, in England, implies wholesome habits of life, daily thrift, and a rank above the lowest. I longed to be acquainted with them, in order to investigate what manner of folks they were, what sort of households they kept, their politics, their religion, their tastes, and whether they were as narrow-minded as their betters. There can be very little doubt of it: an Englishman is English, in whatever rank of life, though no more intensely so, I should imagine, as an artisan or petty shopkeeper, than as a member of Parliament.

The English character, as I conceive it, is by no means a very lofty one; they seem to have a great deal of earth and grimy dust clinging about them, as was probably the case with the stalwart and quarrelsome people who sprouted up out of the soil, after Cadmus had sown the dragon's teeth. And yet, though the individual Englishman is sometimes preternaturally disagreeable, an observer standing aloof has a sense of natural kindness towards them in the lump. They adhere closer to the original simplicity in which mankind was created than we ourselves do; they love, quarrel, laugh, cry, and turn their actual selves inside out with greater freedom than any class of Americans would consider decorous. It was often so with these holiday folks in Greenwich Park; and, ridiculous as it may sound, I fancy myself to have caught very satisfactory glimpses of Arcadian life among the Cockneys there, hardly beyond the scope of Bow-Bells, picnicking in the grass, uncouthly gambolling on the broad slopes, or straying in motley groups or by single pairs of love-making youths and maidens, along the sunstreaked avenues. Even the omnipresent policemen or parkkeepers could not disturb the beatific impression on my mind. One feature, at all events, of the Golden Age was to be seen in the herds of deer that encountered you in the somewhat remoter recesses of the Park, and were readily prevailed upon to nibble a bit of bread out of your hand. But, though no wrong had ever been done them, and no horn had sounded nor hound bayed at the heels of themselves or their antlered progenitors for centuries past, there was still an apprehensiveness lingering in their hearts; so that a slight movement of the hand or a step too near would send a whole squadron of them scampering away, just as a breath scatters the winged seeds of a dandelion.

The aspect of Greenwich Park, with all those festal people wandering through it, resembled that of the Borghese Gardens under the walls of Rome, on a Sunday or Saint's day; but, I am not ashamed to say, it a little disturbed whatever grimly ghost of Puritanic strictness might be lingering in the sombre depths of a New England heart, among severe and sunless remembrances of the Sabbaths of childhood, and pangs of remorse for ill-gotten lessons in the catechism, and for erratic fantasies or hardly suppressed laughter in the middle of long sermons. Occasionally, I tried to take the long-hoarded sting out of these compunctious smarts by attending divine service in the open air. On a cart outside of the Park-wall (and, if I mistake not, at two or three corners and secluded spots within the Park itself) a Methodist preacher uplifts his voice and speedily gathers a congregation, his zeal for whose religious welfare impels the good man to such earnest vociferation and toilsome gesture that his perspiring face is quickly in a stew. His inward flame conspires with the too fervid sun, and makes a positive martyr of him, even in the very exercise of his pious labor; insomuch that he purchases every atom of spiritual increment to his hearers by loss of his own corporeal solidity, and, should his discourse last long enough, must finally exhale before their eyes. If I smile at him, be it understood, it is not in scorn; he performs his sacred office more acceptably than many a prelate. These wayside services attract numbers who would not otherwise listen to prayer, sermon, or hymn, from one year's end to another, and who, for that very reason, are the auditors most likely to be moved by the preacher's eloquence. Yonder Greenwich pensioner, too,—in his costume of three-cornered hat, and old-fashioned, brass-buttoned blue coat with ample skirts, which makes him look like a contemporary of Admiral Benbow,—that tough old mariner may hear a word or two which will go nearer his heart than anything that the chaplain of the Hospital can be expected to deliver. I always noticed, moreover, that a considerable proportion of the audience were soldiers, who came hither with a day's leave from Woolwich,— hardy veterans in aspect, some of whom wore as many as four or five medals, Crimean or East Indian, on the breasts of their scarlet coats. The miscellaneous congregation listen with every appearance of heartfelt interest; and, for my own part, I must frankly acknowledge that I never found it possible to give five minutes' attention to any other English preaching: so cold and commonplace are the homilies

that pass for such, under the aged roofs of churches. And as
for cathedrals, the sermon is an exceedingly diminutive and
unimportant part of the religious services, — if, indeed, it be
considered a part, — among the pompous ceremonies, the into-
nations, and the resounding and lofty-voiced strains of the
choristers. The magnificence of the setting quite dazzles out
what we Puritans look upon as the jewel of the whole affair;
for I presume that it was our forefathers, the Dissenters in
England and America, who gave the sermon its present prominence in the Sabbath exercises.

The Methodists are probably the first and only Englishmen
who have worshipped in the open air since the ancient Britons
listened to the preaching of the Druids; and it reminded me of
that old priesthood, to see certain memorials of their dusky
epoch — not religious, however, but warlike — in the neighborhood of the spot where the Methodist was holding forth.
These were some ancient barrows, beneath or within which
are supposed to lie buried the slain of a forgotten or doubtfully
remembered battle, fought on the site of Greenwich Park as
long ago as two or three centuries after the birth of Christ.
Whatever may once have been their height and magnitude,
they have now scarcely more prominence in the actual scene
than the battle of which they are the sole monuments retains
in history, — being only a few mounds side by side, elevated
a little above the surface of the ground, ten or twelve feet in
diameter, with a shallow depression in their summits. When
one of them was opened, not long since, no bones, nor armor,
nor weapons were discovered, nothing but some small jewels,
and a tuft of hair, — perhaps from the head of a valiant general, who, dying on the field of his victory, bequeathed this
lock, together with his indestructible fame, to after ages. The
hair and jewels are probably in the British Museum, where the
potsherds and rubbish of innumerable generations make the
visitor wish that each passing century could carry off all its
fragments and relics along with it, instead of adding them to
the continually accumulating burden which human knowledge

is compelled to lug upon its back. As for the fame, I know not what has become of it.

After traversing the Park, we come into the neighborhood of Greenwich Hospital, and will pass through one of its spacious gateways for the sake of glancing at an establishment which does more honor to the heart of England than anything else that I am acquainted with, of a public nature. It is very seldom that we can be sensible of anything like kindliness in the acts or relations of such an artificial thing as a National Government. Our own government, I should conceive, is too much an abstraction ever to feel any sympathy for its maimed sailors and soldiers, though it will doubtless do them a severe kind of justice, as chilling as the touch of steel. But it seemed to me that the Greenwich pensioners are the petted children of the nation, and that the government is their dry nurse, and that the old men themselves have a childlike consciousness of their position. Very likely, a better sort of life might have been arranged, and a wiser care bestowed on them; but, such as it is, it enables them to spend a sluggish, careless, comfortable old age, grumbling, growling, gruff, as if all the foul weather of their past years were pent up within them, yet not much more discontented than such weather-beaten and battle-battered fragments of human kind must inevitably be. Their home, in its outward form, is on a very magnificent plan. Its germ was a royal palace, the full expansion of which has resulted in a series of edifices externally more beautiful than any English palace that I have seen, consisting of several quadrangles of stately architecture, united by colonnades and gravel-walks, and enclosing grassy squares, with statues in the centre, the whole extending along the Thames. It is built of marble, or very light-colored stone, in the classic style, with pillars and porticos, which (to my own taste, and, I fancy, to that of the old sailors) produce but a cold and shivery effect in the English climate. Had I been the architect, I would have studied the characters, habits, and predilections of nautical people in Wapping, Rotherhithe, and the neighborhood of the Tower (places

which I visited in affectionate remembrance of Captain Lemuel
Gulliver, and other actual or mythological navigators), and
would have built the hospital in a kind of ethereal similitude
to the narrow, dark, ugly, and inconvenient, but snug and
cosey homeliness of the sailor boarding-houses there. There
can be no question that all the above attributes, or enough of
them to satisfy an old sailor's heart, might be reconciled with
architectural beauty and the wholesome contrivances of modern dwellings, and thus a novel and genuine style of building
be given to the world.

But their countrymen meant kindly by the old fellows in
assigning them the ancient royal site where Elizabeth held her
court and Charles II. began to build his palace. So far as the
locality went, it was treating them like so many kings; and,
with a discreet abundance of grog, beer, and tobacco, there
was perhaps little more to be accomplished in behalf of men
whose whole previous lives have tended to unfit them for old
age. Their chief discomfort is probably for lack of something
to do or think about. But, judging by the few whom I saw,
a listless habit seems to have crept over them, a dim dreami-
ness of mood, in which they sit between asleep and awake, and
find the long day wearing towards bedtime without its having
made any distinct record of itself upon their consciousness.
Sitting on stone benches in the sunshine, they subside into
slumber, or nearly so, and start at the approach of footsteps
echoing under the colonnades, ashamed to be caught napping,
and rousing themselves in a hurry, as formerly on the midnight
watch at sea. In their brightest moments, they gather in
groups and bore one another with endless sea-yarns about their
voyages under famous admirals, and about gale and calm,
battle and chase, and all that class of incident that had its
sphere on the deck and in the hollow interior of a ship, where
their world has exclusively been. For other pastime, they
quarrel among themselves, comrade with comrade, and perhaps
shake paralytic fists in furrowed faces. If inclined for a little
exercise, they can bestir their wooden legs on the long espla-

nade that borders by the Thames, criticising the rig of passing ships, and firing off volleys of malediction at the steamers, which have made the sea another element than that they used to be acquainted with.   All this is but cold comfort for the evening of life, yet may compare rather favorably with the preceding portions of it, comprising little save imprisonment on shipboard, in the course of which they have been tossed all about the world and caught hardly a glimpse of it, forgetting what grass and trees are, and never finding out what woman is, though they may have encountered a painted spectre which they took for her.   A country owes much to human beings whose bodies she has worn out and whose immortal part she has left undeveloped or debased, as we find them here; and having wasted an idle paragraph upon them, let me now suggest that old men have a kind of susceptibility to moral impressions, and even (up to an advanced period) a receptivity of truth, which often appears to come to them after the active time of life is past.   The Greenwich pensioners might prove better subjects for true education now than in their school-boy days; but then where is the Normal School that could educate instructors for such a class?

There is a beautiful chapel for the pensioners, in the classic style, over the altar of which hangs a picture by West.   I never could look at it long enough to make out its design; for this artist (though it pains me to say it of so respectable a countryman) had a gift of frigidity, a knack of grinding ice into his paint, a power of stupefying the spectator's perceptions and quelling his sympathy, beyond any other limner that ever handled a brush.   In spite of many pangs of conscience, I seize this opportunity to wreak a lifelong abhorrence upon the poor, blameless man, for the sake of that dreary picture of Lear, an explosion of frosty fury, that used to be a bugbear to me in the Athenaeum Exhibition.   Would fire burn it, I wonder?

The principal thing that they have to show you, at Greenwich Hospital, is the Painted Hall.   It is a splendid and spacious room, at least a hundred feet long and half as high, with a ceiling painted in fresco by Sir James Thornhill. As a work of art, I presume, this frescoed canopy has little merit, though it produces an exceedingly rich effect by its brilliant coloring and as a specimen of magnificent upholstery. The walls of the grand apartment are entirely covered with pictures, many of them representing battles and other naval incidents that were once fresher in the world's memory than now, but chiefly portraits of old admirals, comprising the whole line of heroes who have trod the quarter-decks of British ships for more than two hundred years back. Next to a tomb in Westminster Abbey, which was Nelson's most elevated object of ambition, it would seem to be the highest meed of a naval warrior to have his portrait hung up in the Painted Hall; but, by dint of victory upon victory, these illustrious personages have grown to be a mob, and by no means a very interesting one, so far as regards the character of the faces here depicted. They are generally commonplace, and often singularly stolid; and I have observed (both in the Painted Hall and elsewhere, and not only in portraits, but in the actual presence of such renowned people as I have caught glimpses of) that the countenances of heroes are not nearly so impressive as those of statesmen, — except, of course, in the rare instances where warlike ability has been but the one-sided manifestation of a profound genius for managing the world's affairs. Nine tenths of these distinguished admirals, for instance, if their faces tell truth, must needs have been blockheads, and might have served better, one would imagine, as wooden figure-heads for their own ships than to direct any difficult and intricate scheme of action from the quarter-deck. It is doubtful whether the same kind of men will hereafter meet with a similar degree of success; for they were victorious chiefly through the old English hardihood, exercised in a field of which modern science had not yet got possession. Rough valor has lost something of its value since their days, and must continue to sink lower and lower in the comparative estimate of warlike qualities. In the next naval war, as between England and France, I would bet, methinks, upon the Frenchman's head.

It is remarkable, however, that the great naval hero of England — the greatest, therefore, in the world, and of all time — had none of the stolid characteristics that belong to his class, and cannot fairly be accepted as their representative man. Foremost in the roughest of professions, he was as delicately organized as a woman, and as painfully sensitive as a poet. More than any other Englishman he won the love and admiration of his country, but won them through the efficacy of qualities that are not English, or, at all events, were intensified in his case and made poignant and powerful by something morbid in the man, which put him otherwise at cross-purposes with life. He was a man of genius; and genius in an Englishman (not to cite the good old simile of a pearl in the oyster) is usually a symptom of a lack of balance in the general making-up of the character; as we may satisfy ourselves by running over the list of their poets, for example, and observing how many of them have been sickly or deformed, and how often their lives have been darkened by insanity. An ordinary Englishman is the healthiest and wholesomest of human beings; an extraordinary one is almost always, in one way or another, a sick man. It was so with Lord Nelson. The wonderful contrast or relation between his personal qualities, the position which he held, and the life that he lived, makes him as interesting a personage as all history has to show; and it is a pity that Southey's biography — so good in its superficial way, and yet so inadequate as regards any real delineation of the man — should have taken the subject out of the hands of some writer endowed with more delicate appreciation and deeper insight than that genuine Englishman possessed. But Southey accomplished his own purpose, which, apparently, was to present his hero as a pattern for England's young midshipmen.

But the English capacity for hero-worship is full to the brim with what they are able to comprehend of Lord Nelson's character. Adjoining the Painted Hall is a smaller room, the walls of which are completely and exclusively adorned with pictures of the great Admiral's exploits. We see the frail, ardent man in all the most noted events of his career, from his encounter with a Polar Bear to his death at Trafalgar, quivering here and there about the room like a blue, lambent flame. No Briton ever enters that apartment without feeling the beef and ale of his composition stirred to its depths, and finding himself changed into a hero for the nonce, however stolid his brain, however tough his heart, however unexcitable his ordinary mood. To confess the truth, I myself, though belonging to another parish, have been deeply sensible to the sublime recollections there aroused, acknowledging that Nelson expressed his life in a kind of symbolic poetry which I had as much right to understand as these burly islanders. Cool and critical observer as I sought to be, I enjoyed their burst of honest indignation when a visitor (not an American, I am glad to say) thrust his walking-stick almost into Nelson's face, in one of the pictures, by way of pointing a remark; and the bystanders immediately glowed like so many hot coals, and would probably have consumed the offender in their wrath, had he not effected his retreat. But the most sacred objects of all are two of Nelson's coats, under separate glass cases. One is that which he wore at the Battle of the Nile, and it is now sadly injured by moths, which will quite destroy it in a few years, unless its guardians preserve it as we do Washington's military suit by occasionally baking it in an oven. The other is the coat in which he received his death-wound at Trafalgar. On its breast are sewed three or four stars and orders of knighthood, now much dimmed by time and damp, but which glittered brightly enough on the battle-day to draw the fatal aim of a French marksman. The bullet-hole is visible on the shoulder, as well as a part of the golden tassels of an epaulet, the rest of which was shot away. Over the coat is laid a white waistcoat, with a great blood-stain on it, out of which all the redness has utterly faded, leaving it of a dingy yellow hue, in the threescore years since that blood gushed out.   Yet it was once the reddest blood in England, — Nelson's blood!

The hospital stands close adjacent to the town of Greenwich, which will always retain a kind of festal aspect in my memory, in consequence of my having first become acquainted with it on Easter Monday.   Till a few years ago, the first three days of Easter were a carnival season in this old town, during which the idle and disreputable part of London poured itself into the streets like an inundation of the Thames, — as unclean as that turbid mixture of the offscourings of the vast city, and overflowing with its grimy pollution whatever rural innocence, if any, might be found in the suburban neighborhood.   This festivity was called Greenwich Fair, the final one of which, in an immemorial succession, it was my fortune to behold.

If I had bethought myself of going through the fair with a note-book and pencil, jotting down all the prominent objects, I doubt not that the result might have been a sketch of English life quite as characteristic and worthy of historical preservation as an account of the Roman Carnival.   Having neglected to do so, I remember little more than a confusion of unwashed and shabbily dressed people, intermixed with some smarter figures, but, on the whole, presenting a mobbish appearance such as we never see in our own country.   It taught me to understand why Shakespeare, in speaking of a crowd, so often alludes to its attribute of evil odor.   The common people of England, I am afraid, have no daily familiarity with even so necessary a thing as a wash-bowl, not to mention a bathing-tub. And, furthermore, it is one mighty difference between them and us, that every man and woman on our side of the water has a working-day suit and a holiday suit, and is occasionally as fresh as a rose, whereas, in the good old country, the griminess of his labor or squalid habits clings forever to the individual, and gets to be a part of his personal substance.   These are broad facts, involving great corollaries and dependencies. There are really, if you stop to think about it, few sadder spectacles in the world than a ragged coat, or a soiled and shabby gown, at a festival.

This unfragrant crowd was exceedingly dense, being welded together, as it were, in the street through which we strove to make our way. On either side were oyster-stands, stalls of oranges (a very prevalent fruit in England, where they give the withered ones a guise of freshness by boiling them), and booths covered with old sail-cloth, in which the commodity that most attracted the eye was gilt gingerbread. It was so completely enveloped in Dutch gilding that I did not at first recognize an old acquaintance, but wondered what those golden crowns and images could be. There were likewise drums and other toys for small children, and a variety of showy and worthless articles for children of a larger growth; though it perplexed me to imagine who, in such a mob, could have the innocent taste to desire playthings, or the money to pay for them. Not that I have a right to accuse the mob, on my own knowledge, of being any less innocent than a set of cleaner and better dressed people might have been; for, though one of them stole my pocket-handkerchief, I could not but consider it fair game, under the circumstances, and was grateful to the thief for sparing me my purse. They were quiet, civil, and remarkably good-humored, making due allowance for the national gruffness; there was no riot, no tumultuous swaying to and fro of the mass, such as I have often noted in an American crowd; no noise of voices, except frequent bursts of laughter, hoarse or shrill, and a widely diffused, inarticulate murmur, resembling nothing so much as the rumbling of the tide among the arches of London Bridge. What immensely perplexed me was a sharp, angry sort of rattle, in all quarters, far off and close at hand, and sometimes right at my own back, where it sounded as if the stout fabric of my English surtout had been ruthlessly rent in twain; and everybody's clothes, all over the fair, were evidently being torn asunder in the same way. By and by, I discovered that this strange noise was produced by a little instrument called "The Fun of the Fair," — a sort of rattle, consisting of a wooden wheel, the cogs of which turn against a thin slip of wood, and so produce a rasping sound when drawn smartly against a person's back. The ladies draw their rattles against the backs of their male friends (and everybody passes for a friend at Greenwich Fair), and the young men return the compliment on the broad British backs of the ladies; and all are bound by immemorial custom to take it in good part and be merry at the joke. As it was one of my prescribed official duties to give an account of such mechanical contrivances as might be unknown in my own country, I have thought it right to be thus particular in describing the Fun of the Fair.

But this was far from being the sole amusement. There were theatrical booths, in front of which were pictorial representations of the scenes to be enacted within; and anon a drummer emerged from one of them, thumping on a terribly lax drum, and followed by the entire *dramatis personae,* who ranged themselves on a wooden platform in front of the theatre. They were dressed in character, but wofully shabby, with very dingy and wrinkled white tights, threadbare cottonvelvets, crumpled silks, and crushed muslin, and all the gloss and glory gone out of their aspect and attire, seen thus in the broad daylight and after a long series of performances. They sang a song together, and withdrew into the theatre, whither the public were invited to follow them at the inconsiderable cost of a penny a ticket. Before another booth stood a pair of brawny fighting-men, displaying their muscle, and soliciting patronage for an exhibition of the noble British art of pugilism. There were pictures of giants, monsters, and outlandish beasts, most prodigious, to be sure, and worthy of all admiration, unless the artist had gone incomparably beyond his subject. Jugglers proclaimed aloud the miracles which they were prepared to work; and posture-makers dislocated every joint of their bodies and tied their limbs into inextricable knots, wherever they could find space to spread a little square of carpet on the ground. In the midst of the confusion, while everybody was treading on his neighbor's toes, some little boys were very solicitous to brush your boots. These lads, I believe, are a product of modern society, — at least, no older than the time of Gay, who celebrates their origin in his "Trivia"; but in most other respects the scene reminded me of Bunyan's description of Vanity Fair, — nor is it at all improbable that the Pilgrim may have been a merry-maker here in his wild youth.

It seemed very singular — though, of course, I immediately classified it as an English characteristic — to see a great many portable weighing-machines, the owners of which cried out continually and amain, "Come, know your weight! Come, come, know your weight to-day! Come, know your weight!" and a multitude of people, mostly large in girth, were moved by this vociferation to sit down in the machines. I know not whether they valued themselves on their beef, and estimated their standing as members of society at so much a pound; but I shall set it down as a national peculiarity, and a symbol of the prevalence of the earthly over the spiritual element, that Englishmen are wonderfully bent on knowing how solid and physically ponderous they are.

On the whole, having an appetite for the brown bread and the tripe and sausages of life, as well as for its nicer cates and dainties, I enjoyed the scene, and was amused at the sight of a gruff old Greenwich pensioner, who, forgetful of the sailor-frolics of his young days, stood looking with grim disapproval at all these vanities. Thus we squeezed our way through the mob-jammed town, and emerged into the Park, where, likewise, we met a great many merry-makers, but with freer space for their gambols than in the streets. We soon found ourselves the targets for a cannonade with oranges (most of them in a decayed condition), which went humming past our ears from the vantage-ground of neighboring hillocks, sometimes hitting our sacred persons with an inelastic thump. This was one of the privileged freedoms of the time, and was nowise to be resented, except by returning the salute. Many persons were running races, hand in hand, down the declivities, especially that steepest one on the summit of which stands the world-central Observatory, and (as in the race of life) the partners were usually male and female, and often caught a tumble together before reaching the bottom of the hill. Hereabouts we were pestered and haunted by two young girls, the eldest not more than thirteen, teasing us to buy matches; and finding no market for their commodity, the taller one suddenly turned a somerset before our faces, and rolled heels over head from top to bottom of the hill on which we stood. Then, scrambling up the acclivity, the topsy-turvy trollop offered us her matches again, as demurely as if she had never flung aside her equilibrium; so that, dreading a repetition of the feat, we gave her sixpence and an admonition, and enjoined her never to do so any more.

The most curious amusement that we witnessed here — or anywhere else, indeed — was an ancient and hereditary pastime called "Kissing in the Ring." I shall describe the sport exactly as I saw it, although an English friend assures me that there are certain ceremonies with a handkerchief, which make it much more decorous and graceful. A handkerchief, indeed! There was no such thing in the crowd, except it were the one which they had filched out of my pocket. It is one of the simplest kinds of games, needing little or no practice to make the player altogether perfect; and the manner of it is this. A ring is formed (in the present case, it was of large circumference and thickly gemmed around with faces, mostly on the broad grin), into the centre of which steps an adventurous youth, and, looking round the circle, selects whatever maiden may most delight his eye. He presents his hand (which she is bound to accept), leads her into the centre, salutes her on the lips, and retires, taking his stand in the expectant circle. The girl, in her turn, throws a favorable regard on some fortunate young man, offers her hand to lead him forth, makes him happy with a maidenly kiss, and withdraws to hide her blushes, if any there be, among the simpering faces in the ring; while the favored swain loses no time in transferring her salute to the prettiest and plumpest among the many mouths that are primming themselves in anticipation. And thus the thing goes on, till all the festive throng are inwreathed and intertwined into an endless and inextricable chain of kisses; though, indeed, it smote me with compassion to reflect that some forlorn pair of lips might be left out, and never know the triumph of a salute, after throwing aside so many delicate reserves for the sake of winning it. If the young men had any chivalry, there was a fair chance to display it by kissing the homeliest damsel in the circle.

To be frank, however, at the first glance, and to my American eye, they looked all homely alike, and the chivalry that I suggest is more than I could have been capable of, at any period of my life. They seemed to be country-lasses, of sturdy and wholesome aspect, with coarse-grained, cabbage-rosy cheeks, and, I am willing to suppose, a stout texture of moral principle, such as would bear a good deal of rough usage without suffering much detriment. But how unlike the trim little damsels of my native land! I desire above all things to be courteous; but, since the plain truth must be told, the soil and climate of England produces feminine beauty as rarely as they do delicate fruit; and though admirable specimens of both are to be met with, they are the hot-house ameliorations of refined society, and apt, moreover, to relapse into the coarseness of the original stock. The men are manlike, but the women are not beautiful, though the female Bull be well enough adapted to the male. To return to the lasses of Greenwich Fair, their charms were few, and their behavior, perhaps, not altogether commendable; and yet it was impossible not to feel a degree of faith in their innocent intentions, with such a half-bashful zest and entire simplicity did they keep up their part of the game. It put the spectator in good-humor to look at them, because there was still something of the old Arcadian life, the secure freedom of the antique age, in their way of surrendering their lips to strangers, as if there were no evil or impurity in the world. As for the young men, they were chiefly specimens of the vulgar sediment of London life, often shabbily genteel, rowdyish, pale, wearing the unbrushed coat, unshifted linen, and unwashed faces of yesterday, as well as the haggardness of last night's jollity in a gin-shop. Gathering their character from these tokens, I wondered whether there were any reasonable prospect of their fair partners returning to their rustic homes with as much innocence (whatever were its amount or quality) as they brought to Greenwich Fair, in spite of the perilous familiarity established by Kissing in the Ring.

The manifold disorders resulting from the fair, at which a vast city was brought into intimate relations with a comparatively rural district, have at length led to its suppression; this was the very last celebration of it, and brought to a close the broad-mouthed merriment of many hundred years. Thus my poor sketch, faint as its colors are, may acquire some little value in the reader's eyes from the consideration that no observer of the coming time will ever have an opportunity to give a better. I should find it difficult to believe, however, that the queer pastime just described, or any moral mischief to which that and other customs might pave the way, can have led to the overthrow of Greenwich Fair; for it has often seemed to me that Englishmen of station and respectability, unless of a peculiarly philanthropic turn, have neither any faith in the feminine purity of the lower orders of their countrywomen, nor the slightest value for it, allowing its possible existence. The distinction of ranks is so marked, that the English cottage damsel holds a position somewhat analogous to that of the negro girl in our Southern States. Hence comes inevitable detriment to the moral condition of those men themselves, who forget that the humblest woman has a right and a duty to hold herself in the same sanctity as the highest. The subject cannot well be discussed in these pages; but I offer it as a serious conviction, from what I have been able to observe, that the England of today is the unscrupulous old England of Tom Jones and Joseph Andrews, Humphrey Clinker and Roderick Random; and in our refined era, just the same as at that more free-spoken epoch, this singular people has a certain contempt for any fine-strained purity, any special squeamishness, as they consider it, on the part of an ingenuous youth. They appear to look upon it as a suspicious phenomenon in the masculine character.

Nevertheless, I by no means take upon me to affirm that English morality, as regards the phase here alluded to, is really at a lower point that our own. Assuredly, I hope so, because, making a higher pretension, or, at all events, more carefully hiding whatever may be amiss, we are either better than they, or necessarily a great deal worse. It impressed me that their open avowal and recognition of immoralities served to throw the disease to the surface, where it might be more effectually dealt with, and leave a sacred interior not utterly profaned, instead of turning its poison back among the inner vitalities of the character, at the imminent risk of corrupting them all. Be that as it may, these Englishmen are certainly a franker and simpler people than ourselves, from peer to peasant; but if we can take it as compensatory on our part (which I leave to be considered) that they owe those noble and manly qualities to a coarser grain in their nature, and that, with a finer one in ours, we shall ultimately acquire a marble polish of which they are unsusceptible, I believe that this may be the truth.

Up the Thames

...THE aspect of London along the Thames, below Bridge, as it is called, is by no means so impressive as it ought to be, considering what peculiar advantages are offered for the display of grand and stately architecture by the passage of a river through the midst of a great city. It seems, indeed, as if the heart of London had been cleft open for the mere purpose of showing how rotten and drearily mean it had become. The shore is lined with the shabbiest, blackest, and ugliest buildings that can be imagined, decayed warehouses with blind windows, and wharves that look ruinous; insomuch that, had I known nothing more of the world's metropolis, I might have fancied that it had already experienced the downfall which I have heard commercial and financial prophets predict for it, within the century. And the muddy tide of the Thames, reflecting nothing, and hiding a million of unclean secrets within its breast, — a sort of guilty conscience, as it were, unwholesome with the rivulets of sin that constantly flow into it, — is just the dismal stream to glide by such a city. The surface, to be sure, displays no lack of activity, being fretted by the passage of a hundred steamers and covered with a good deal of shipping, but mostly of a clumsier build than I had been accustomed to see in the

Mersey: a fact which I complacently attributed to the smaller number of American clippers in the Thames, and the less prevalent influence of American example in refining away the broad-bottomed capacity of the old Dutch or English models.

About midway between Greenwich and London Bridge, at a rude landing-place on the left bank of the river, the steamer rings its bell and makes a momentary pause in front of a large circular structure, where it may be worth our while to scramble ashore. It indicates the locality of one of those prodigious practical blunders that would supply John Bull with a topic of inexhaustible ridicule, if his cousin Jonathan had committed them, but of which he himself perpetrates ten to our one in the mere wantonness of wealth that lacks better employment. The circular building covers the entrance to the Thames Tunnel, and is surmounted by a dome of glass, so as to throw daylight down into the great depth at which the passage of the river commences. Descending a wearisome succession of staircases, we at last find ourselves, still in the broad noon, standing before a closed door, on opening which we behold the vista of an arched corridor that extends into everlasting midnight. In these days, when glass has been applied to so many new purposes, it is a pity that the architect had not thought of arching portions of his abortive tunnel with immense blocks of the lucid substance, over which the dusky Thames would have flowed like a cloud, making the sub-fluvial avenue only a little gloomier than a street of upper London. At present, it is illuminated at regular intervals by jets of gas, not very brilliantly, yet with lustre enough to show the damp plaster of the ceiling and walls, and the massive stone pavement, the crevices of which are oozy with moisture, not from the incumbent river, but from hidden springs in the earth's deeper heart. There are two parallel corridors, with a wall between, for the separate accommodation of the double throng of foot-passengers, equestrians, and vehicles of all kinds, which was expected to roll and reverberate continually through the Tunnel. Only one of them has ever been opened, and its echoes are but feebly awakened by infrequent foot-falls.

Yet there seem to be people who spend their lives here, and who probably blink like owls, when, once or twice a year, perhaps, they happen to climb into the sunshine. All along the corridor, which I believe to be a mile in extent, we see stalls or shops in little alcoves, kept principally by women; they were of a ripe age, I was glad to observe, and certainly robbed England of none of its very moderate supply of feminine loveliness by their deeper than tomb-like interment. As you approach (and they are so accustomed to the dusky gaslight that they read all your characteristics afar of), they assail you with hungry entreaties to buy some of their merchandise, holding forth views of the Tunnel put up in cases of Derbyshire spar, with a magnifying-glass at one end to make the vista more effective. They offer you, besides, cheap jewelry, sunny topazes and resplendent emeralds for sixpence, and diamonds as big as the Koh-i-noor at a not much heavier cost, together with a multifarious trumpery which has died out of the upper world to reappear in this Tartarean bazaar. That you may fancy yourself still in the realms of the living, they urge you to partake of cakes, candy, ginger-beer, and such small refreshment, more suitable, however, for the shadowy appetite of ghosts than for the sturdy stomachs of Englishmen. The most capacious of the shops contains a dioramic exhibition of cities and scenes in the daylight world, with a dreary glimmer of gas among them all; so that they serve well enough to represent the dim, unsatisfactory remembrances that dead people might be supposed to retain from their past lives, mixing them up with the ghastliness of their unsubstantial state. I dwell the more upon these trifles, and do my best to give them a mockery of importance, because, if these are nothing, then all this elaborate contrivance and mighty piece of work has been wrought in vain.

The Englishman has burrowed under the bed of his great river, and set ships of two or three thousand tons a-rolling over his head, only to provide new sites for a few old women to sell cakes and ginger-beer!

Yet the conception was a grand one; and though it has proved an absolute failure, swallowing an immensity of toil and money, with annual returns hardly sufficient to keep the pavement free from the ooze of subterranean springs, yet it needs, I presume only an expenditure three or four (or, for aught I know, twenty) times as large, to make the enterprise brilliantly successful. The descent is so great from the bank of the river to its surface, and the Tunnel dips so profoundly under the river's bed, that the approaches on either side must commence a long way off, in order to render the entrance accessible to horsemen or vehicles; so that the larger part of the cost of the whole affair should have been expended on its margins. It has turned out a sublime piece of folly; and when the New Zealander of distant ages shall have moralized sufficiently among the ruins of London Bridge, he will bethink himself that somewhere thereabout was the marvellous Tunnel, the very existence of which will seem to him as incredible as that of the hanging gardens of Babylon. But the Thames will long ago have broken through the massive arch, and choked up the corridors with mud and sand and with the large stones of the structure itself, intermixed with skeletons of drowned people, the rusty ironwork of sunken vessels, and the great many such precious and curious things as a river always contrives to hide in its bosom; the entrance will have been obliterated, and its very site forgotten beyond the memory of twenty generations of men, and the whole neighborhood be held a dangerous spot on account of the malaria; insomuch that the traveller will make but a brief and careless inquisition for the traces of the old wonder, and will stake his credit before the public, in some Pacific Monthly of that day, that the story of it is but a myth, though enriched with a spiritual profundity which he will proceed to unfold.

Yet it is impossible (for a Yankee, at least) to see so much magnificent ingenuity thrown away, without trying to endow the unfortunate result with some kind of usefulness, though perhaps widely different from the purpose of its original conception. In former ages, the mile-long corridors, with their numerous alcoves, might have been utilized as a series of dungeons, the fittest of all possible receptacles for prisoners of state. Dethroned monarchs and fallen statesmen would not have needed to remonstrate against a domicile so spacious, so deeply secluded from the world's scorn, and so admirably in accordance with their thenceforward sunless fortunes. An alcove here might have suited Sir Walter Raleigh better than that darksome hiding-place communicating with the great chamber in the Tower, pacing from end to end of which he meditated upon his "History of the World." His track would here have been straight and narrow, indeed, and would therefore have lacked somewhat of the freedom that his intellect demanded; and yet the length to which his footsteps might have travelled forth and retraced themselves would partly have harmonized his physical movement with the grand curves and planetary returns of his thought, through cycles of majestic periods. Having it in his mind to compose the world's history, methinks he could have asked no better retirement than such a cloister as this, insulated from all the seductions of mankind and womankind, deep beneath their mysteries and motives, down into the heart of things, full of personal reminiscences in order to the comprehensive measurement and verification of historic records, seeing into the secrets of human nature, — secrets that daylight never yet revealed to mortal, — but detecting their whole scope and purport with the infallible eyes of unbroken solitude and night. And then the shades of the old mighty men might have risen from their still profounder abodes and joined him in the dim corridor, treading beside him with an antique stateliness of mien, telling him in melancholy tones, grand, but always melancholy, of the greater ideas and purposes which their most renowned performances so imperfectly carried out, that, magnificent successes in the view of all posterity, they were but failures to those who planned them. As Raleigh was a navigator, Noah would have explained to him the peculiarities of construction that made the ark so seaworthy; as Raleigh was a statesman, Moses would have discussed with him the principles of laws and government; as Raleigh was a soldier, Caesar and Hannibal would have held debate in his presence, with his martial student for their umpire; as Raleigh was a poet, David, or whatever most illustrious bard he might call up, would have touched his harp, and made manifest all the true significance of the past by means of song and the subtle intelligences of music.

Meanwhile, I had forgotten that Sir Walter Raleigh's century knew nothing of gaslight, and that it would require a prodigious and wasteful expenditure of tallow-candles to illuminate the Tunnel sufficiently to discern even a ghost. On this account, however, it would be all the more suitable place of confinement for a metaphysician, to keep him from bewildering mankind with his shadowy speculations; and, being shut off from external converse, the dark corridor would help him make rich discoveries in those cavernous regions and mysterious by-paths of the intellect, which he had so long accustomed himself to explore. But how would every successive age rejoice in so secure a habitation for its reformers, and especially for each best and wisest man that happened to be then alive! He seeks to burn up our whole system of society, under pretence of purifying it from its abuses! Away with him into the Tunnel, and let him begin by setting the Thames on fire, if he is able!

If not precisely these, yet akin to these were some of the fantasies that haunted me as I passed under the river: for the place is suggestive of such idle and irresponsible stuff by its own abortive character, its lack of whereabout on

upper earth, or any solid foundation of realities. Could I
have looked forward a few years, I might have regretted
that American enterprise had not provided a similar tunnel,
under the Hudson or the Potomac, for the convenience of
our National Government in times hardly yet gone by. It
would be delightful to clap up all the enemies of our peace
and Union in the dark together, and there let them abide,
listening to the monotonous roll of the river above their
heads, or perhaps in a state of miraculously suspended animation, until, — be it after months, years, or centuries, —
when the turmoil shall be all over, the Wrong washed away
in blood (since that must needs be the cleansing fluid), and
the Right firmly rooted in the soil which that blood will have
enriched, they might crawl forth again and catch a single
glimpse at their redeemed country, and feel it to be a better
land than they deserve, and die!

I was not sorry when the daylight reached me after a much
briefer abode in the nether regions than, I fear, would await
the troublesome personages just hinted at. . . .

The next notable group of objects is an assemblage of
ancient walls, battlements, and turrets, out of the midst of
which rises prominently one great square tower, of a grayish
hue, bordered with white stone, and having a small turret
at each corner of the roof. This central structure is the
White Tower, and the whole circuit of ramparts and enclosed edifices constitutes what is known in English history,
and still more widely and impressively in English poetry, as
the Tower. A crowd of river-craft are generally moored
in front of it; but if we look sharply at the right moment
under the base of the rampart, we may catch a glimpse of
an arched water-entrance, half submerged, past which the
Thames glides as indifferently as if it were the mouth of a
city-kennel. Nevertheless, it is the Traitor's Gate, a dreary
kind of triumphal passageway (now supposed to be shut up
and barred forever), through which a multitude of noble
and illustrious personages have entered the Tower and found

it a brief resting-place on their way to heaven. Passing it
many times, I never observed that anybody glanced at this
shadowy and ominous trap-door, save myself. It is well that
America exists, if it were only that her vagrant children may
be impressed and affected by the historical monuments of
England in a degree of which the native inhabitants are
evidently incapable. These matters are too familiar, too real,
and too hopelessly built in amongst and mixed up with the
common objects and affairs of life, to be easily susceptible
of imaginative coloring in their minds; and even their poets
and romancers feel it a toil, and almost a delusion, to extract
poetic material out of what seems embodied poetry itself to
an American. An Englishman cares nothing about the Tower,
which to us is a haunted castle in dreamland. That honest
and excellent gentleman, the late Mr. G. P. R. James (whose
mechanical ability, one might have supposed, would nour-
ish itself by devouring every old stone of such a structure),
once assured me that he had never in his life set eyes upon
the Tower, though for years an historic novelist in London.

Not to spend a whole summer's day upon the voyage, we
will suppose ourselves to have reached London Bridge, and
thence to have taken another steamer for a farther passage
up the river. But here the memorable objects succeed each
other so rapidly that I can spare but a single sentence even
for the great Dome, though I deem it more picturesque, in
that dusky atmosphere, than St. Peter's in its clear blue sky.
I must mention, however (since everything connected with
royalty is especially interesting to my dear countrymen), that
I once saw a large and beautiful barge, splendidly gilded
and ornamented, and overspread with a rich covering, lying
at the pier nearest to St. Paul's Cathedral; it had the royal
banner of Great Britain displayed, besides being decorated
with a number of other flags; and many footmen (who are
universally the grandest and gaudiest objects to be seen in
England at this day, and these were regal ones, in a bright
scarlet livery bedizened with gold-lace, and white silk stock-

ings) were in attendance. I know not what festive or ceremonial occasion may have drawn out this pageant; after
all, it might have been merely a city-spectacle, appertaining
to the Lord Mayor; but the sight had its value in bringing
vividly before me the grand old times when the sovereign
and nobles were accustomed to use the Thames as the high
street of the metropolis, and join in pompous processions
upon it; whereas, the desuetude of such customs, nowadays,
has caused the whole show of river-life to consist in a multitude of smoke-begrimed steamers. An analogous change
has taken place in the streets, where cabs and the omnibus
have crowded out a rich variety of vehicles; and thus life
gets more monotonous in hue from age to age, and appears
to seize every opportunity to strip off a bit of its gold-lace
among the wealthier classes, and to make itself decent in the
lower ones.

Yonder is Whitefriars, the old rowdy Alsatia, now wearing as decorous a face as any other portion of London; and,
adjoining it, the avenues and brick squares of the Temple,
with that historic garden, close upon the river-side, and
still rich in shrubbery and flowers, where the partisans of
York and Lancaster plucked the fatal roses, and scattered
their pale and bloody petals over so many English battle-fields.
Hard by, we see the long white front or rear of Somerset
House, and, farther on, rise the two new Houses of Parliament, with a huge unfinished tower already hiding its imperfect summit in the smoky canopy, — the whole vast and
cumbrous edifice a specimen of the best that modern architecture can effect, elaborately imitating the masterpieces of
those simple ages when men "builded better than they knew."
Close by it, we have a glimpse of the roof and upper towers of
the holy Abbey; while that gray, ancestral pile on the opposite side of the river is Lambeth Palace, a venerable group
of halls and turrets, chiefly built of brick, but with at least
one large tower of stone. In our course, we have passed beneath half a dozen bridges, and, emerging out of the black

heart of London, shall soon reach a cleanly suburb, where old Father Thames, if I remember, begins to put on an aspect of unpolluted innocence. And now we look back upon the mass of innumerable roofs, out of which rise steeples, towers, columns, and the great crowning Dome, — look back, in short, upon that mystery of the world's proudest city, amid which a man so longs and loves to be; not, perhaps, because it contains much that is positively admirable and enjoyable, but because, at all events, the world has nothing better. The cream of external life is there; and whatever merely intellectual or material good we fail to find perfect in London, we may as well content ourselves to seek that unattainable thing no farther on this earth.

The steamer terminates its trip at Chelsea, an old town endowed with a prodigious number of pothouses, and some famous gardens, called the Cremorne, for public amusement. The most noticeable thing, however, is Chelsea Hospital, which, like that of Greenwich, was founded, I believe, by Charles II. (whose bronze statue, in the guise of an old Roman, stands in the centre of the quadrangle), and appropriated as a home for aged and infirm soldiers of the British army. The edifices are of three stories, with windows in the high roofs, and are built of dark, sombre brick, with stone edgings and facings. The effect is by no means that of grandeur (which is somewhat disagreeably an attribute of Greenwich Hospital), but a quiet and venerable neatness. . . .

The chapel consists of a great hall with a vaulted roof, and over the altar is a large painting in fresco, the subject of which I did not trouble myself to make out. More appropriate adornments of the place, dedicated as well to martial reminiscences as religious worship, are the long ranges of dusty and tattered banners, that hang from their staves all round the ceiling of the chapel. They are trophies of battles fought and won in every quarter of the world, comprising the captured flags of all the nations with whom the British lion has waged war since James II.'s time, — French,

Dutch, East Indian, Prussian, Russian, Chinese, and American, — collected together in this consecrated spot, not to
symbolize that there shall be no more discord upon earth,
but drooping over the aisle in sullen, though peaceable
humiliation. Yes, I said "American" among the rest; for
the good old pensioner mistook me for an Englishman, and
failed not to point out (and, methought, with an especial
emphasis of triumph) some flags that had been taken at
Bladensburg and Washington. I fancied, indeed, that they
hung a little higher and drooped a little lower than any of
their companions in disgrace. It is a comfort, however, that
their proud devices are already indistinguishable, or nearly
so, owing to dust and tatters and the kind offices of the moths,
and that they will soon rot from the banner-staves and be
swept out in unrecognized fragments from the chapel-door.

It is a good method of teaching a man how imperfectly
cosmopolitan he is, to show him his country's flag occupying
a position of dishonor in a foreign land. But, in truth, the
whole system of a people crowing over its military triumphs
had far better be dispensed with, both on account of the
ill-blood that it helps to keep fermenting among the nations,
and because it operates as an accumulative inducement to
future generations to aim at a kind of glory, the gain of
which has generally proved more ruinous than its loss. I
heartily wish that every trophy of victory might crumble
away, and that every reminiscence or tradition of a hero,
from the beginning of the world to this day, could pass out
of all men's memories at once and forever. I might feel
very differently, to be sure, if we Northerners had anything
especially valuable to lose by the fading of those illuminated
names. . . .

Crossing Battersea Bridge, in the neighborhood of Chelsea,
I remember seeing a distant gleam of the Crystal Palace,
glimmering afar in the afternoon sunshine like an imaginary
structure, — an air-castle by chance descended upon earth,
and resting there one instant before it vanished, as we some-

times see a soap-bubble touch unharmed on the carpet, — a thing of only momentary visibility and no substance, destined to be overburdened and crushed down by the first cloud-shadow that might fall upon that spot. Even as I looked, it disappeared. Shall I attempt a picture of this exhalation of modern ingenuity, or what else shall I try to paint? Everything in London and its vicinity has been depicted innumerable times, but never once translated into intelligible images; it is an "old, old story," never yet told, nor to be told. . . .

On a Sunday afternoon, I passed through a side-entrance in the time-blackened wall of a place of worship, and found myself among a congregation assembled in one of the transepts and the immediately contiguous portion of the nave. It was a vast old edifice, spacious enough, within the extent covered by its pillared roof and overspread by its stone pavement, to accommodate the whole church-going London, and with a far wider and loftier concave than any human power of lungs could fill with audible prayer. Oaken benches were arranged in the transept, on one of which I seated myself, and joined, as well as I knew how, in the sacred business that was going forward. But when it came to the sermon, the voice of the preacher was puny, and so were his thoughts, and both seemed impertinent at such a time and place, where he and all of us were bodily included within a sublime act of religion, which could be seen above and around us and felt beneath our feet. The structure itself was the worship of the devout men of long ago, miraculously preserved in stone without losing an atom of its fragrance and fervor; it was a kind of anthem-strain that they had sung and poured out of the organ in centuries gone by; and being so grand and sweet, the Divine benevolence had willed it to be prolonged for the behoof of auditors unborn. I therefore came to the conclusion, that, in my individual case, it would be better and more reverent to let my eyes wander about the edifice than to fasten them and my thoughts on the evidently uninspired mortal who was venturing — and felt it no venture at all — to speak here above his breath.

The interior of Westminster Abbey (for the reader recognized it, no doubt, the moment we entered) is built of rich brown stone; and the whole of it — the lofty roof, the tall, clustered pillars, and the pointed arches — appears to be in consummate repair. At all points where decay has laid its finger, the structure is clamped with iron or otherwise carefully protected; and being thus watched over, — whether as a place of ancient sanctity, a noble specimen of Gothic art, or an object of national interest and pride, — it may reasonably be expected to survive for as many ages as have passed over it already. It was sweet to feel its venerable quietude, its long-enduring peace, and yet to observe how kindly and even cheerfully it received the sunshine of to-day, which fell from the great windows into the fretted aisles and arches that laid aside somewhat of their aged gloom to welcome it. Sunshine always seems friendly to old abbeys, churches, and castles, kissing them, as it were, with a more affectionate, though still reverential familiarity, than it accords to edifices of later date. A square of golden light lay on the sombre pavement of the nave, afar off, falling through the grand western entrance, the folding leaves of which were wide open, and afforded glimpses of people passing to and fro in the outer world, while we sat dimly enveloped in the solemnity of antique devotion. In the south transept, separated from us by the full breadth of the minister, there were painted glass windows, of which the uppermost appeared to be a great orb of many-colored radiance, being, indeed, a cluster of saints and angels whose glorified bodies formed the rays of an aureole emanating from a cross in the midst. These windows are modern, but combine softness with wonderful brilliancy of effect. Through the pillars and arches, I saw that the walls in that distant region of the edifice were almost wholly incrusted with marble, now grown yellow with time, no blank, unlettered slabs, but memorials of such

men as their respective generations deemed wisest and bravest.
Some of them were commemorated merely by inscriptions on
mural tablets, others by sculptured bas-reliefs, others (once
famous, but now forgotten, generals or admirals, these) by
ponderous tombs that aspired towards the roof of the aisle,
or partly curtained the immense arch of a window. These
mountains of marble were peopled with the sisterhood of
Allegory, winged trumpeters, and classic figures in full-bot-
tomed wigs; but it was strange to observe how the old Abbey
melted all such absurdities into the breadth of its own
grandeur, even magnifying itself by what would elsewhere
have been ridiculous. Methinks it is the test of Gothic
sublimity to overpower the ridiculous without deigning to
hide it; and these grotesque monuments of the last century
answer a similar purpose with the grinning faces which the
old architects scattered among their most solemn conceptions.

From these distant wanderings (it was my first visit to Westminster Abbey, and I would gladly have taken it all in at a
glance) my eyes came back and began to investigate what
was immediately about me in the transept. Close at my
elbow was the pedestal of Canning's statue. Next beyond
it was a massive tomb, on the spacious tablet of which re-
posed the full-length figures of a marble lord and lady, whom
an inscription announced to be the Duke and Duchess of
Newcastle, — the historic Duke of Charles I.'s time, and the
fantastic Duchess, traditionally remembered by her poems
and plays. She was of a family, as the record on her tomb
proudly informed us, of which all the brothers had been
valiant and all the sisters virtuous. A recent statue of Sir
John Malcolm, the new marble as white as snow, held the
next place; and near by was a mural monument and bust of
Sir Peter Warren. The round visage of this old British
admiral has a certain interest for a New-Englander, because
it was by no merit of his own (though he took care to assume it as such), but by the valor and warlike enterprise of
our colonial forefathers, especially the stout men of Massa-

chusetts, that he won rank and renown, and a tomb in Westminster Abbey.   Lord Mansfield, a huge mass of marble done
into the guise of a judicial gown and wig, with a stern face
in the midst of the latter, sat on the other side of the transept;
and on the pedestal beside him was a figure of Justice, holding forth, instead of the customary grocer's scales, an actual
pair of brass steelyards.   It is an ancient and classic instrument, undoubtedly; but I had supposed that Portia (when
Shylock's pound of flesh was to be weighed) was the only
judge that ever really called for it in a court of justice.   Pitt
and Fox were in the same distinguished company; and John
Kemble, in Roman costume, stood not far off, but strangely
shorn of the dignity that is said to have enveloped him like
a mantle in his lifetime.   Perhaps the evanescent majesty
of the stage is incompatible with the long endurance of marble
and the solemn reality of the tomb; though, on the other
hand, almost every illustrious personage here represented
has been invested with more or less of stage-trickery by his
sculptor.   In truth, the artist (unless there be a divine efficacy
in his touch, making evident a heretofore hidden dignity in
the actual form) feels it an imperious law to remove his
subject as far from the aspect of ordinary life as may be
possible without sacrificing every trace of resemblance.   The
absurd effect of the contrary course is very remarkable in
the statue of Mr. Wilberforce, whose actual self, save for
the lack of color, I seemed to behold, seated just across the
aisle.

This excellent man appears to have sunk into himself
in a sitting posture, with a thin leg crossed over his knee,
a book in one hand, and a finger of the other under his
chin, I believe, or applied to the side of his nose, or to some
equally familiar purpose; while his exceedingly homely and
wrinkled face, held a little on one side, twinkles at you with
the shrewdest complacency, as if he were looking right into
your eyes, and twigged something there which you had half
a mind to conceal from him.   He keeps this look so pertina-

ciously that you feel it to be insufferably impertinent, and
bethink yourself what common ground there may be between
yourself and a stone image, enabling you to resent it. I
have no doubt that the statue is as like Mr. Wilberforce as
one pea to another, and you might fancy, that, at some ordinary moment, when he least expected it, and before he had
time to smooth away his knowing complication of wrinkles,
he had seen the Gorgon's head, and whitened into marble, —
not only his personal self, but his coat and small-clothes,
down to a button and the minutest crease of the cloth. The
ludicrous result marks the impropriety of bestowing the
age-long duration of marble upon small, characteristic in-
dividualities, such as might come within the province of
waxen imagery. The sculptor should give permanence to
the figure of a great man in his mood of broad and grand
composure, which would obliterate all mean peculiarities; for,
if the original were unaccustomed to such a mood, or if
his features were incapable of assuming the guise, it seems
questionable whether he could really have been entitled to a
marble immortality. In point of fact, however, the English
face and form are seldom statuesque, however illustrious the
individual.

It ill becomes me, perhaps, to have lapsed into this mood
of half-jocose criticism in describing my first visit to Westminster Abbey, a spot which I had dreamed about more
reverentially, from my childhood upward, than any other in
the world, and which I then beheld, and now look back upon,
with profound gratitude to the men who built it, and a kindly
interest, I may add, in the humblest personage that has contributed his little all to its impressiveness, by depositing his
dust or his memory there. But it is a characteristic of this
grand edifice that it permits you to smile as freely under
the roof of its central nave as if you stood beneath the yet
grander canopy of heaven. Break into laughter, if you feel
inclined, provided the vergers do not hear it echoing among
the arches. In an ordinary church you would keep your coun-

tenance for fear of disturbing the sanctities or proprieties of the place; but you need leave no honest and decorous portion of your human nature outside of these benign and truly hospitable walls. Their mild awfulness will take care of itself. Thus it does no harm to the general impression, when you come to be sensible that many of the monuments are ridiculous, and commemorate a mob of people who are mostly forgotten in their graves, and few of whom ever deserved any better boon from posterity. You acknowledge the force of Sir Godfrey Kneller's objection to being buried in Westminster Abbey, because "they do bury fools there!" Nevertheless, these grotesque carvings of marble, that break out in dingy-white blotches on the old freestone of the interior walls, have come there by as natural a process as might cause mosses and ivy to cluster about the external edifice; for they are the historical and biographical record of each successive age, written with its own hand, and all the truer for the inevitable mistakes, and none the less solemn for the occasional absurdity. Though you entered the Abbey expecting to see the tombs only of the illustrious, you are content at last to read many names, both in literature and history, that have now lost the reverence of mankind, if indeed they ever really possessed it. Let these men rest in peace. Even if you miss a name or two that you hoped to find there, they may well be spared. It matters little a few more or less, or whether Westminster Abbey contains or lacks any one man's grave, so long as the Centuries, each with the crowd of personages that it deemed memorable, have chosen it as their place of honored sepulture, and laid themselves down under its pavement. The inscriptions and devices on the walls are rich with evidences of the fluctuating tastes, fashions, manners, opinions, prejudices, follies, wisdoms of the past, and thus they combine into a more truthful memorial of their dead times than any individual epitaph-maker ever meant to write.

When the services were over, many of the audience seemed

inclined to linger in the nave or wander away among the
mysterious aisles; for there is nothing in this world so fas-
cinating as a Gothic minster, which always invites you deeper
and deeper into its heart both by vast revelations and shadowy
concealments. Through the open-work screen that divides
the nave from the chancel and choir, we could discern the
gleam of a marvellous window, but were debarred from entrance into that more sacred precinct of the Abbey by the
vergers. The vigilant officials (doing their duty all the more
strenuously because no fees could be exacted from Sunday
visitors) flourished their staves, and drove us towards the grand
entrance like a flock of sheep. Lingering through one of
the aisles, I happened to look down, and found my foot upon
a stone inscribed with this familiar exclamation, *"O rare Ben
Jonson!"* and remembered the story of stout old Ben's burial
in that spot, standing upright, — not, I presume, on account
of any unseemly reluctance on his part to lie down in the
dust, like other men, but because standing-room was all that
could reasonably be demanded for a poet among the slum-
berous notabilities of his age. It made me weary to think of
it! — such a prodigious length of time to keep one's feet!
— apart from the honor of the thing, it would certainly have
been better for Ben to stretch himself at ease in some country
churchyard. To this day, however, I fancy that there is a
contemptuous alloy mixed up with the admiration which
the higher classes of English society profess for their literary
men.

Another day — in truth, many other days — I sought out
Poet's Corner, and found a sign-board and pointed finger
directing the visitor to it, on the corner house of a little
lane leading towards the rear of the Abbey. The entrance
is at the southeastern end of the south transept, and it is used,
on ordinary occasions, as the only free mode of access to the
building. It is no spacious arch, but a small, lowly door,
passing through which, and pushing aside an inner screen
that partly keeps out an exceedingly chill wind, you find

yourself in a dim nook of the Abbey, with the busts of poets
gazing at you from the otherwise bare stone-work of the
walls. Great poets, too; for Ben Jonson is right behind the
door, and Spenser's tablet is next, and Butler's on the same
side of the transept, and Milton's (whose bust you know at
once by its resemblance to one of his portraits, though older,
more wrinkled, and sadder than that) is close by, and a profile-
medallion of Gray beneath it. A window high aloft sheds
down a dusky daylight on these and many other sculptured
marbles, now as yellow as old parchment, that cover the
three walls of the nook up to an elevation of about twenty
feet above the pavement. It seemed to me that I had always
been familiar with the spot. Enjoying a humble intimacy —
and how much of my life had else been a dreary solitude! —
with many of its inhabitants, I could not feel myself a stranger
there. It was delightful to be among them. There was a
genial awe, mingled with a sense of kind and friendly presences about me; and I was glad, moreover, at finding so
many of them there together, in fit companionship, mutually
recognized and duly honored, all reconciled now, whatever
distant generations, whatever personal hostility or other miserable impediment, had divided them far asunder while they
lived. I have never felt a similar interest in any other tombstones, nor have I ever been deeply moved by the imaginary
presence of other famous dead people. A poet's ghost is the
only one that survives for his fellow-mortals, after his bones
are in the dust, — and he not ghostly, but cherishing many
hearts with his own warmth in the chillest atmosphere of life.
What other fame is worth aspiring for? Or, let me speak it
more boldly, what other long-enduring fame can exist? We
neither remember nor care anything for the past, except as
the poet has made it intelligibly noble and sublime to our
comprehension. The shades of the mighty have no substance; they flit ineffectually about the darkened stage where
they performed their momentary parts, save when the poet
has thrown his own creative soul into them, and imparted

a more vivid life than ever they were able to manifest to mankind while they dwelt in the body. And therefore — though he cunningly disguises himself in their armor, their robes of state, or kingly purple — it is not the statesman, the warrior, or the monarch that survives, but the despised poet, whom they may have fed with their crumbs, and to whom they owe all that they now are or have, — a name!

In the foregoing paragraph I seem to have been betrayed into a flight above or beyond the customary level that best agrees with me; but it represents fairly enough the emotions with which I passed from Poets' Corner into the chapels, which contain the sepulchres of kings and great people. They are magnificent even now, and must have been inconceivably so when the marble slabs and pillars wore their new polish, and the statues retained the brilliant colors with which they were originally painted, and the shrines their rich gilding, of which the sunlight still shows a glimmer or a streak, though the sunbeam itself looks tarnished with antique dust. Yet this recondite portion of the Abbey presents few memorials of personages whom we care to remember. The shrine of Edward the Confessor has a certain interest, because it was so long held in religious reverence, and because the very dust that settled upon it was formerly worth gold. The helmet and war-saddle of Henry V., worn at Agincourt, and now suspended above his tomb, are memorable objects, but more for Shakespeare's sake than the victor's own. Rank has been the general passport to admission here. Noble and regal dust is as cheap as dirt under the pavement. I am glad to recollect, indeed (and it is too characteristic of the right English spirit not to be mentioned), one or two gigantic statues of great mechanicians, who contributed largely to the material welfare of England, sitting familiarly in their marble chairs among forgotten kings and queens. Otherwise, the quaintness of the earlier monuments, and the antique beauty of some of them, are what chiefly gives them value. Nevertheless, Addison is buried among the men of rank; not on the plea of his literary fame, however, but because he was connected with nobility by marriage, and had been a Secretary of State. His gravestone is inscribed with a resounding verse from Tickell's lines to his memory, the only lines by which Tickell himself is now remembered, and which (as I discovered a little while ago) he mainly filched from an obscure versifier of somewhat earlier date.

Returning to Poets' Corner, I looked again at the walls, and wondered how the requisite hospitality can be shown to poets of our own and the succeeding ages. There is hardly a foot of space left, although room has lately been found for a bust of Southey and a full-length statue of Campbell. At best, only a little portion of the Abbey is dedicated to poets, literary men, musical composers, and others of the gentle artist breed, and even into that small nook of sanctity men of other pursuits have thought it decent to intrude themselves. Methinks the tuneful throng, being at home here, should recollect how they were treated in their lifetime, and turn the cold shoulder, looking askance at nobles and official personages, however worthy of honorable interment elsewhere. Yet it shows aptly and truly enough what portion of the world's regard and honor has heretofore been awarded to literary eminence in comparison with other modes of greatness, — this dimly lighted corner (nor even that quietly to themselves) in the vast minster, the walls of which are sheathed and hidden under marble that has been wasted upon the illustrious obscure. Nevertheless, it may not be worth while to quarrel with the world on this account; for, to confess the very truth, their own little nook contains more than one poet whose memory is kept alive by his monument, instead of imbuing the senseless stone with a spiritual immortality, — men of whom you do not ask, "Where is he?" but, "Why is he here?" I estimate that all the literary people who really make an essential part of one's inner life, including the period since English literature first existed, might have ample elbow-room to sit down and quaff their draughts

of Castaly round Chaucer's broad, horizontal tombstone.
These divinest poets consecrate the spot, and throw a re-
flected glory over the humblest of their companions.   And
as for the latter, it is to be hoped that they may have long
outgrown the characteristic jealousies and morbid sensibilities of their craft, and have found out the little value (probably not amounting to sixpence in immortal currency) of
the posthumous renown which they once aspired to win.
It would be a poor compliment to a dead poet to fancy him
leaning out of the sky and snuffing up the impure breath
of earthly praise.

Yet we cannot easily rid ourselves of the notion that those
who have bequeathed us the inheritance of an undying song
would fain be conscious of its endless reverberations in the
hearts of mankind, and would delight, among sublimer enjoyments, to see their names emblazoned in such a treasure-
place of great memories as Westminster Abbey.   There are
some men, at all events, — true and tender poets, moreover,
and fully deserving of the honor, — whose spirits, I feel
certain, would linger a little while about Poets' Corner, for
the sake of witnessing their own apotheosis among their
kindred.   They have had a strong natural yearning, not so
much for applause as sympathy, which the cold fortune of
their lifetime did but scantily supply; so that this unsatisfied
appetite may make itself felt upon sensibilities at once so
delicate and retentive, even a step or two beyond the grave.
Leigh Hunt, for example, would be pleased, even now, if he
could learn that his bust had been reposited in the midst of
the old poets whom he admired and loved; though there is
hardly a man among the authors of to-day and yesterday whom
the judgment of Englishmen would be less likely to place
there.   He deserves it, however, if not for his verse (the value
of which I do not estimate, never having been able to read
it), yet for his delightful prose, his unmeasured poetry, the
inscrutable happiness of his touch, working soft miracles by
a life-process like the growth of grass and flowers.   As with

all such gentle writers, his page sometimes betrayed a vestige
of affectation, but, the next moment, a rich, natural luxuriance
overgrew and buried it out of sight. I knew him a little,
and (since, Heaven be praised, few English celebrities whom I
chanced to meet have enfranchised my pen by their decease,
and as I assume no liberties with living men) I will conclude this rambling article by sketching my first interview
with Leigh Hunt....

I have met no Englishman whose manners seemed to me
so agreeable, soft, rather than polished, wholly unconven-
tional, the natural growth of a kindly and sensitive disposition without any reference to rule, or else obedient to some
rule so subtle that the nicest observer could not detect the
application of it....

There was not an English trait in him from head to foot,
morally, intellectually, or physically. Beef, ale, or stout,
brandy or port-wine, entered not at all into his composition.
In his earlier life, he appears to have given evidences of
courage and sturdy principle, and of a tendency to fling himself into the rough struggle of humanity on the liberal side.
It would be taking too much upon myself to affirm that this
was merely a projection of his fancy world into the actual,
and that he never could have hit a downright blow, and was
altogether an unsuitable person to receive one. I beheld him
not in his armor, but in his peacefulest robes. Nevertheless,
drawing my conclusion merely from what I saw, it would
have occurred to me that his main deficiency was a lack of
grit. Though anything but a timid man, the combative and
defensive elements were not prominently developed in his
character, and could have been made available only when
he put an unnatural force upon his instincts. It was on
this account, and also because of the fineness of his nature
generally, that the English appreciated him no better, and
left this sweet and delicate poet poor, and with scanty
laurels, in his declining age.

It was not, I think, from his American blood that Leigh

Hunt derived either his amiability or his peaceful inclinations; at least, I do not see how we can reasonably claim the former quality as a national characteristic, though the latter might have been fairly inherited from his ancestors on the mother's side, who were Pennsylvania Quakers. But the kind of excellence that distinguished him — his fineness, subtilty, and grace — was that which the richest cultivation has heretofore tended to develop in the happier examples of American genius, and which (though I say it a little reluctantly) is perhaps what our future intellectual advancement may make general among us. His person, at all events, was thoroughly American, and of the best type, as were likewise his manners; for we are the best as well as the worst mannered people in the world. . . .

Outside Glimpses of English Poverty

BECOMING an inhabitant of a great English town, I often turned aside from the prosperous thoroughfares (where the edifices, the shops, and the bustling crowd differed not so much from scenes with which I was familiar in my own country), and went designedly astray among precincts that reminded me of some of Dickens's grimiest pages. There I caught glimpses of a people and a mode of life that were comparatively new to my observation, a sort of sombre phantasmagoric spectacle, exceedingly undelightful to behold, yet involving a singular interest and even fascination in its ugliness.

Dirt, one would fancy, is plenty enough all over the world, being the symbolic accompaniment of the foul incrustation which began to settle over and bedim all earthly things as soon as Eve had bitten the apple; ever since which hapless epoch, her daughters have chiefly been engaged in a desperate and unavailing struggle to get rid of it. But the dirt of a poverty-stricken English street is a monstrosity unknown on our side of the Atlantic. It reigns supreme within its own limits, and is inconceivable everywhere beyond them. We enjoy the great advantage, that the brightness and dryness of our atmosphere keep everything clean that the sun shines upon, converting the larger portion of our impurities into transitory dust which the next wind can sweep away, in contrast with the damp, adhesive grime that incorporates itself with all surfaces (unless continually and painfully cleansed) in the chill moisture of the English air. Then the all-pervading smoke of the city, abundantly intermingled with the sable snow-flakes of bituminous coal, hovering overhead, descending, and alighting on pavements and rich architectural fronts, on the snowy muslin of the ladies, and the gentlemen's starched collars and shirt-bosoms, invests even the better streets in a half-mourning garb. It is beyond the resources of Wealth to keep the smut away from its premises or its own fingers' ends; and as for Poverty, it surrenders itself to the dark influence without a struggle. Along with disastrous circumstances, pinching need, adversity so lengthened out as to constitute the rule of life, there comes a certain chill depression of the spirits which seems especially to shudder at cold water. In view of so wretched a state of things, we accept the ancient Deluge not merely as an insulated phenomenon, but as a periodical necessity, and acknowledge that nothing less than such a general washing-day could suffice to cleanse the slovenly old world of its moral and material dirt.

Gin-shops, or what the English call spirit-vaults, are numerous in the vicinity of these poor streets, and are set off with the magnificence of gilded door-posts, tarnished by contact with the unclean customers who haunt there. Ragged children come thither with old shaving-mugs, or broken-nosed teapots, or any such makeshift receptacle, to get a little poison or madness for their parents, who deserve no better requital at their hands for having engendered them. Inconceivably sluttish women enter at noonday and stand at the counter among boon-companions of both sexes, stirring up misery and jollity in a bumper together, and quaffing off the mixture with a relish. As for the men, they lounge there continually, drinking till they are drunken, — drinking as long as they have a halfpenny left, and then, as it seemed to me, waiting for a sixpenny miracle to be wrought in their pockets so as to enable them to be drunken again. Most of these establishments have a

significant advertisement of "Beds," doubtless for the accommodation of their customers in the interval between one in-
toxication and the next.   I never could find it in my heart,
however, utterly to condemn these sad revellers, and should
certainly wait till I had some better consolation to offer before
depriving them of their dram of gin, though death itself were
in the glass; for methought their poor souls needed such fiery
stimulant to lift them a little way out of the smothering squalor
of both their outward and interior life, giving them glimpses
and suggestions, even if bewildering ones, of a spiritual existence that limited their present misery.   The temperance-
reformers unquestionably derive their commission from the
Divine Beneficence, but have never been taken fully into its
counsels.   All may not be lost, though those good men fail.

Pawnbrokers' establishments, distinguished by the mystic
symbol of the three golden balls, were conveniently accessible;
though what personal property these wretched people could
possess, capable of being estimated in silver or copper, so as
to afford a basis for a loan, was a problem that still perplexes
me.   Old clothesmen, likewise, dwelt hard by, and hung out
ancient garments to dangle in the wind.   There were butchers'
shops, too, of a class adapted to the neighborhood, presenting
no such generously fattened carcasses as Englishmen love to
gaze at in the market, no stupendous halves of mighty beeves,
no dead hogs, or muttons ornamented with carved bas-reliefs
of fat on their ribs and shoulders, in a peculiarly British style
of art, — not these, but bits and gobbets of lean meat, selvages
snipt off from steaks, tough and stringy morsels, bare bones
smitten away from joints by the cleaver; tripe, liver, bullocks'
feet, or whatever else was cheapest and divisible into the smallest lots.   I am afraid that even such delicacies came to many
of their tables hardly oftener than Christmas.   In the windows
of other little shops you saw half a dozen wizened herrings;
some eggs in a basket, looking so dingily antique that your
imagination smelt them; fly-speckled biscuits, segments of a
hungry cheese, pipes and papers of tobacco.   Now and then

a sturdy milk-woman passed by with a wooden yoke over her shoulders, supporting a pail on either side, filled with a whitish fluid, the composition of which was water and chalk and the milk of a sickly cow, who gave the best she had, poor thing! but could scarcely make it rich or wholesome, spending her life in some close city-nook and pasturing on strange food. I have seen, once or twice, a donkey coming into one of these streets with panniers full of vegetables, and departing with a return cargo of what looked like rubbish and street-sweepings. No other commerce seemed to exist, except, possibly, a girl might offer you a pair of stockings or a worked collar, or a man whisper something mysterious about wonderfully cheap cigars. And yet I remember seeing female hucksters in those regions, with their wares on the edge of the sidewalk and their own seats right in the carriage-way, pretending to sell half-decayed oranges and apples, toffy, Ormskirk cakes, combs, and cheap jewelry, the coarsest kind of crockery, and little plates of oysters, — knitting patiently all day long, and removing their undiminished stock in trade at nightfall. All indispensable importations from other quarters of the town were on a remarkably diminutive scale: for example, the wealthier inhabitants purchased their coal by the wheelbarrow-load, and the poorer ones by the peck-measure. It was a curious and melancholy spectacle, when an overladen coal-cart happened to pass through the street and drop a handful or two of its burden in the mud, to see half a dozen women and children scrambling for the treasure-trove, like a flock of hens and chickens gobbling up some spilt corn. In this connection I may as well mention a commodity of boiled snails (for such they appeared to me, though probably a marine production) which used to be peddled from door to door, piping hot, as an article of cheap nutriment.

The population of these dismal abodes appeared to consider the sidewalks and middle of the street as their common hall. In a drama of low life, the unity of place might be arranged rigidly according to the classic rule, and the street be the one locality in which every scene and incident should occur. Courtship, quarrels, plot and counterplot, conspiracies for robbery and murder, family difficulties or agreements, — all such matters, I doubt not, are constantly discussed or transacted in this sky-roofed saloon, so regally hung with its sombre canopy of coal-smoke.   Whatever the disadvantages of the English climate, the only comfortable or wholesome part of life, for the city poor, must be spent in the open air.   The stifled and squalid rooms where they lie down at night, whole families and neighborhoods together, or sulkily elbow one another in the daytime, when a settled rain drives them within doors, are worse horrors than it is worth while (without a practical object in view) to admit into one's imagination.   No wonder that they creep forth from the foul mystery of their interiors, stumble down from their garrets, or scramble up out of their cellars, on the upper step of which you may see the grimy housewife, before the shower is ended, letting the raindrops gutter down her visage; while her children (an impish progeny of cavernous recesses below the common sphere of humanity) swarm into the daylight and attain all that they know of personal purification in the nearest mud-puddle.   It might almost make a man doubt the existence of his own soul to observe how Nature has flung these little wretches into the street and left them there, so evidently regarding them as nothing worth, and how all mankind acquiesce in the great mother's estimate of her offspring.   For, if they are to have no immortality, what superior claim can I assert for mine?   And how difficult to believe that anything so precious as a germ of immortal growth can have been buried under this dirt-heap, plunged into this cesspool of misery and vice!   As often as I beheld the scene, it affected me with surprise and loathsome interest, much resembling, though in a far intenser degree, the feeling with which, when a boy, I used to turn over a plank or an old log that had long lain on the damp ground, and found a vivacious multitude of unclean and devilish-looking insects scampering to and fro beneath it.   Without an infinite faith, there seemed

as much prospect of a blessed futurity for those hideous bugs
and many-footed worms as for these brethren of our humanity
and co-heirs of all our heavenly inheritance. Ah, what a
mystery! Slowly, slowly, as after groping at the bottom of a
deep, noisome, stagnant pool, my hope struggles upward to
the surface, bearing the half-drowned body of a child along
with it, and heaving it aloft for its life, and my own life, and
all our lives. Unless these slime-clogged nostrils can be made
capable of inhaling celestial air, I know not how the purest
and most intellectual of us can reasonably expect ever to taste
a breath of it. The whole question of eternity is staked there.
If a single one of those helpless little ones be lost, the world
is lost!

The women and children greatly preponderate in such
places; the men probably wandering abroad in quest of that
daily miracle, a dinner and a drink, or perhaps slumbering in
the daylight that they may the better follow out their cat-like
rambles through the dark. Here are women with young figures, but old, wrinkled, yellow faces, tanned and blear-eyed
with the smoke which they cannot spare from their scanty fires,
— it being too precious for its warmth to be swallowed by the
chimney. Some of them sit on the doorsteps, nursing their
unwashed babies at bosoms which we will glance aside from,
for the sake of our mothers and all womanhood, because the
fairest spectacle is here the foulest. Yet motherhood, in these
dark abodes, is strangely identical with what we have all known
it to be in the happiest homes. Nothing, as I remember, smote
me with more grief and pity (all the more poignant because
perplexingly entangled with an inclination to smile) than to
hear a gaunt and ragged mother priding herself on the pretty
ways of her ragged and skinny infant, just as a young matron
might, when she invites her lady friends to admire her plump,
white-robed darling in the nursery. Indeed, no womanly characteristic seemed to have altogether perished out of these poor
souls. It was the very same creature whose tender torments
make the rapture of our young days, whom we love, cherish,

and protect, and rely upon in life and death, and whom we delight to see beautify her beauty with rich robes and set it off with jewels, though now fantastically masquerading in a garb of tatters, wholly unfit for her to handle. I recognized her, over and over again, in the groups round a doorstep or in the descent of a cellar, chatting with prodigious earnestness about intangible trifles, laughing for a little jest, sympathizing at almost the same instant with one neighbor's sunshine and another's shadow; wise, simple, sly, and patient, yet easily perturbed, and breaking into small feminine ebullitions of spite, wrath, and jealousy, tornadoes of a moment, such as vary the social atmosphere of her silken-skirted sisters, though smothered into propriety by dint of a well-bred habit. Not that there was an absolute deficiency of good-breeding, even here. It often surprised me to witness a courtesy and deference among these ragged folks, which, having seen it, I did not thoroughly believe in, wondering whence it should have come. I am persuaded, however, that there were laws of intercourse which they never violated, — a code of the cellar, the garret, the common staircase, the doorstep, and the pavement, which perhaps had as deep a foundation in natural fitness as the code of the drawing-room.

Yet again I doubt whether I may not have been uttering folly in the last two sentences, when I reflect how rude and rough these specimens of feminine character generally were. They had a readiness with their hands that reminded me of Molly Seagrim and other heroines in Fielding's novels. For example, I have seen a woman meet a man in the street, and, for no reason perceptible to me, suddenly clutch him by the hair and cuff his ears, — an infliction which he bore with exemplary patience, only snatching the very earliest opportunity to take to his heels. Where a sharp tongue will not serve the purpose, they trust to the sharpness of their finger-nails, or incarnate a whole vocabulary of vituperative words in a resounding slap, or the downright blow of a doubled fist. All English people, I imagine, are influenced in a far greater degree than ourselves by this simple and honest tendency, in cases of disagreement, to batter one another's persons; and whoever has seen a crowd of English ladies (for instance, at the door of the Sistine Chapel, in Holy Week) will be satisfied that their belligerent propensities are kept in abeyance only by a merciless rigor on the part of society. It requires a vast deal of refinement to spiritualize their large physical endowments. Such being the case with the delicate ornaments of the drawing-room, it is less to be wondered at that women who live mostly in the open air, amid the coarsest kind of companionship and occupation, should carry on the intercourse of life with a freedom unknown to any class of American females, though still, I am resolved to think, compatible with a generous breadth of natural propriety. It shocked me, at first, to see them (of all ages, even elderly, as well as infants that could just toddle across the street alone) going about in the mud and mire, or through the dusky snow and slosh of a severe week in winter, with petticoats high uplifted above bare, red feet and legs; but I was comforted by observing that both shoes and stockings generally reappeared with better weather, having been thriftily kept out of the damp for the convenience of dry feet within doors. Their hardihood was wonderful, and their strength greater than could have been expected from such spare diet as they probably lived upon. I have seen them carrying on their heads great burdens under which they walked as freely as if they were fashionable bonnets; or sometimes the burden was huge enough almost to cover the whole person, looked at from behind, — as in Tuscan villages you may see the girls coming in from the country with great bundles of green twigs upon their backs, so that they resemble locomotive masses of verdure and fragrance. But these poor English women seemed to be laden with rubbish, incongruous and indescribable, such as bones and rags, the sweepings of the house and of the street, a merchandise gathered up from what poverty itself had thrown away, a heap of filthy stuff analogous to Christian's bundle of sin.

Sometimes, though very seldom, I detected a certain graceful-ness among the younger women that was altogether new to my observation. It was a charm proper to the lowest class. One girl I particularly remember, in a garb none of the cleanest and nowise smart, and herself exceedingly coarse in all respects, but yet endowed with a sort of witchery, a native charm, a robe of simple beauty and suitable behavior that she was born in and had never been tempted to throw off, because she had really nothing else to put on. Eve herself could not have been more natural. Nothing was affected, nothing imitated; no proper grace was vulgarized by an effort to assume the man-ners or adornments of another sphere. This kind of beauty, arrayed in a fitness of its own, is probably vanishing out of the world, and will certainly never be found in America, where all the girls, whether daughters of the upper-tendom, the medi-ocrity, the cottage, or the kennel, aim at one standard of dress and deportment, seldom accomplishing a perfectly triumphant hit or an utterly absurd failure. Those words, "genteel" and "ladylike," are terrible ones, and do us infinite mischief, but it is because (at least, I hope so) we are in a transition state, and shall emerge into a higher mode of simplicity than has ever been known to past ages.

In such disastrous circumstances as I have been attempting to describe, it was beautiful to observe what a mysterious effi-cacy still asserted itself in character. A woman, evidently poor as the poorest of her neighbors, would be knitting or sewing on the doorstep, just as fifty other women were; but round about her skirts (though wofully patched) you would be sensible of a certain sphere of decency, which, it seemed to me, could not have been kept more impregnable in the cosiest little sitting-room, where the teakettle on the hob was humming its good old song of domestic peace. Maidenhood had a similar power. The evil habit that grows upon us in this harsh world makes me faithless to my own better perceptions; and yet I have seen girls in these wretched streets, on whose virgin purity, judging merely from their impression on my instincts as they passed by,

I should have deemed it safe, at the moment, to stake my life. The next moment, however, as the surrounding flood of moral uncleanness surged over their footsteps, I would not have staked a spike of thistle-down on the same wager. Yet the miracle was within the scope of Providence, which is equally wise and equally beneficent (even to those poor girls, though I acknowledge the fact without the remotest comprehension of the mode of it), whether they were pure or what we fellow-sinners call vile.   Unless your faith be deep-rooted and of most vigorous growth, it is the safer way not to turn aside into this region so suggestive of miserable doubt.   It was a place "with dreadful faces thronged," wrinkled and grim with vice and wretchedness; and, thinking over the line of Milton here quoted, I come to the conclusion that those ugly lineaments which startled Adam and Eve, as they looked backward to the closed gate of Paradise, were no fiends from the pit, but the more terrible foreshadowings of what so many of their descendants were to be.   God help them, and us likewise, their brethren and sisters!   Let me add, that, forlorn, ragged, careworn, hopeless, dirty, haggard, hungry, as they were, the most pitiful thing of all was to see the sort of patience with which they accepted their lot, as if they had been born into the world for that and nothing else.   Even the little children had this characteristic in as perfect development as their grandmothers.

The children, in truth, were the ill-omened blossoms from which another harvest of precisely such dark fruitage as I saw ripened around me was to be produced.   Of course you would imagine these to be lumps of crude iniquity, tiny vessels as full as they could hold of naughtiness; nor can I say a great deal to the contrary.   Small proof of parental discipline could I discern, save when a mother (drunken, I sincerely hope) snatched her own imp out of a group of pale, half-naked, humor-eaten abortions that were playing and squabbling together in the mud, turned up its tatters, brought down her heavy hand on its poor little tenderest part, and let it go again with a shake. If the child knew what the punishment was for, it was wiser than I pretend to be.   It yelled and went back to its playmates in the mud.   Yet let me bear testimony to what was beautiful, and more touching than anything that I ever witnessed before in the intercourse of happier children.   I allude to the superintendence which some of these small people (too small, one would think, to be sent into the street alone, had there been any other nursery for them) exercised over still smaller ones. Whence they derived such a sense of duty, unless immediately from God, I cannot tell; but it was wonderful to observe the expression of responsibility in their deportment, the anxious fidelity with which they discharged their unfit office, the tender patience with which they linked their less pliable impulses to the wayward footsteps of an infant, and let it guide them whithersoever it liked.   In the hollow-cheeked, large-eyed girl of ten, whom I saw giving a cheerless oversight to her baby-brother, I did not so much marvel at it.   She had merely come a little earlier than usual to the perception of what was to be her business in life.   But I admired the sickly-looking little boy, who did violence to his boyish nature by making himself the servant of his little sister, — she too small to walk, and he too small to take her in his arms, — and therefore working a kind of miracle to transport her from one dirt-heap to another. Beholding such works of love and duty, I took heart again, and deemed it not so impossible, after all, for these neglected children to find a path through the squalor and evil of their circumstances up to the gate of heaven.   Perhaps there was this latent good in all of them, though generally they looked brutish, and dull even in their sports; there was little mirth among them, nor even a fully awakened spirit of blackguardism.   Yet sometimes, again, I saw, with surprise and a sense as if I had been asleep and dreaming, the bright intelligent, merry face of a child whose dark eyes gleamed with vivacious expression through the dirt that incrusted its skin, like sunshine struggling through a very dusty window-pane.

In these streets the belted and blue-coated policeman appears seldom in comparison with the frequency of his occurrence in more reputable thoroughfares. I used to think that the inhabitants would have ample time to murder one another, or any stranger, like myself, who might violate the filthy sanctities of the place, before the law could bring up its lumbering assistance. Nevertheless, there is a supervision; nor does the watchfulness of authority permit the populace to be tempted to any outbreak. Once, in a time of dearth, I noticed a balladsinger going through the street hoarsely chanting some discordant strain in a provincial dialect, of which I could only make out that it addressed the sensibilities of the auditors on the score of starvation; but by his side stalked the policeman, offering no interference, but watchful to hear what this rough minstrel said or sang, and silence him, if his effusion threatened to prove too soul-stirring. In my judgment, however, there is little or no danger of that kind: they starve patiently, sicken patiently, die patiently, not through resignation, but a diseased flaccidity of hope. If ever they should do mischief to those above them, it will probably be by the communication of some destructive pestilence; for, so the medical men affirm, they suffer all the ordinary diseases with a degree of virulence elsewhere unknown, and keep among themselves traditionary plagues that have long ceased to afflict more fortunate societies. Charity herself gathers her robe about her to avoid their contact. It would be a dire revenge, indeed, if they were to prove their claims to be reckoned of one blood and nature with the noblest and wealthiest by compelling them to inhale death through the diffusion of their own poverty-poisoned atmosphere.

A true Englishman is a kind man at heart, but has an unconquerable dislike to poverty and beggary. Beggars have heretofore been so strange to an American that he is apt to become their prey, being recognized through his national peculiarities, and beset by them in the streets. The English smile at him, and say that there are ample public arrangements for every pauper's possible need, that street charity promotes idleness and vice, and that yonder personification of misery on the pavement will lay up a good day's profit, besides supping more luxuriously than the dupe who gives him a shilling. By and by the stranger adopts their theory and begins to practise upon it, much to his own temporary freedom from annoyance, but not entirely without moral detriment or sometimes a too late contrition. Years afterwards, it may be, his memory is still haunted by some vindictive wretch whose cheeks were pale and hunger-pinched, whose rags fluttered in the east-wind, whose right arm was paralyzed and his left leg shrivelled into a mere nerveless stick, but whom he passed by remorselessly because an Englishman chose to say that the fellow's misery looked too perfect, was too artistically got up, to be genuine. Even allowing this to be true (as, a hundred chances to one, it was), it would still have been a clear case of economy to buy him off with a little loose silver, so that his lamentable figure should not limp at the heels of your conscience all over the world. To own the truth, I provided myself with several such imaginary persecutors in England, and recruited their number with at least one sickly-looking wretch whose acquaintance I first made at Assisi, in Italy, and, taking a dislike to something sinister in his aspect, permitted him to beg early and late, and all day long, without getting a single baiocco. At my latest glimpse of him, the villain avenged himself, not by a volley of horrible curses as any other Italian beggar would, but by taking an expression so grief-stricken, want-wrung, hopeless, and withal resigned, that I could paint his lifelike portrait at this moment. Were I to go over the same ground again, I would listen to no man's theories, but buy the little luxury of beneficence at a cheap rate, instead of doing myself a moral mischief by exuding a stony incrustation over whatever natural sensibility I might possess.

On the other hand, there were some mendicants whose utmost efforts I even now felicitate myself on having withstood. Such was a phenomenon abridged of his lower half, who beset me for two or three years together, and, in spite of his deficiency of locomotive members, had some supernatural method of transporting himself (simultaneously, I believe) to all quarters

of the city. He wore a sailor's jacket (possibly, because skirts
would have been a superfluity to his figure), and had a remarkably broad-shouldered and muscular frame, surmounted by a
large, fresh-colored face, which was full of power and intelligence. His dress and linen were the perfection of neatness.
Once a day, at least, wherever I went, I suddenly became aware
of this trunk of a man on the path before me, resting on his
base, and looking as if he had just sprouted out of the pavement, and would sink into it again and reappear at some other
spot the instant you left him behind. The expression of his
eye was perfectly respectful, but terribly fixed, holding your
own as by fascination, never once winking, never wavering
from its point-blank gaze right into your face, till you were
completely beyond the range of his battery of one immense
rifled cannon. This was his mode of soliciting alms; and he
reminded me of the old beggar who appealed so touchingly
to the charitable sympathies of Gil Blas, taking aim at him
from the roadside with a long-barrelled musket. The intent-
ness and directness of his silent appeal, his close and unrelent-
ing attack upon your individuality, respectful as it seemed,
was the very flower of insolence; or, if you give it a possibly
truer interpretation, it was the tyrannical effort of a man endowed with great natural force of character to constrain your
reluctant will to his purpose. Apparently, he had staked his
salvation upon the ultimate success of a daily struggle between
himself and me, the triumph of which would compel me to
become a tributary to the hat that lay on the pavement beside
him. Man or fiend, however, there was a stubbornness in his
intended victim which this massive fragment of a mighty personality had not altogether reckoned upon, and by its aid I
was enabled to pass him at my customary pace hundreds of
times over, quietly meeting his terribly respectful eye, and
allowing him the fair chance which I felt to be his due, to
subjugate me, if he really had the strength for it. He never
succeeded, but, on the other hand, never gave up the contest;
and should I ever walk those streets again, I am certain that

the truncated tyrant will sprout up through the pavement and look me fixedly in the eye, and perhaps get the victory.

I should think all the more highly of myself, if I had shown equal heroism in resisting another class of beggarly depredators, who assailed me on my weaker side and won an easy spoil. Such was the sanctimonious clergyman, with his white cravat, who visited me with a subscription-paper, which he himself had drawn up, in a case of heart-rending distress; — the respectable and ruined tradesman, going from door to door, shy and silent in his own person, but accompanied by a sympathizing friend, who bore testimony to his integrity, and stated the unavoidable misfortunes that had crushed him down; — or the delicate and prettily dressed lady, who had been bred in affluence, but was suddenly thrown upon the perilous charities of the world by the death of an indulgent, but secretly insolvent father, or the commercial catastrophe and simultaneous suicide of the best of husbands; — or the gifted, but unsuccessful author, appealing to my fraternal sympathies, generously rejoicing in some small prosperities which he was kind enough to term my own triumphs in the field of letters, and claiming to have largely contributed to them by his unbought notices in the public journals. England is full of such people, and a hundred other varieties of peripatetic tricksters, higher than these, and lower, who act their parts tolerably well, but seldom with an absolutely illusive effect.   I knew at once, raw Yankee as I was, that they were humbugs, almost without an exception, — rats that nibble at the honest bread and cheese of the community, and grow fat by their petty pilferings, — yet often gave them what they asked, and privately owned myself a simpleton. There is a decorum which restrains you (unless you happen to be a police-constable) from breaking through a crust of plausible respectability, even when you are certain that there is a knave beneath it.

After making myself as familiar as I decently could with the poor streets, I became curious to see what kind of a home was provided for the inhabitants at the public expense, fearing

that it must needs be a most comfortless one, or else their
choice (if choice it were) of so miserable a life outside was truly
difficult to account for. Accordingly, I visited a great almshouse, and was glad to observe how unexceptionably all the
parts of the establishment were carried on, and what an orderly
life, full-fed, sufficiently reposeful, and undisturbed by the arbi-
trary exercise of authority, seemed to be led there. Possibly,
indeed, it was that very orderliness, and the cruel necessity of
being neat and clean, and even the comfort resulting from these
and other Christian-like restraints and regulations, that
constituted the principal grievance on the part of the poor,
shiftless inmates, accustomed to a lifelong luxury of dirt and
harum-scarumness. The wild life of the streets has perhaps
as unforgetable a charm, to those who have once thoroughly
imbibed it, as the life of the forest or the prairie. But I
conceive rather that there must be insuperable difficulties, for
the majority of the poor, in the way of getting admittance to
the almshouse, than that a merely aesthetic preference for the
street would incline the pauper class to fare scantily and pre-
cariously, and expose their raggedness to the rain and snow,
when such a hospitable door stood wide open for their entrance. It might be that the roughest and darkest side of the
matter was not shown me, there being persons of eminent
station and of both sexes in the party which I accompanied;
and, of course, a properly trained public functionary would
have deemed it a monstrous rudeness, as well as a great shame,
to exhibit anything to people of rank that might too painfully
shock their sensibilities.

The women's ward was the portion of the establishment
which we especially examined. It could not be questioned
that they were treated with kindness as well as care. No doubt,
as has been already suggested, some of them felt the irksome-
ness of submission to general rules of orderly behavior, after
being accustomed to that perfect freedom from the minor
proprieties, at least, which is one of the compensations of
absolutely hopeless poverty, or of any circumstances that set

us fairly below the decencies of life.   I asked the governor of the house whether he met with any difficulty in keeping peace and order among his inmates; and he informed me that his troubles among the women were incomparably greater than with the men.   They were freakish, and apt to be quarrelsome, inclined to plague and pester one another in ways that it was impossible to lay hold of, and to thwart his own authority by the like intangible methods.   He said this with the utmost good-nature, and quite won my regard by so placidly resigning himself to the inevitable necessity of letting the women throw dust into his eyes.   They certainly looked peaceable and sisterly enough as I saw them, though still it might be faintly perceptible that some of them were consciously playing their parts before the governor and his distinguished visitors.

This governor seemed to me a man thoroughly fit for his position.   An American, in an office of similar responsibility, would doubtless be a much superior person, better educated, possessing a far wider range of thought, more naturally acute, with a quicker tact of external observation and a readier faculty of dealing with difficult cases.   The women would not succeed in throwing half so much dust into his eyes.   Moreover, his black coat, and thin, sallow visage, would make him look like a scholar, and his manners would indefinitely approximate to those of a gentleman.   But I cannot help questioning whether, on the whole, these higher endowments would produce decidedly better results.   The Englishman was thoroughly plebeian both in aspect and behavior, a bluff, ruddy-faced, hearty, kindly, yeoman-like personage, with no refinement whatever, nor any superfluous sensibility, but gifted with a native wholesomeness of character which must have been a very beneficial element in the atmosphere of the almshouse.   He spoke to his pauper family in loud, good-humored, cheerful tones, and treated them with a healthy freedom that probably caused the forlorn wretches to feel as if they were free and healthy likewise.   If he had understood them a little better, he would not have treated them half so wisely.   We are apt to make

sickly people more morbid, and unfortunate people more miserable, by endeavoring to adapt our deportment to their
especial and individual needs.   They eagerly accept our well-
meant efforts; but it is like returning their own sick breath
back upon themselves, to be breathed over and over again,
intensifying the inward mischief at every reception.   The sympathy that would really do them good is of a kind that recognizes their sound and healthy parts, and ignores the part
affected by disease, which will thrive under the eye of a too
close observer like a poisonous weed in the sunshine.   My
good friend the governor had no tendencies in the latter direc-
tion, and abundance of them in the former, and was con-
sequently as wholesome and invigorating as the west-wind with
a little spice of the north in it, brightening the dreary visages
that encountered us as if he had carried a sunbeam in his hand.
He expressed himself by his whole being and personality, and
by works more than words, and had the not unusual English
merit of knowing what to do much better than how to talk
about it.

   The women, I imagine, must have felt one imperfection in
their state, however comfortable otherwise.   They were forbid-
den, or, at all events, lacked the means, to follow out their
natural instinct of adorning themselves; all were well dressed
in one homely uniform of blue-checked gowns, with such caps
upon their heads as English servants wear.   Generally, too,
they had one dowdy English aspect, and a vulgar type of
features so nearly alike that they seemed literally to constitute
a sisterhood.   We have few of these absolutely unilluminated
faces among our native American population, individuals of
whom must be singularly unfortunate, if, mixing as we do, no
drop of gentle blood has contributed to refine the turbid element, no gleam of hereditary intelligence has lighted up the
stolid eyes, which their forefathers brought from the Old
Country.   Even in this English almshouse, however, there was
at least one person who claimed to be intimately connected
with rank and wealth.   The governor, after suggesting that

this person would probably be gratified by our visit, ushered us into a small parlor, which was furnished a little more like a room in a private dwelling than others that we entered, and had a row of religious books and fashionable novels on the mantel-piece.   An old lady sat at a bright coal-fire, reading a romance, and rose to receive us with a certain pomp of manner and elaborate display of ceremonious courtesy, which, in spite of myself, made me inwardly question the genuineness of her aristocratic pretensions.   But, at any rate, she looked like a respectable old soul, and was evidently gladdened to the very core of her frost-bitten heart by the awful punctiliousness with which we responded to her gracious and hospitable, though unfamiliar welcome.   After a little polite conversation, we retired; and the governor, with a lowered voice and an air of deference, told us that she had been a lady of quality, and had ridden in her own equipage, not many years before, and now lived in continual expectation that some of her rich relatives would drive up in their carriages to take her away.   Meanwhile, he added, she was treated with great respect by her fellow-paupers.   I could not help thinking, from a few criticisable peculiarities in her talk and manner, that there might have been a mistake on the governor's part, and perhaps a venial exaggeration on the old lady's, concerning her former position in society; but what struck me was the forcible instance of that most prevalent of English vanities, the pretension to aristocratic connection, on one side, and the submission and reverence with which it was accepted by the governor and his household, on the other.   Among ourselves, I think, when wealth and eminent position have taken their departure, they seldom leave a pallid ghost behind them, — or, if it sometimes stalks abroad, few recognize it.

We went into several other rooms, at the doors of which, pausing on the outside, we could hear the volubility, and sometimes the wrangling, of the female inhabitants within, but invariably found silence and peace when we stepped over the threshold.   The women were grouped together in their sitting-rooms, sometimes three or four, sometimes a larger number, classified by their spontaneous affinities, I suppose, and all busied, so far as I can remember, with the one occupation of knitting coarse yarn stockings. Hardly any of them, I am sorry to say, had a brisk or cheerful air, though it often stirred them up to a momentary vivacity to be accosted by the governor, and they seemed to like being noticed, however slightly, by the visitors. The happiest person whom I saw there (and running hastily through my experiences, I hardly recollect to have seen a happier one in my life, if you take a careless flow of spirits as happiness) was an old woman that lay in bed among ten or twelve heavy-looking females, who plied their knitting-work round about her. She laughed, when we entered, and immediately began to talk to us, in a thin, little, spirited quaver, claiming to be more than a century old; and the governor (in whatever way he happened to be cognizant of the fact) confirmed her age to be a hundred and four. Her jauntiness and cackling merriment were really wonderful. It was as if she had got through with all her actual business in life two or three generations ago, and now, freed from every responsibility for herself or others, had only to keep up a mirthful state of mind till the short time, or long time (and, happy as she was, she appeared not to care whether it were long or short), before Death, who had misplaced her name in his list, might remember to take her away. She had gone quite round the circle of human existence, and come back to the play-ground again. And so she had grown to be a kind of miraculous old pet, the plaything of people seventy or eighty years younger than herself, who talked and laughed with her as if she were a child, finding great delight in her wayward and strangely playful responses, into some of which she cunningly conveyed a gibe that caused their ears to tingle a little. She had done getting out of bed in this world, and lay there to be waited upon like a queen or a baby.

In the same room sat a pauper who had once been an actress of considerable repute, but was compelled to give up her profession by a softening of the brain. The disease seemed to have stolen the continuity out of her life, and disturbed all healthy relationship between the thoughts within her and the world without. On our first entrance, she looked cheerfully at us, and showed herself ready to engage in conversation; but suddenly, while we were talking with the century-old crone, the poor actress began to weep, contorting her face with extravagant stage-grimaces, and wringing her hands for some inscrutable sorrow. It might have been a reminiscence of actual calamity in her past life, or, quite as probably, it was but a dramatic woe, beneath which she had staggered and shrieked and wrung her hands with hundreds of repetitions in the sight of crowded theatres, and been as often comforted by thunders of applause. But my idea of the mystery was, that she had a sense of wrong in seeing the aged woman (whose empty vivacity was like the rattling of dry peas in a bladder) chosen as the central object of interest to the visitors, while she herself, who had agitated thousands of hearts with a breath, sat starving for the admiration that was her natural food. I appeal to the whole society of artists of the Beautiful and the Imaginative, — poets, romancers, painters, sculptors, actors, — whether or no this is a grief that may be felt even amid the torpor of a dissolving brain!

We looked into a good many sleeping-chambers, where were rows of beds, mostly calculated for two occupants, and provided with sheets and pillow-cases that resembled sackcloth. It appeared to me that the sense of beauty was insufficiently regarded in all the arrangements of the almshouse; a little cheap luxury for the eye, at least, might do the poor folks a substantial good. But, at all events, there was the beauty of perfect neatness and orderliness, which, being heretofore known to few of them, was perhaps as much as they could well digest in the remnant of their lives. We were invited into the laundry, where a great washing and drying were in process, the whole atmosphere being hot and vaporous with the steam of wet garments and bedclothes. This atmosphere

was the pauper-life of the past week or fortnight resolved into
a gaseous state, and breathing it, however fastidiously, we were
forced to inhale the strange element into our inmost being.
Had the Queen been there, I know not how she could have
escaped the necessity.   What an intimate brotherhood is this
in which we dwell, do what we may to put an artificial remoteness between the high creature and the low one!   A poor man's
breath, borne on the vehicle of tobacco-smoke, floats into a
palace-window and reaches the nostrils of a monarch.   It is
but an example, obvious to the sense, of the innumerable and
secret channels by which, at every moment of our lives, the
flow and reflux of a common humanity pervade us all.   How
superficial are the niceties of such as pretend to keep aloof!
Let the whole world be cleansed, or not a man or woman of
us all can be clean.

By and by we came to the ward where the children were kept,
on entering which, we saw, in the first place, several unlovely
and unwholesome little people lazily playing together in a
court-yard.   And here a singular incommodity befell one member of our party.*   Among the children was a wretched, pale,
half-torpid little thing (about six years old, perhaps, but I know
not whether a girl or a boy), with a humor in its eyes and face,
which the governor said was the scurvy, and which appeared
to bedim its powers of vision, so that it toddled about groping-
ly, as if in quest of it did not precisely know what.   This
child — this sickly, wretched, humor-eaten infant, the offspring
of unspeakable sin and sorrow, whom it must have required
several generations of guilty progenitors to render so pitiable
an object as we beheld it — immediately took an unaccountable fancy to the gentleman just hinted at.   It prowled about
him like a pet kitten, rubbing against his legs, following everywhere at his heels, pulling at his coat-tails, and, at last, exerting
all the speed that its poor limbs were capable of, got directly
before him and held forth its arms, mutely insisting on being

*[Hawthorne himself, as his *Note-Books* prove.]

taken up. It said not a word, being perhaps under-witted and incapable of prattle. But it smiled up in his face, — a sort of woful gleam was that smile, through the sickly blotches that covered its features, — and found means to express such a perfect confidence that it was going to be fondled and made much of, that there was no possibility in a human heart of balking its expectation. It was as if God had promised the poor child this favor on behalf of that individual, and he was bound to fulfil the contract, or else no longer call himself a man among men. Nevertheless, it could be no easy thing for him to do, he being a person burdened with more than an Englishman's customary reserve, shy of actual contact with human beings, afflicted with a peculiar distaste for whatever was ugly, and, furthermore, accustomed to that habit of observation from an insulated stand-point which is said (but, I hope, erroneously) to have the tendency of putting ice into the blood.

So I watched the struggle in his mind with a good deal of interest, and am seriously of opinion that he did an heroic act, and effected more than he dreamed of towards his final salvation, when he took up the loathsome child and caressed it as tenderly as if he had been its father. To be sure, we all smiled at him, at the time, but doubtless would have acted pretty much the same in a similar stress of circumstances. The child, at any rate, appeared to be satisfied with his behavior; for when he had held it a considerable time, and set it down, it still favored him with its company, keeping fast hold of his forefinger till we reached the confines of the place. And on our return through the court-yard, after visiting another part of the establishment, here again was this same little Wretchedness waiting for its victim, with a smile of joyful, and yet dull recognition about its scabby mouth and in its rheumy eyes. No doubt, the child's mission in reference to our friend was to remind him that he was responsible, in his degree, for all the sufferings and misdemeanors of the world in which he lived, and was not entitled to look upon a particle of its dark calamity as if it were none of his concern: the offspring of a brother's iniquity being his own blood-relation, and the guilt, likewise, a burden on him, unless he expiated it by better deeds.

All the children in this ward seemed to be invalids, and, going up stairs, we found more of them in the same or a worse condition than the little creature just described, with their mothers (or more probably other women, for the infants were mostly foundlings) in attendance as nurses. The matron of the ward, a middle-aged woman, remarkably kind and mother-ly in aspect, was walking to and fro across the chamber — on that weary journey in which careful mothers and nurses travel so continually and so far, and gain never a step of progress — with an unquiet baby in her arms. She assured us that she enjoyed her occupation, being exceedingly fond of children; and, in fact, the absence of timidity in all the little people was a sufficient proof that they could have had no experience of harsh treatment, though, on the other hand, none of them appeared to be attracted to one individual more than another. In this point they differed widely from the poor child below stairs. They seemed to recognize a universal motherhood in womankind, and cared not which individual might be the mother of the moment. I found their tameness as shocking as did Alexander Selkirk* that of the brute subjects of his else solitary kingdom. It was a sort of tame familiarity, a perfect indifference to the approach of strangers, such as I never noticed in other children. I accounted for it partly by their nerveless, unstrung state of body, incapable of the quick thrills of delight and fear which play upon the lively harp-strings of a healthy child's nature, and partly by their woful lack of ac-quaintance with a private home, and their being therefore destitute of the sweet home-bred shyness, which is like the sanctity of heaven about a mother-petted child. Their condi-tion was like that of chickens hatched in an oven, and growing up without the especial guardianship of a matron hen: both the chicken and the child, methinks, must needs want some-thing that is essential to their respective characters.

*[Scottish sailor whose adventures suggested *Robinson Crusoe* to Defoe.]

In this chamber (which was spacious, containing a large number of beds) there was a clear fire burning on the hearth, as in all the other occupied rooms; and directly in front of the blaze sat a woman holding a baby, which, beyond all reach of comparison, was the most horrible object that ever afflicted my sight.   Days afterwards — nay, even now, when I bring it up vividly before my mind's eye — it seemed to lie upon the floor of my heart, polluting my moral being with the sense of something grievously amiss in the entire conditions of humanity.   The holiest man could not be otherwise than full of wickedness, the chastest virgin seemed impure, in a world where such a babe was possible.   The governor whispered me, apart, that, like nearly all the rest of them, it was the child of unhealthy parents.   Ah, yes!   There was the mischief.   This spectral infant, a hideous mockery of the visible link which Love creates between man and woman, was born of disease and sin.   Diseased Sin was its father, and Sinful Disease its mother, and their offspring lay in the woman's arms like a nursing Pestilence, which, could it live and grow up, would make the world a more accursed abode than ever heretofore. Thank Heaven, it could not live!   This baby, if we must give it that sweet name, seemed to be three or four months old, but, being such an unthrifty changeling, might have been considerably older.   It was all covered with blotches, and preternaturally dark and discolored; it was withered away, quite shrunken and fleshless; it breathed only amid pantings and gaspings, and moaned painfully at every gasp.   The only comfort in reference to it was the evident impossibility of its surviving to draw many more of those miserable, moaning breaths; and it would have been infinitely less heart-depressing to see it die, right before my eyes, than to depart and carry it alive in my remembrance, still suffering the incalculable torture of its little life. I can by no means express how horrible this infant was, neither ought I to attempt it.   And yet I must add one final touch. Young as the poor little creature was, its pain and misery had endowed it with a premature intelligence, insomuch that its eyes seemed to stare at the by-standers out of their sunken sockets knowingly and appealingly, as if summoning us one and all to witness the deadly wrong of its existence. At least, I so interpreted its look, when it positively met and responded to my own awe-stricken gaze, and therefore I lay the case, as far as I am able, before mankind, on whom God has imposed the necessity to suffer in soul and body till this dark and dreadful wrong be righted.

Thence we went to the school-rooms, which were underneath the chapel. The pupils, like the children whom we had just seen, were, in large proportion, foundlings. Almost without exception, they looked sickly, with marks of eruptive trouble in their doltish faces, and a general tendency to diseases of the eye. Moreover, the poor little wretches appeared to be uneasy within their skins, and screwed themselves about on the benches in a disagreeably suggestive way, as if they had inherited the evil habits of their parents as an innermost garment of the same texture and material as the shirt of Nessus, and must wear it with unspeakable discomfort as long as they lived. I saw only a single child that looked healthy; and on my pointing him out, the governor informed me that this little boy, the sole exception to the miserable aspect of his school-fellows, was not a foundling, nor properly a work-house child, being born of respectable parentage, and his father one of the officers of the institution. As for the remainder, — the hundred pale abortions to be counted against one rosy-cheeked boy, — what shall we say or do? Depressed by the sight of so much misery, and uninventive of remedies for the evils that force themselves on my perception, I can do little more than recur to the idea already hinted at in the early part of this article, regarding the speedy necessity of a new deluge. So far as these children are concerned, at any rate, it would be a blessing to the human race, which they will contribute to enervate and corrupt, — a greater blessing to themselves, who inherit no patrimony but disease and vice, and in whose souls, if there be a spark of God's life, this seems the only possible mode of keeping it aglow, —

if every one of them could be drowned to-night, by their best friends, instead of being put tenderly to bed. This heroic method of treating human maladies, moral and material, is certainly beyond the scope of man's discretionary rights, and probably will not be adopted by Divine Providence until the opportunity of milder reformation shall have been offered us again and again, through a series of future ages.

It may be fair to acknowledge that the humane and excellent governor, as well as other persons better acquainted with the subject than myself, took a less gloomy view of it, though still so dark a one as to involve scanty consolation. They remarked that individuals of the male sex, picked up in the streets and nurtured in the work-house, sometimes succeed tolerably well in life, because they are taught trades before being turned into the world, and, by dint of immaculate behavior and good luck, are not unlikely to get employment and earn a livelihood. The case is different with the girls. They can only go to service, and are invariably rejected by families of respectability on account of their origin, and for the better reason of their unfitness to fill satisfactorily even the meanest situations in a well-ordered English household. Their resource is to take service with people only a step or two above the poorest class, with whom they fare scantily, endure harsh treatment, lead shifting and precarious lives, and finally drop into the slough of evil, through which, in their best estate, they do but pick their slimy way on stepping-stones.

From the schools we went to the bake-house, and the brew-house (for such cruelty is not harbored in the heart of a true Englishman as to deny a pauper his daily allowance of beer), and through the kitchens, where we beheld an immense pot over the fire, surging and walloping with some kind of a savory stew that filled it up to its brim. We also visited a tailor's shop, and a shoemaker's shop, in both of which a number of men, and pale, diminutive apprentices, were at work, diligently enough, though seemingly with small heart in the business. Finally, the governor ushered us into a shed, inside of which was piled up an immense quantity of new coffins. They were of the plainest description, made of pine boards, probably of American growth, not very nicely smoothed by the plane, neither painted nor stained with black, but provided with a loop of rope at either end for the convenience of lifting the rude box and its inmate into the cart that shall carry them to the burial ground. There, in holes ten feet deep, the paupers are buried one above another, mingling their relics indistinguishably. In another world may they resume their individuality, and find it a happier one than here!

As we departed, a character came under our notice which I have met with in all almshouses, whether of the city or village, or in England or America. It was the familiar simpleton, who shuffled across the courtyard, clattering his wooden-soled shoes, to greet us with a howl or a laugh, I hardly know which, holding out his hand for a penny, and chuckling grossly when it was given him. All under-witted persons, so far as my experience goes, have this craving for copper coin, and appear to estimate its value by a miraculous instinct, which is one of the earliest gleams of human intelligence while the nobler faculties are yet in abeyance. There may come a time, even in this world, when we shall all understand that our tendency to the individual appropriation of gold and broad acres, fine houses, and such good and beautiful things as are equally enjoyable by a multitude, is but a trait of imperfectly developed intelligence, like the simpleton's cupidity of a penny. When that day dawns, — and probably not till then, — I imagine that there will be no more poor streets nor need of almshouses.

I was once present at the wedding of some poor English people, and was deeply impressed by the spectacle, though by no means with such proud and delightful emotions as seem to have affected all England on the recent occasion of the marriage of its Prince. It was in the Cathedral at Manchester, a particularly black and grim old structure, into which I had stepped to examine some ancient and curious wood-carvings within the choir. The woman in attendance greeted me with a smile (which always glimmers forth on the feminine visage, I know not why, when a wedding is in question), and asked me to take a seat in the nave till some poor parties were married, it being the Easter holidays, and a good time for them to marry, because no fees would be demanded by the clergyman. I sat down accordingly, and soon the parson and his clerk appeared at the altar, and a considerable crowd of people made their entrance at a side-door, and ranged themselves in a long, huddled line across the chancel. They were my acquaintances of the poor streets, or persons in a precisely similar condition of life, and were now come to their marriage-ceremony in just such garbs as I had always seen them wear: the men in their loafer's coats, out at elbows, or their laborers' jackets, defaced with grimy toil; the women drawing their shabby shawls tighter about their shoulders, to hide the raggedness beneath; all of them unbrushed, unshaven, unwashed, uncombed, and wrinkled with penury and care; nothing virgin-like in the brides, nor hopeful or energetic in the bridegrooms; — they were, in short, the mere rags and tatters of the human race, whom some east-wind of evil omen, howling along the streets, had chanced to sweep together into an unfragrant heap. Each and all of them, conscious of his or her individual misery, had blundered into the strange miscalculation of supposing that they could lessen the sum of it by multiplying it into the misery of another person. All the couples (and it was difficult, in such a confused crowd, to compute exactly their number) stood up at once, and had execution done upon them in the lump, the clergyman addressing only small parts of the service to each individual pair, but so managing the larger portion as to include the whole company without the trouble of repetition. By this compendious contrivance, one would apprehend, he came dangerously near making every man and woman the husband or wife of every other; nor, perhaps, would he have perpetrated much additional mischief by the mistake; but, after receiving a benediction in common, they assorted themselves in their own fashion, as they only knew how, and departed to the garrets, or the cellars, or the unsheltered street-corners, where their honeymoon and subsequent lives were to be spent. The parson smiled decorously, the clerk and the sexton grinned broadly, the female attendant tittered almost aloud, and even the married parties seemed to see something exceedingly funny in the affair; but for my part, though generally apt enough to be tickled by a joke, I laid it away in my memory as one of the saddest sights I ever looked upon.

Not very long afterwards, I happened to be passing the same venerable Cathedral, and heard a clang of joyful bells, and beheld a bridal party coming down the steps towards a carriage and four horses, with a portly coachman and two postilions, that waited at the gate. One parson and one service had amalgamated the wretchedness of a score of paupers; a Bishop and three or four clergymen had combined their spiritual might to forge the golden links of this other marriage-bond. The bridegroom's mien had a sort of careless and kindly English pride; the bride floated along in her white drapery, a creature so nice and delicate that it was a luxury to see her, and a pity that her silk slippers should touch anything so grimy as the old stones of the churchyard avenue. The crowd of ragged people, who always cluster to witness what they may of an aristocratic wedding, broke into audible admiration of the bride's beauty and the bridegroom's manliness, and uttered prayers and ejaculations (possibly paid for in alms) for the happiness of both. If the most favorable of earthly conditions could make them happy, they had every prospect of it. They were going to live on their abundance in one of those stately and delightful English homes, such as no other people ever created or inherited, a hall set far and safe within its own private grounds, and surrounded with venerable trees, shaven lawns, rich shrubbery, and trimmest pathways, the whole so artfully contrived and tended that summer rendered it a paradise, and even winter would hardly disrobe it of its beauty; and all this fair property seemed more exclusively and inalienably their own, because of its descent through many forefathers, each of whom had added an improvement or a charm, and thus transmitted it with a stronger stamp of rightful possession to his heir. And is it possible, after all, that there may be a flaw in the title-deeds? Is, or is not, the system wrong that gives one married pair so immense a superfluity of luxurious home, and shuts out a million others from any home whatever? One day or another, safe as they deem themselves, and safe as the hereditary temper of the people really tends to make them, the gentlemen of England will be compelled to face this question.

Civic Banquets

IT has often perplexed me to imagine how an Englishman will be able to reconcile himself to any future state of existence from which the earthly institution of dinner shall be excluded. Even if he fail to take his appetite along with him (which it seems to me hardly possible to believe, since this endowment is so essential to his composition), the immortal day must still admit an interim of two or three hours during which he will be conscious of a slight distaste, at all events, if not an absolute repugnance, to merely spiritual nutriment. The idea of dinner has so imbedded itself among his highest and deepest characteristics, so illuminated itself with intellect and softened itself with the kindest emotions of his heart, so linked itself with Church and State, and grown so majestic with long hereditary customs and ceremonies, that, by taking it utterly away, Death, instead of putting the final touch to his perfection, would leave him infinitely less complete than we have already known him. He could not be roundly happy. Paradise, among all its enjoyments, would lack one daily felicity which his sombre little island possessed. Perhaps it is not irreverent to conjecture that a provision may have been made, in this particular, for the Englishman's exceptional necessities. It strikes me that Milton was of the opinion here suggested, and may have intended to throw out a delightful and consolatory hope for his countrymen, when he represents the genial archangel as playing his part with such excellent appetite at Adam's dinner-table, and confining himself to fruit and vegetables only because, in those early days of her housekeeping, Eve had no more acceptable viands to set before him. Milton, indeed, had a true English taste for the pleasures of the table, though refined by the lofty and poetic discipline to which he had subjected himself. It is delicately implied in the refection in Paradise, and more substantially, though still elegantly, betrayed in the sonnet proposing to "Laurence, of virtuous father virtuous son," a series of nice little dinners in midwinter; and it blazes fully out in that untasted banquet which, elaborate as it was, Satan tossed up in a trice from the kitchen-ranges of Tartarus.

Among this people, indeed, so wise in their generation, dinner has a kind of sanctity quite independent of the dishes that may be set upon the table; so that, if it be only a mutton-chop, they treat it with due reverence, and are rewarded with a degree of enjoyment which such reckless devourers as ourselves do not often find in our richest abundance. It is good to see how stanch they are after fifty or sixty years of heroic eating, still relying upon their digestive powers and indulging a vigorous appetite; whereas an American has generally lost the one and learned to distrust the other long before reaching the earliest decline of life; and thenceforward he makes little account of his dinner, and dines at his peril, if at all. I know not whether my countrymen will allow me to tell them, though I think it scarcely too much to affirm, that on this side of the water, people never dine. At any rate, abundantly as Nature has provided us with most of the material requisites, the highest possible dinner has never yet been eaten in America. It is the consummate flower of civilization and refinement; and our inability to produce it, or to appreciate its admirable beauty if a happy inspiration should bring it into bloom, marks fatally the limit of culture which we have attained.

It is not to be supposed, however, that the mob of cultivated Englishmen know how to dine in this elevated sense. The unpolishable ruggedness of the national character is still an impediment to them, even in that particular line where they are best qualified to excel. Though often present at good men's feasts, I remember only a single dinner, which, while lamentably conscious that many of its higher excellences were thrown away upon me, I yet could feel to be a perfect work of art. It could not, without unpardonable coarseness, be styled a matter of animal enjoyment, because, out of the very perfection of that lower bliss, there had arisen a dream-like development of spiritual happiness. As in the masterpieces of painting and poetry, there was a something intangible, a final deliciousness that only fluttered about your comprehension, vanishing whenever you tried to detain it, and compelling you to recognize it by faith rather than sense. It seemed as if a diviner set of senses were requisite, and had been partly supplied, for the special fruition of this banquet, and that the guests around the table (only eight in number) were becoming so educated, polished, and softened, by the delicate influences of what they ate and drank, as to be now a little more than mortal for the nonce. And there was that gentle, delicious sadness, too, which we find in the very summit of our most exquisite enjoyments, and feel it a charm beyond all the gayety through which it keeps breathing its undertone. In the present case, it was worth a heavier sigh to reflect that such a festal achievement — the production of so much art, skill, fancy, invention, and perfect taste, — the growth of all the ages, which appeared to have been ripening for this hour, since man first began to eat and to moisten his food with wine — must lavish its happiness upon so brief a moment, when other beautiful things can be made a joy forever. Yet a dinner like this is no better than we can get, any day, at the rejuvenescent Cornhill Coffee-House, unless the whole man, with soul, intellect, and stomach, is ready to appreciate it, and unless, moreover, there is such a harmony in all the circumstances and accompaniments, and especially such a pitch of well-according minds, that nothing shall jar rudely against the guest's thoroughly awakened sensibilities. The world, and especially our part of it, being the rough, ill-assorted, and tumultuous place we find it, a beefsteak is about as good as any other dinner.

The foregoing reminiscence, however, has drawn me aside from the main object of my sketch, in which I purposed to give a slight idea of those public, or partially public banquets, the custom of which so thoroughly prevails among the English people, that nothing is ever decided upon, in matters of peace and war, until they have chewed upon it in the shape of roast-beef, and talked it fully over in their cups. Nor are these festivities merely occasional, but of stated recurrence in all considerable municipalities and associated bodies. The most ancient times appear to have been as familiar with them as the Englishmen of to-day. In many of the old English towns, you find some stately Gothic hall or chamber in which the Mayor and other authorities of the place have long held their sessions; and always, in convenient contiguity, there is a dusky kitchen, with an immense fireplace where an ox might lie roasting at his ease, though the less gigantic scale of modern cookery may now have permitted the cobwebs to gather in its chimney. . . .

The Mayor's dinner-parties occur as often as once a fortnight, and, inviting his guests by fifty or sixty at a time, his Worship probably assembles at his board most of the eminent citizens and distinguished personages of the town and neighborhood more than once during his year's incumbency, and very much, no doubt, to the promotion of good feeling among individuals of opposite parties and diverse pursuits in life. A miscellaneous party of Englishmen can always find more comfortable ground to meet upon than as many Americans, their differences of opinion being incomparably less radical than ours, and it being the sincerest wish of all their hearts, whether they call themselves Liberals or what not, that nothing in this world shall ever be greatly altered from what it has been and is.

Thus there is seldom such a virulence of political hostility that it may not be dissolved in a glass or two of wine, without making the good liquor any more dry or bitter than accords with English taste.

The first dinner of this kind at which I had the honor to be present took place during assize-time, and included among the guests the judges and the prominent members of the bar. Reaching the Town Hall at seven o'clock, I communicated my name to one of several splendidly dressed footmen, and he repeated it to another on the first staircase, by whom it was passed to a third, and thence to a fourth at the door of the reception-room, losing all resemblance to the original sound in the course of these transmissions; so that I had the advantage of making my entrance in the character of a stranger, not only to the whole company, but to myself as well. His Worship, however, kindly recognized me, and put me on speaking-terms with two or three gentlemen, whom I found very affable, and all the more hospitably attentive on the score of my nationality. It is very singular how kind an Englishman will almost invariably be to an individual American, without ever bating a jot of his prejudice against the American character in the lump. My new acquaintances took evident pains to put me at my ease; and, in requital of their good-nature, I soon began to look round at the general company in a critical spirit, making my crude observations apart, and drawing silent inferences, of the correctness of which I should not have been half so well satisfied a year afterwards as at that moment.

There were two judges present, a good many lawyers, and a few officers of the army in uniform. The other guests seemed to be principally of the mercantile class, and among them was a ship-owner from Nova Scotia, with whom I coalesced a little, inasmuch as we were born with the same sky over our heads, and an unbroken continuity of soil between his abode and mine. There was one old gentleman, whose character I never made out, with powdered hair, clad in black breeches and silk stockings, and wearing a rapier at his side; otherwise, with the exception of the military uniforms, there was little or no pretence of official costume. It being the first considerable assemblage of Englishmen that I had seen, my honest impression about them was, that they were a heavy and homely set of people, with a remarkable roughness of aspect and behavior, not repulsive, but beneath which it required more familiarity with the national character than I then possessed always to detect the good breeding of a gentleman. Being generally middle-aged, or still further advanced, they were by no means graceful in figure; for the comeliness of the youthful Englishman rapidly diminishes with years, his body appearing to grow longer, his legs to abbreviate themselves, and his stomach to assume the dignified prominence which justly belongs to that metropolis of his system. His face (what with the acridity of the atmosphere, ale at lunch, wine at dinner, and a well-digested abundance of succulent food) gets red and mottled, and develops at least one additional chin, with a promise of more; so that, finally, a stranger recognizes his animal part at the most superficial glance, but must take time and a little pains to discover the intellectual. Comparing him with an American, I really thought that our national paleness and lean habit of flesh gave us greatly the advantage in an aesthetic point of view. It seemed to me, moreover, that the English tailor had not done so much as he might and ought for these heavy figures, but had gone on wilfully exaggerating their uncouthness by the roominess of their garments; he had evidently no idea of accuracy of fit, and smartness was entirely out of his line. But, to be quite open with the reader, I afterwards learned to think that this aforesaid tailor has a deeper art than his brethren among ourselves, knowing how to dress his customers with such individual propriety that they look as if they were born in their clothes, the fit being to the character rather than the form. If you make an Englishman smart (unless he be a very exceptional one, of whom I have seen a few), you make him a monster; his best aspect is that of ponderous respectability.

To make an end of these first impressions, I fancied that not merely the Suffolk bar, but the bar of any inland county in New England, might show a set of thin-visaged men looking wretchedly worn, sallow, deeply wrinkled across the forehead, and grimly furrowed about the mouth, with whom these heavy-cheeked English lawyers, slow-paced and fat-witted as they must needs be, would stand very little chance in a professional contest. How that matter might turn out, I am unqualified to decide. But I state these results of my earliest glimpses at Englishmen, not for what they are worth, but because I ultimately gave them up as worth little or nothing. In course of time, I came to the conclusion that Englishmen of all ages are a rather good-looking people, dress in admirable taste from their own point of view, and, under a surface never silken to the touch, have a refinement of manners too thorough and genuine to be thought of as a separate endowment, — that is to say, if the individual himself be a man of station, and has had gentlemen for his father and grandfather. The sturdy Anglo-Saxon nature does not refine itself short of the third generation. The tradesmen, too, and all other classes, have their own proprieties. The only value of my criticisms, therefore, lay in their exemplifying the proneness of a traveller to measure one people by the distinctive characteristics of another, — as English writers invariably measure us, and take upon themselves to be disgusted accordingly, instead of trying to find out some principle of beauty with which we may be in conformity.

In due time we were summoned to the table, and went thither in no solemn procession, but with a good deal of jostling, thrusting behind, and scrambling for places when we reached our destination. The legal gentlemen, I suspect, were responsible for this indecorous zeal, which I never afterwards remarked in a similar party. The dining-hall was of noble size, and, like the other rooms of the suite, was gorgeously painted and gilded and brilliantly illuminated. There was a splendid table-service, and a noble array of footmen, some of them in

plain clothes, and others wearing the town-livery, richly decorated with gold-lace, and themselves excellent specimens of
the blooming young manhood of Britain.   When we were fairly seated, it was certainly an agreeable spectacle to look up and
down the long vista of earnest faces, and behold them so resolute, so conscious that there was an important business in hand,
and so determined to be equal to the occasion.   Indeed, Englishman or not, I hardly know what can be prettier than a
snow-white table-cloth, a huge heap of flowers as a central
decoration, bright silver, rich china, crystal glasses, decanters
of Sherry at due intervals, a French roll and an artistically
folded napkin at each plate, all that airy portion of a banquet,
in short, that comes before the first mouthful, the whole illuminated by a blaze of artificial light, without which a dinner
of made-dishes looks spectral, and the simplest viands are the
best.   Printed bills-of-fare were distributed, representing an
abundant feast, no part of which appeared on the table until
called for in separate plates.   I have entirely forgotten what it
was, but deem it no great matter, inasmuch as there is a pervading commonplace and identicalness in the composition of
extensive dinners, on account of the impossibility of supplying
a hundred guests with anything particularly delicate or rare.
It was suggested to me that certain juicy old gentlemen had a
private understanding what to call for, and that it would be
good policy in a stranger to follow in their footsteps through
the feast.   I did not care to do so, however, because, like San-
cho Panza's dip out of Camacho's caldron, any sort of potluck
at such a table would be sure to suit my purpose; so I chose
a dish or two on my own judgment, and, getting through my
labors betimes, had great pleasure in seeing the Englishmen
toil onward to the end.

They drank rather copiously, too, though wisely; for I observed that they seldom took Hock, and let the Champagne
bubble slowly away out of the goblet, solacing themselves with
Sherry, but tasting it warily before bestowing their final confidence.   Their taste in wines, however, did not seem so ex-

quisite, and certainly was not so various, as that to which many Americans pretend.   This foppery of an intimate acquaintance with rare vintages does not suit a sensible Englishman, as he is very much in earnest about his wines, and adopts one or two as his lifelong friends, seldom exchanging them for any Delilahs of a moment, and reaping the reward of his constancy in an unimpaired stomach, and only so much gout as he deems wholesome and desirable.   Knowing well the measure of his powers, he is not apt to fill his glass too often.   Society, indeed, would hardly tolerate habitual imprudences of that kind, though, in my opinion, the Englishmen now upon the stage could carry off their three bottles, at need, with as steady a gait as any of their forefathers.   It is not so very long since the three-bottle heroes sank finally under the table.   It may be (at least, I should be glad if it were true) that there was an occult sympathy between our temperance reform, now somewhat in abeyance, and the almost simultaneous disappearance of hard-drinking among the respectable classes in England.   I remember a middle-aged gentleman telling me (in illustration of the very slight importance attached to breaches of temperance within the memory of men not yet old) that he had seen a certain magistrate, Sir John Linkwater, or Drinkwater, — but I think the jolly old knight could hardly have staggered under so perverse a misnomer as this last, — while sitting on the magisterial bench, pull out a crown-piece and hand it to the clerk.   "Mr. Clerk," said Sir John, as if it were the most indifferent fact in the world, "I was drunk last night.   There are my five shillings."

During the dinner, I had a good deal of pleasant conversation with the gentlemen on either side of me.   One of them, a lawyer, expatiated with great unction on the social standing of the judges.   Representing the dignity and authority of the Crown, they take precedence, during assize-time, of the highest military men in the kingdom, of the Lord Lieutenant of the county, of the Archbishops, of the royal Dukes, and even of the Prince of Wales.   For the nonce, they are the greatest men in England. With a glow of professional complacency that amounted to enthusiasm, my friend assured me, that, in case of a royal dinner, a judge, if actually holding an assize, would be expected to offer his arm and take the Queen herself to the table. Happening to be in company with some of these elevated personages, on subsequent occasions, it appeared to me that the judges are fully conscious of their paramount claims to respect, and take rather more pains to impress them on their ceremonial inferiors than men of high hereditary rank are apt to do. Bishops, if it be not irreverent to say so, are sometimes marked by a similar characteristic. Dignified position is so sweet to an Englishman, that he needs to be born in it, and to feel it thoroughly incorporated with his nature from its original germ, in order to keep him from flaunting it obtrusively in the faces of innocent by-standers.

My companion on the other side was a thick-set, middle-aged man, uncouth in manners, and ugly where none were handsome, with a dark, roughly hewn visage, that looked grim in repose, and seemed to hold within itself the machinery of a very terrific frown. He ate with resolute appetite, and let slip few opportunities of imbibing whatever liquids happened to be passing by. I was meditating in what way this grisly featured table-fellow might most safely be accosted, when he turned to me with a surly sort of kindness, and invited me to take a glass of wine. We then began a conversation that abounded, on his part, with sturdy sense, and, somehow or other, brought me closer to him than I had yet stood to an Englishman. I should hardly have taken him to be an educated man, certainly not a scholar of accurate training; and yet he seemed to have all the resources of education and trained intellectual power at command. My fresh Americanism, and watchful observation of English characteristics, appeared either to interest or amuse him, or perhaps both. Under the mollifying influences of abundance of meat and drink, he grew very gracious (not that I ought to use such a phrase to describe his evidently genuine good-will), and by and by expressed a wish for further acquaintance, asking me to call at his rooms in London and inquire for Sergeant Wilkins, — throwing out the name forcibly, as if he had no occasion to be ashamed of it. I remembered Dean Swift's retort to Sergeant Bettesworth on a similar announcement, — "Of what regiment, pray, sir?" — and fancied that the same question might not have been quite amiss, if applied to the rugged individual at my side. But I heard of him subsequently as one of the prominent men at the English bar, a rough customer, and a terribly strong champion in criminal cases; and it caused me more regret than might have been expected, on so slight an acquaintanceship, when, not long afterwards, I saw his death announced in the newspapers. Not rich in attractive qualities, he possessed, I think, the most attractive one of all, — thorough manhood.

After the cloth was removed, a goodly group of decanters were set before the Mayor, who sent them forth on their outward voyage, full freighted with Port, Sherry, Madeira, and Claret, of which excellent liquors, methought, the latter found least acceptance among the guests. When every man had filled his glass, his Worship stood up and proposed a toast. It was, of course, "Our gracious Sovereign," or words to that effect; and immediately a band of musicians, whose preliminary tootings and thrummings I had already heard behind me, struck up "God save the Queen!" and the whole company rose with one impulse to assist in singing that famous national anthem. It was the first time in my life that I had ever seen a body of men, or even a single man, under the active influence of the sentiment of Loyalty; for, though we call ourselves loyal to our country and institutions, and prove it by our readiness to shed blood and sacrifice life in their behalf, still the principle is as cold and hard, in an American bosom, as the steel spring that puts in motion a powerful machinery. In the Englishman's system, a force similar to that of our steel spring is generated by the warm throbbings of human hearts. He clothes our bare abstraction in flesh and blood, — at present, in the flesh and blood of a woman, — and manages to combine love, awe, and intellectual reverence, all in one emotion, and to embody his mother, his wife, his children, the whole idea of kindred, in a single person, and make her the representative of his country and its laws. We Americans smile superior, as I did at the Mayor's table; and yet, I fancy, we lose some very agreeable titillations of the heart in consequence of our proud prerogative of caring no more about our President than for a man of straw, or a stuffed scarecrow straddling in a cornfield.

But, to say the truth, the spectacle struck me rather ludicrously, to see this party of stout middle-aged and elderly gentlemen, in the fulness of meat and drink, their ample and ruddy faces glistening with wine, perspiration, and enthusiasm, rumbling out those strange old stanzas from the very bottom of their hearts and stomachs, which two organs, in the English interior arrangements, lie closer together than in ours. The song seemed to me the rudest old ditty in the world; but I could not wonder at its universal acceptance and indestructible popularity, considering how inimitably it expresses the national faith and feeling as regards the inevitable righteousness of England, the Almighty's consequent respect and partiality for that redoubtable little island, and his presumed readiness to strengthen its defence against the contumacious wickedness and knavery of all other principalities or republics. Tennyson himself, though evidently English to the very last prejudice, could not write half so good a song for the purpose. Finding that the entire dinner-table struck in, with voices of every pitch between rolling thunder and the squeak of a cart-wheel, and that the strain was not of such delicacy as to be much hurt by the harshest of them, I determined to lend my own assistance in swelling the triumphant roar. It seemed but a proper courtesy to the first Lady in the land, whose guest, in the largest sense, I might consider myself. Accordingly, my first tuneful efforts (and probably my last, for I purpose not to sing any more, unless it be "Hail Columbia" on the restoration of the Union) were poured freely forth in honor of Queen Victoria. The Sergeant smiled like the carved head of a Swiss nutcracker, and the other gentlemen in my neighborhood, by nods and gestures, evinced grave approbation of so suitable a tribute to English superiority; and we finished our stave and sat down in an extremely happy frame of mind.

Other toasts followed in honor of the great institutions and interests of the country, and speeches in response to each were made by individuals whom the Mayor designated or the company called for. None of them impressed me with a very high idea of English postprandial oratory. It is inconceivable, indeed, what ragged and shapeless utterances most Englishmen are satisfied to give vent to, without attempting anything like artistic shape, but clapping on a patch here and another there, and ultimately getting out what they want to say, and generally wih a result of sufficiently good sense, but in some such disorganized mass as if they had thrown it up rather than spoken it. It seemed to me that this was almost as much by choice as necessity. An Englishman, ambitious of public favor, should not be too smooth. If an orator is glib, his countrymen distrust him. They dislike smartness. The stronger and heavier his thoughts, the better, provided there be an element of commonplace running through them; and any rough, yet never vulgar force of expression, such as would knock an opponent down if it hit him, only it must not be too personal, is altogether to their taste; but a studied neatness of language, or other such superficial graces, they cannot abide. They do not often permit a man to make himself a fine orator of malice aforethought, that is, unless he be a nobleman (as, for example, Lord Stanley, of the Derby family), who, as an hereditary legislator and necessarily a public speaker, is bound to remedy a poor natural delivery in the best way he can. On the whole, I partly agree with them, and, if I cared for any oratory whatever, should be as likely to applaud theirs as our own. When an English speaker sits down, you feel that you have been listening to a real man, and not to an actor; his sentiments have a wholesome earth-smell in them, though, very likely, this apparent naturalness is as much an art as what we expend in rounding a sentence or elaborating a peroration. . . .

This slight article on the civic banquets of England would be too wretchedly imperfect without an attempted description of a Lord Mayor's dinner at the Mansion House in London. I should have preferred the annual feast at Guildhall, but never had the good fortune to witness it. Once, however, I was honored with an invitation to one of the regular dinners, and gladly accepted it, — taking the precaution, nevertheless, though it hardly seemed necessary, to inform the City-King, through a mutual friend, that I was no fit representative of American eloquence, and must humbly make it a condition that I should not be expected to open my mouth, except for the reception of his Lordship's bountiful hospitality. The reply was gracious and acquiescent; so that I presented myself in the great entrance-hall of the Mansion House, at half-past six o'clock, in a state of most enjoyable freedom from the pusillanimous apprehensions that often tormented me at such times. The Mansion House was built in Queen Anne's days, in the very heart of old London, and is a palace worthy of its inhabitant, were he really as great a man as his traditionary state and pomp would seem to indicate. Times are changed, however, since the days of Whittington, or even of Hogarth's Industrious Apprentice, to whom the highest imaginable reward of life-long integrity was a seat in the Lord Mayor's chair. People nowadays say that the real dignity and importance have perished out of the office, as they do, sooner or later, out of all earthly institutions, leaving only a painted and gilded shell like that of an Easter egg, and that it is only second-rate and third-rate men who now condescend to be ambitious of the Mayoralty. I felt a little grieved at this; for the original emigrants of New England had strong sympathies with the people of London, who were mostly Puritans in religion and Parliamentarians in politics, in the early days of our country; so that the Lord Mayor was a potentate of huge dimensions in the estimation of our forefathers, and held to be hardly second to the prime minister of the throne. The true great men of the city now appear to have aims beyond city greatness, connecting themselves with national politics, and seeking to be identified with the aristocracy of the country.

In the entrance-hall I was received by a body of footmen dressed in a livery of blue coats and buff breeches, in which they looked wonderfully like American Revolutionary generals, only bedizened with far more lace and embroidery than those simple and grand old heroes ever dreamed of wearing. There were likewise two very imposing figures, whom I should have taken to be military men of rank, being arrayed in scarlet coats and large silver epaulets; but they turned out to be officers of the Lord Mayor's household, and were now employed in assigning to the guests the places which they were respectively to occupy at the dinner-table. Our names (for I had included myself in a little group of friends) were announced; and ascending the staircase, we met his Lordship in the doorway of the first reception-room, where, also, we had the advantage of a presentation to the Lady Mayoress. As this distinguished couple retired into private life at the termination of their year of office, it is inadmissible to make any remarks, critical or laudatory, on the manners and bearing of two personages suddenly emerging from a position of respectable mediocrity into one of preëminent dignity within their own sphere. Such individuals almost always seem to grow nearly or quite to the full size of their office. If it were desirable to write an essay on the latent aptitude of ordinary people for grandeur, we have an exemplification in our own country, and on a scale incomparably greater than that of the Mayoralty, though invested with nothing like the outward magnificence that gilds and embroiders the latter. If I have been correctly informed, the Lord Mayor's salary is exactly double that of the President of the United States, and yet is found very inadequate to his necessary expenditure.

There were two reception-rooms, thrown into one by the opening of wide folding-doors; and though in an old style, and not yet so old as to be venerable, they are remarkably handsome apartments, lofty as well as spacious, with carved ceilings and walls, and at either end a splendid fireplace of white marble, ornamented with sculptured wreaths of flowers and foliage. The company were about three hundred, many of them celebrities in politics, war, literature, and science, though I recollect none preëminently distinguished in either department. But it is certainly a pleasant mode of doing honor to men of literature, for example, who deserve well of the public, yet do not often meet it face to face, thus to bring them together under genial auspices, in connection with persons of note in other lines. I know not what may be the Lord Mayor's mode or principle of selecting his guests, nor whether, during his official term, he can proffer his hospitality to every man of noticeable talent in the wide world of London, nor, in fine, whether his Lordship's invitation is much sought for or valued; but it seemed to me that this periodical feast is one of the many sagacious methods which the English have contrived for keeping up a good understanding among different sorts of people. Like most other distinctions of society, however, I presume that the Lord Mayor's card does not often seek out modest merit, but comes at last when the recipient is conscious of the bore, and doubtful about the honor.

One very pleasant characteristic, which I never met with at any other public or partially public dinner, was the presence of ladies. No doubt, they were principally the wives and daughters of city magnates; and if we may judge from the many sly allusions in old plays and satirical poems, the city of London has always been famous for the beauty of its women and the reciprocal attractions between them and the men of quality. Be that as it might, while straying hither and thither through those crowded apartments, I saw much reason for modifying certain heterodox opinions which I had imbibed, in my Transatlantic newness and rawness, as regarded the delicate character and frequent occurrence of English beauty. To state the entire truth (being, at this period, some years old in English life), my taste, I fear, had long since begun to be deteriorated by acquaintance with other models of feminine loveliness than it was my happiness to know in America. I often found, or seemed to find, if I may dare to confess it, in the persons of such of my dear countrywomen as I now occasionally met, a certain meagreness, (Heaven forbid that I should call it scrawniness!) a deficiency of physical development, a scantiness, so to speak, in the pattern of their material make, a paleness of complexion, a thinness of voice, — all of which characteristics, nevertheless, only made me resolve so much the more sturdily to uphold these fair creatures as angels, because I was sometimes driven to a half-acknowledgment that the English ladies, looked at from a lower point of view, were perhaps a little finer animals than they. The advantages of the latter, if any they could really be said to have, were all comprised in a few additional lumps of clay on their shoulders and other parts of their figures. It would be a pitiful bargain to give up the ethereal charm of American beauty in exchange for half a hundred-weight of human clay!

At a given signal we all found our way into an immense room, called the Egyptian Hall, I know not why, except that the architecture was classic, and as different as possible from the ponderous style of Memphis and the Pyramids. A powerful band played inspiringly as we entered, and a brilliant profusion of light shone down on two long tables, extending the whole length of the hall, and a cross-table between them, occuping nearly its entire breadth. Glass gleamed and silver glistened on an acre or two of snowy damask, over which were set out all the accompaniments of a stately feast. We found our places without much difficulty, and the Lord Mayor's chaplain implored a blessing on the food, — a ceremony which the English never omit, at a great dinner or a small one, yet consider, I fear, not so much a religious rite as a sort of preliminary relish before the soup. . . .

Nearly opposite to me, on the other side of the table, sat a young lady in white, whom I am sorely tempted to describe, but dare not, because not only the supereminence of her beauty, but its peculiar character, would cause the sketch to be recognized, however rudely it might be drawn. I hardly thought that there existed such a woman outside of a picture-frame, or the covers of a romance: not that I had ever met with her resemblance even there, but, being so distinct and singular an apparition, she seemed likelier to find her sisterhood in poetry and picture than in real life. Let us turn away from her, lest a touch too apt should compel her stately and cold and soft and womanly grace to gleam out upon my page with a strange repulsion and unattainableness in the very spell that made her beautiful.* At her side, and familiarly attentive to her, sat a gentleman of whom I remember only a hard outline of the nose and forehead, and such a monstrous portent of a beard that you could discover no symptom of a mouth, except when he opened it to speak, or to put in a morsel of food. Then, indeed, you suddenly became aware of a cave hidden behind the impervious and darksome shrubbery. There could be no doubt who this gentleman and lady were. Any child would have recognized them at a glance. It was Bluebeard and a new wife (the loveliest of the series, but with already a mysterious gloom overshadowing her fair young brow) travelling in their honeymoon, and dining, among other distinguished strangers, at the Lord Mayor's table.

After an hour or two of valiant achievement with knife and fork came the dessert; and at the point of the festival where finger-glasses are usually introduced, a large silver basin was carried round to the guests, containing rose-water, into which we dipped the ends of our napkins and were conscious of a delightful fragrance, instead of that heavy and weary odor, the hateful ghost of a defunct dinner. This seems to be an ancient custom of the city, not confined to the Lord Mayor's table, but never met with westward of Temple Bar.

---

*[In his journal Hawthorne described her as a blend of Judith, Bathsheba, and Eve — a prototype for the painter Miriam Schaefer in *The Marble Faun*.]

During all the feast, in accordance with another ancient custom, the origin or purport of which I do not remember to have heard, there stood a man in armor, with a helmet on his head, behind his Lordship's chair. When the after-dinner wine was placed on the table, still another official personage appeared behind the chair, and proceeded to make a solemn and sonorous proclamation (in which he enumerated the principal guests, comprising three or four noblemen, several baronets, and plenty of generals, members of Parliament, aldermen, and other names of the illustrious, one of which sounded strangely familiar to my ears), ending in some such style as this: "and other gentlemen and ladies, here present, the Lord Mayor drinks to you all in a loving-cup," — giving a sort of sentimental twang to the two words, — "and sends it round among you!" And forthwith the loving-cup — several of them, indeed, on each side of the tables — came slowly down with all the antique ceremony.

The fashion of it is thus. The Lord Mayor, standing up and taking the covered cup in both hands, presents it to the guest at his elbow, who likewise rises, and removes the cover for his Lordship to drink, which being successfully accomplished, the guest replaces the cover and receives the cup into his own hands. He then presents it to his next neighbor, that the cover may be again removed for himself to take a draught, after which the third person goes through a similar manoeuvre with a fourth, and he with a fifth, until the whole company find themselves inextricably intertwisted and entangled in one complicated chain of love. When the cup came to my hands, I examined it critically, both inside and out, and perceived it to be an antique and richly ornamented silver goblet, capable of holding about a quart of wine. Considering how much trouble we all expended in getting the cup to our lips, the guests appeared to content themselves with wonderfully moderate potations. In truth, nearly or quite the original quart of wine being still in the goblet, it seemed doubtful whether any of the company had more than barely touched the silver

rim before passing it to their neighbors, — a degree of ab-
stinence that might be accounted for by a fastidious repugnance to so many compotators in one cup, or possibly by a
disapprobation of the liquor. Being curious to know all
about these important matters, with a view of recommending
to my countrymen whatever they might usefully adopt, I
drank an honest sip from the loving-cup, and had no occasion
for another, — ascertaining it to be Claret of a poor original
quality, largely mingled with water, and spiced and sweetened.
It was good enough, however, for a merely spectral or ceremonial drink, and could never have been intended for any
better purpose.

The toasts now began in the customary order, attended
with speeches neither more nor less witty and ingenious than
the specimens of table eloquence which had heretofore delighted me. As preparatory to each new display, the herald, or
whatever he was, behind the chair of state, gave awful notice
that the Right Honorable the Lord Mayor was about to pro-
pose a toast. His Lordship being happily delivered thereof, together with some accompanying remarks, the band played an
appropriate tune, and the herald again issued proclamation
to the effect that such or such a nobleman, or gentleman, general, dignified clergyman, or what not, was going to respond
to the Right Honorable the Lord Mayor's toast; then, if I
mistake not, there was another prodigious flourish of trumpets
and twanging of stringed instruments; and, finally, the doomed
individual, waiting all this while to be decapitated, got up and
proceeded to make a fool of himself. A bashful young earl
tried his maiden oratory on the good citizens of London, and,
having evidently got every word by heart (even including, however he managed it, the most seemingly casual improvisations
of the moment), he really spoke like a book, and made incomparably the smoothest speech I ever heard in England.

The weight and gravity of the speakers, not only on this
occasion, but all similar ones, was what impressed me as most
extraordinary, not to say absurd. Why should people eat a

good dinner, and put their spirits into festive trim with Champagne, and afterwards mellow themselves into a most enjoyable state of quietude with copious libations of Sherry and old Port, and then disturb the whole excellent result by listening to speeches as heavy as an after-dinner nap, and in no degree so refreshing? If the Champagne had thrown its sparkle over the surface of these effusions, or if the generous Port had shone through their substance with a ruddy glow of the old English humor, I might have seen a reason for honest gentlemen prattling in their cups, and should undoubtedly have been glad to be a listener. But there was no attempt nor impulse of the kind on the part of the orators, nor apparent expectation of such a phenomenon on that of the audience. In fact, I imagine that the latter were best pleased when the speaker embodied his ideas in the figurative language of arithmetic, or struck upon any hard matter of business or statistics, as a heavy-laden bark bumps upon a rock in mid-ocean. The sad severity, the too earnest utilitarianism, of modern life, have wrought a radical and lamentable change, I am afraid, in this ancient and goodly institution of civic banquets. People used to come to them, a few hundred years ago, for the sake of being jolly; they come now with an odd notion of pouring sober wisdom into their wine by way of wormwood-bitters, and thus make such a mess of it that the wine and wisdom reciprocally spoil one another.

Possibly, the foregoing sentiments have taken a spice of acridity from a circumstance that happened about this stage of the feast, and very much interrupted my own further enjoyment of it. Up to this time, my condition had been exceedingly felicitous, both on account of the brilliancy of the scene, and because I was in close proximity with three very pleasant English friends. One of them was a lady, whose honored name my readers would recognize as a household word, if I dared write it; another, a gentleman, likewise well known to them, whose fine taste, kind heart, and genial cultivation are qualities seldom mixed in such happy proportion as in him. The third was the man to whom I owed most in England, the warm benignity of whose nature was never weary of doing me good, who led me to many scenes of life, in town, camp, and country, which I never could have found out for myself, who knew precisely the kind of help a stranger needs, and gave it as freely as if he had not had a thousand more important things to live for. Thus I never felt safer or cosier at anybody's fireside, even my own, than at the dinner-table of the Lord Mayor.

Out of this serene sky came a thunderbolt. His Lordship got up and proceeded to make some very eulogistic remarks upon "the literary and commercial" — I question whether those two adjectives were ever before married by a copulative conjunction, and they certainly would not live together in illicit intercourse, of their own accord — "the literary and commercial attainments of an eminent gentleman there present," and then went on to speak of the relations of blood and interest between Great Britain and the aforesaid eminent gentleman's native country. Those bonds were more intimate than had ever before existed between two great nations, throughout all history, and his Lordship felt assured that that whole honorable company would join him in the expression of a fervent wish that they might be held inviolably sacred, on both sides of the Atlantic, now and forever. Then came the same wearisome old toast, dry and hard to chew upon as a musty sea-biscuit, which had been the text of nearly all the oratory of my public career. The herald sonorously announced that Mr. So-and-so would now respond to his Right Honorable Lordship's toast and speech, the trumpets sounded the customary flourish for the onset, there was a thunderous rumble of anticipatory applause, and finally a deep silence sank upon the festive hall.

All this was a horrid piece of treachery on the Lord Mayor's part, after beguiling me within his lines on a pledge of safe-conduct; and it seemed very strange that he could not let an unobtrusive individual eat his dinner in peace, drink a small sample of the Mansion House wine, and go away grateful at heart for the old English hospitality. If his Lordship had sent

me an infusion of ratsbane in the loving-cup, I should have
taken it much more kindly at his hands. But I suppose the
secret of the matter to have been somewhat as follows.

All England, just then, was in one of those singular fits of
panic excitement (not fear, though as sensitive and tremulous
as that emotion), which, in consequence of the homogeneous
character of the people, their intense patriotism, and their
dependence for their ideas in public affairs on other sources
than their own examination and individual thought, are more
sudden, pervasive, and unreasoning than any similar mood of
our own public. In truth, I have never seen the American
public in a state at all similar, and believe that we are incapable of it. Our excitements are not impulsive, like theirs, but,
right or wrong, are moral and intellectual. For example, the
grand rising of the North, at the commencement of this war,
bore the aspect of impulse and passion only because it was so
universal, and necessarily done in a moment, just as the quiet
and simultaneous getting-up of a thousand people out of their
chairs would cause a tumult that might be mistaken for a
storm. We were cool then, and have been cool ever since,
and shall remain cool to the end, which we shall take coolly,
whatever it may be. There is nothing which the English find
it so difficult to understand in us as this characteristic. They
imagine us, in our collective capacity, a kind of wild beast,
whose normal condition is savage fury, and are always looking
for the moment when we shall break through the slender barriers of international law and comity, and compel the reasonable part of the world, with themselves at the head, to combine
for the purpose of putting us into a stronger cage. At times
this apprehension becomes so powerful (and when one man
feels it, a million do), that it resembles the passage of the wind
over a broad field of grain, where you see the whole crop bend-
ing and swaying beneath one impulse, and each separate stalk
tossing with the selfsame disturbance as its myriad companions.
At such periods all Englishmen talk with a terrible identity of
sentiment and expression. You have the whole country in

each man; and not one of them all, if you put him strictly to the question, can give a reasonable ground for his alarm. There are but two nations in the world — our own country and France — that can put England into this singular state. It is the united sensitiveness of a people extremely well-to-do, careful of their country's honor, most anxious for the preservation of the cumbrous and moss-grown prosperity which they have been so long in consolidating, and incompetent (owing to the national half-sightedness, and their habit of trusting to a few leading minds for their public opinion) to judge when that prosperity is really threatened.

If the English were accustomed to look at the foreign side of any international dispute, they might easily have satisfied themselves that there was very little danger of a war at that particular crisis, from the simple circumstance that their own Government had positively not an inch of honest ground to stand upon, and could not fail to be aware of the fact. Neither could they have met Parliament with any show of a justification for incurring war. It was no such perilous juncture as exists now, when law and right are really controverted on sustainable or plausible grounds, and a naval commander may at any moment fire off the first cannon of a terrible contest. If I remember it correctly, it was a mere diplomatic squabble, in which the British ministers, with the politic generosity which they are in the habit of showing towards their official subordinates, had tried to browbeat us for the purpose of sustaining an ambassador in an indefensible proceeding; and the American Government (for God had not denied us an administration of statesmen then) had retaliated with stanch courage and exquisite skill, putting inevitably a cruel mortification upon their opponents, but indulging them with no pretence whatever for active resentment.

Now the Lord Mayor, like any other Englishman, probably fancied that War was on the western gale, and was glad to lay hold of even so insignificant an American as myself, who might be made to harp on the rusty old strings of national sympathies,

identity of blood and interest, and community of language and
literature, and whisper peace where there was no peace, in however weak an utterance.   And possibly his Lordship thought,
in his wisdom, that the good feeling which was sure to be
expressed by a company of well-bred Englishmen, at his august
and far-famed dinner-table, might have an appreciable influence on the grand result.   Thus, when the Lord Mayor invited
me to his feast, it was a piece of strategy.   He wanted to induce
me to fling myself, like a lesser Curtius, with a larger object of
self-sacrifice, into the chasm of discord between England and
America, and, on my ignominious demur, had resolved to shove
me in with his own right-honorable hands, in the hope of
closing up the horrible pit forever.   On the whole, I forgive
his Lordship.   He meant well by all parties, — himself, who
would share the glory, and me, who ought to have desired
nothing better than such an heroic opportunity, — his own
country, which would continue to get cotton and breadstuffs,
and mine, which would get everything that men work with
and wear.

As soon as the Lord Mayor began to speak, I rapped upon
my mind, and it gave forth a hollow sound, being absolutely
empty of appropriate ideas.   I never thought of listening to
the speech, because I knew it all beforehand in twenty repetitions from other lips, and was aware that it would not offer
a single suggestive point.   In this dilemma, I turned to one
of my three friends, a gentleman whom I knew to possess an
enviable flow of silver speech, and obtested him, by whatever
he deemed holiest, to give me at least an available thought or
two to start with, and, once afloat, I would trust my guardian-
angel for enabling me to flounder ashore again.   He advised
me to begin with some remarks complimentary to the Lord
Mayor, and expressive of the hereditary reverence in which his
office was held, — at least, my friend thought that there would
be no harm in giving his Lordship this little sugar-plum,
whether quite the fact or no, — was held by the descendants of
the Puritan forefathers.   Thence, if I liked, getting flexible

with the oil of my own eloquence, I might easily slide off into the momentous subject of the relations between England and America, to which his Lordship had made such weighty allusion.

Seizing this handful of straw with a death-grip, and bidding my three friends bury me honorably, I got upon my legs to save both countries, or perish in the attempt. The tables roared and thundered at me, and suddenly were silent again. But, as I have never happened to stand in a position of greater dignity and peril, I deem it a stratagem of sage policy here to close these Sketches, leaving myself still erect in so heroic an attitude.

Passages from *The English Note-Books*

A Gothic Eye

COVENTRY (1855)

I admire this in Gothic architecture, — that you cannot master it all at once, that it is not a naked outline; but, as deep and rich as human nature itself, always revealing new ideas. It is as if the builder had built himself and his age up into it, and as if the edifice had life.   Grecian temples are less interesting to me, being so cold and crystalline. . . .   We certainly know nothing of church-building in America, and of all English things that I have seen, methinks the churches disappoint me least.   I feel, too, that there is something much more wonderful in them than I have yet had time to know and experience.

SMITHELL'S HALL (1855)

The peculiarity of this house is what is called "The Bloody Footstep."   In the time of Bloody Mary, a Protestant clergyman — George Marsh, by name — was examined before the then proprietor of the Hall, Sir Roger Barton, I think, and committed to prison for his heretical opinions, and was ultimately burned at the stake.   As his guards were conducting him from the justice-room, through the stone-paved passage that leads from front to rear of Smithell's Hall, he stamped his foot upon one of the flagstones in earnest protestation against the wrong which he was undergoing. The foot, as some say, left a bloody mark in the stone; others have it, that the stone yielded like wax under his foot, and that there has been a shallow cavity ever since.... The blood-stained version of the story is more consistent with the appearance of the mark than the imprint would be; for if the martyr's blood oozed out through his shoe and stocking, it might have made his foot slide along the stone, and thus have lengthened the shape. Of course it is all a humbug.... But, even if it had been always there, the footprint might, after the fact, be looked upon as a prophecy.... At any rate, the legend is a good one.*

---

*[In one version of Hawthorne's "abortive project" on the ancestral-footstep theme, the stained mark, in which the hero fits his foot, has been made by a regicide who trod in the King's blood. One of the Cromwellian regicides who fled to New England in 1660 married a Middleton—the name of Hawthorne's hero, whose ancestry is connected with the legendary imprint. The coincidence may have been deliberate.]

A Sentimental Journey

Adjoining the drawing-room is the dining-room, in one corner of which, between two windows, Scott died.   It was now a quarter of a century since his death; but it seemed to me that we spoke with a sort of hush in our voices, as if he were still dying here, or had but just departed.... On the whole, there is no simple and great impression left by Abbotsford; and I felt angry and dissatisfied with myself for not feeling something which I did not and could not feel.   But it is just like going to a museum, if you look into particulars; and one learns from it, too, that Scott could not have been really a wise man, nor an earnest one, nor one that grasped the truth of life; he did but play, and the play grew very sad toward its close.   In a certain way, however, I understand his romances the better for having seen his house; and his house the better for having read his romances.   They throw light on one another....

Bidding farewell to Abbotsford, I cannot but confess a sentiment of remorse for having visited the dwelling-place — as just before I visited the grave — of the mighty minstrel and romancer with so cold a heart and in so critical a mood, — *his* dwelling-place and *his* grave whom I had so admired and loved, and who had done so much for my happiness when I was young. But I, and the world generally, now look at him from a different point of view.... As for Scott, I still cherish him in a warm place, and I do not know that I have any pleasanter anticipation, as regards books, than that of reading all his novels over again after we get back to the Wayside.

A More Attractive Face

THE LAKES (1855)

I question whether any part of the world looks so beautiful as England — this part of England, at least — on a fine summer morning. It makes one think the more cheerfully of human life to see such a bright universal verdure; such sweet, rural, peaceful, flower-bordered cottages, — not cottages of gentility, but dwellings of the laboring poor; such nice villas along the roadside, so tastefully contrived for comfort and beauty, and adorned more and more, year after year, with the care and after-thought of people who mean to live in them a great while, and feel as if their children might live in them also, — and so they plant trees to overshadow their walks, and train ivy and all beautiful vines up against their walls, and thus live for the future in another sense than we Americans do. And the climate helps them out, and makes everything moist, and green, and full of tender life, instead of dry and arid, as human life and vegetable life is so apt to be with us. Certainly, England can present a more attractive face than we can; even in its humbler modes of life, to say nothing of the beautiful lives that might be led, one would think, by the higher classes, whose gateways, with broad, smooth gravelled drives leading through them, one sees every mile or two along the road, winding into some proud seclusion. All this is passing away, and society must assume new relations; but there is no harm in believing that there has been something very good in English life, — good for all classes while the world was in a state out of which these forms naturally grew.

HAMPTON COURT (1856)

How beautifully the royal robe of a monarchy is embroidered! Palaces, pictures, parks! They do enrich life; and kings and aristocracies cannot keep these things to themselves; they merely take care of them for others. Even a king, with all the glory that can be shed around him, is but the liveried and bedizened footman of his people, and the toy of their delight. I am very glad that I came to this country while the English are still playing with such a toy.

A Difference of Manners

I don't know any place that brings all classes into contiguity on equal ground so completely as the waiting-room at Rock Ferry on these frosty days.... This morning, when I looked into the room, there were one or two gentlemen and other respectable persons; but in the best place, close to the fire, and crouching almost into it, was an elderly beggar, with the raggedest of overcoats, two great rents in the shoulders of it disclosing the dingy lining, all bepatched with various stuff covered with dirt, and on his shoes and trousers the mud of an interminable pilgrimage.... He did just as he pleased, took the best place by the fire, nor would have cared though a nobleman were forced to stand aside for him.... It was an Englishman's spirit; but in our country, I imagine, a beggar considers himself a kind of outlaw, and would hardly assume the privileges of a man in any place of public resort. Here beggary is a system, and beggars are a numerous class, and make themselves, in a certain way, respected as such. Nobody evinced the slightest disapprobation of the man's proceedings. In America, I think, we should see many aristocratic airs on such provocation, and probably the ferry people would there have rudely thrust the beggar aside; giving him a shilling, however, which no Englishman would ever think of doing. There would also have been a great deal of fun made of his squalid and ragged figure; whereas nobody smiled at him this morning, nor in any way showed the slightest disrespect. This is good; but it is the result of a state of things by no means good. . . .

Somehow or other, different classes seem to encounter one another in an easier manner than with us; the shock is less palpable. I suppose the reason is that the distinctions are real, and therefore need not be continually asserted.

LIVERPOOL (1854)

It appears to be customary for people of decent station, but in distressed circumstances, to go round among their neighbors and the public, accompanied by a friend, who explains the case. . . .   The whole matter is very foreign to American habits. No respectable American would think of retrieving his affairs by such means, but would prefer ruin ten times over; no friend would take up his cause; no public would think it worth while to prevent the small catastrophe. And yet the custom is not without its good side, as indicating a closer feeling of brotherhood, a more efficient sense of neighborhood, than exists among ourselves, although, perhaps, we are more careless of a fellow-creature's ruin, because ruin with us is by no means the fatal and irretrievable event that it is in England.

LONDON (1856)

Mr. ——— is a self-made man, and a strong instance of the difference between the Englishman and the American, when self-made, and without early education. He is no more a gentleman now than when he began life, — not a whit more refined, either outwardly or inwardly; while the American would have been, after the same experience, not distinguishable outwardly, and perhaps as refined within, as nine tenths of the gentlemen born, in the House of Commons. And, besides, an American comes naturally to any distinctions to which success

in life may bring him; he takes them as if they were his proper
inheritance, and in no wise to be wondered at.   Mr. ———, on
the other hand, took evidently a childish delight in his position,
and felt a childish wonder in having arrived at it; nor did it
seem real to him, after all.

NEWCASTLE (1856)

An old Newcastle gentleman and his friend came into the
smoking-room, and drank three glasses of hot whiskey-toddy
apiece, and were still going on to drink more when we left
them.   These respectable persons probably went away drunk
that night, yet thought none the worse of themselves or of one
another for it.   It is like returning to times twenty years gone
by for a New-Englander to witness such simplicity of manners.

LIVERPOOL (1855)

I have grown wofully aristocratic in my tastes, I fear, since
coming to England; at all events, I am conscious of a certain
disgust at going to dine in a house with a small entrance-hall
and a narrow staircase, parlor with chintz curtains, and all
other arrangements on a similar scale.   This is pitiable.   However, I really do not think I should mind these things, were it
not for the bustle, the affectation, the intensity, of the mistress
of the house.   It is certain that a woman in England is either
decidedly a lady or decidedly not a lady.   There seems to be no
respectable medium.

KENILWORTH (1857)

The distance from Leamington is less than five miles, and at
the Kenilworth station we found a little bit of an omnibus,
into which we packed ourselves, together with two ladies, one
of whom, at least, was an American.   I begin to agree partly
with the English, that we are not a people of elegant manners.
At all events, there is sometimes a bare, hard, meagre sort of

deportment, especially in our women, that has not its parallel elsewhere. But perhaps what sets off this kind of behavior, and brings it into *alto relievo,* is the fact of such uncultivated persons travelling abroad, and going to see sights that would not be interesting except to people of some education and refinement.

SMITHELL'S HALL (1855)

In the morning, before breakfast, we had prayers, read by Mr. ———, in the oak dining-room, all the servants coming in, and everybody kneeling down. I should like to know how much true religious feeling is indicated by this regular observance of religious rites in English families. In America, if people kneel down to pray, it is pretty certain that they feel a genuine interest in the matter, and their daily life is supposed to be in accordance with their devotions. If an American is an infidel, he knows it; but an Englishman is often so without suspecting it, — being kept from that knowledge by this formality of family prayer, and his other regularities of external worship.

YORK (1857)

The services of Easter Sunday comprehend more than the ordinary quantity of singing and chanting; at all events, nearly an hour and a half were thus employed, with some intermixture of prayers and reading of Scriptures; and being almost congealed with cold, I thought it would never come to an end. The spirit of my Puritan ancestors was mighty within me, and I did not wonder at their being out of patience with all this mummery, which seemed to me worse than papistry because it was a corruption of it. At last a canon gave out the text, and preached a sermon about twenty minutes long, — the coldest, driest, most superficial rubbish; for this gorgeous setting of the magnificent cathedral, the elaborate music, and the rich ceremonies seem inevitably to take the life out of the sermon, which, to be anything, must be all.

An Enormous City

LONDON (1857)

It is human life; it is this material world; it is a grim and heavy reality. I have never had the same sense of being surrounded by materialisms and hemmed in with the grossness of this earthly existence anywhere else; these broad, crowded streets are so evidently the veins and arteries of an enormous city. . . .

We think of going to the Crystal Palace to spend the festival day, and eat our Christmas dinner; but, do what we may, we shall have no home feeling or fireside enjoyment. I am weary, weary of London and of England, and can judge now how the old Loyalists must have felt, condemned to pine out their lives here, when the Revolution had robbed them of their native country. And yet there is still a pleasure in being in this dingy, smoky, midmost haunt of men; and I trudge through Fleet Street and Ludgate Street and along Cheapside with an enjoyment as great as I ever felt in a wood-path at home; and I have come to know these streets as well, I believe, as I ever knew Washington Street in Boston, or even Essex Street in my stupid old native town.

LONDON (1858)

We are now making preparations for our departure...and yesterday I went to our Minister's to arrange about the passport. The very moment I rang at his door, it swung open, and the porter ushered me with great courtesy into the anteroom; not that he knew me, or anything about me, except that I was an American citizen. This is the deference which an American servant of the public finds it expedient to show to his sovereigns. Thank heaven, I am a sovereign again, and no longer a servant....

I did not see, and, in fact, declined seeing the Minister himself, but only his son, the Secretary of the Legation, and a Dr. P——, an American traveller just from the Continent. He gave a fearful account of the difficulties that beset a person landing with much luggage in Italy, and especially at Città Vecchia, the very port at which we intended to debark. I have been so long in England that it seems a cold and shivery thing to go anywhere else.